Meeting the
Ethical Challenges
of LEADERSHIP
Second Edition

Meeting the Ethical Challenges *of* LEADERSHIP

Second Edition

CASTING LIGHT OR SHADOW

Craig E. Johnson

George Fox University

SAGE Publications
Thousand Oaks ▪ London ▪ New Delhi

For information:

Sage Publications, Inc.
2455 Teller Road
Thousand Oaks, California 91320
E-mail: order@sagepub.com

Sage Publications Ltd.
1 Oliver's Yard
55 City Road
London EC1Y 1SP
United Kingdom

Sage Publications India Pvt. Ltd.
B-42, Panchsheel Enclave
Post Box 4109
New Delhi 110 017 India

Printed in the United States of America

Library of Congress Cataloging-in-Publication Data

Johnson, Craig E. (Craig Edward), 1952-
Meeting the ethical challenges of leadership: Casting light or shadow /
Craig E. Johnson.—2nd ed.
    p. cm.
Includes bibliographical references and index.
ISBN 1-4129-4129-6 (pbk.)
   1. Leadership—Moral and ethical aspects. I. Title.
HM1261.J64 2005
303.3'4—dc22   2004014908

This book is printed on acid-free paper.

05   06   07   10   9 8 7 6 5 4 3 2

Acquisitions Editor:	Al Bruckner
Editorial Assistant:	MaryAnn Vail
Production Editor:	Diane S. Foster
Copy Editor:	Robert Holm
Typesetter:	C&M Digitals (P) Ltd.
Proofreader:	Eileen Delaney
Indexer:	Teri Greenberg
Cover Designer:	Michelle Lee Kenny

Contents

Acknowledgments

C olleagues and students provided practical and emotional support during the writing of the second edition of this text, just as they did for the first. Research librarians Janis Tyhurst and Louise Newswanger helped locate sources and double-check facts. Richard Engnell and Phil Smith helped clarify my understanding of Rawls's justice as fairness theory. Student assistants, ably supervised by Deborah Hawblitzel, checked out books and articles and photocopied materials. Those enrolled in my leadership seminar and leadership communication classes helped shape this second edition by responding to chapter content, exercises, and cases.

My special thanks go to instructors from around the country who adopted the first edition of *Meeting the Ethical Challenges of Leadership* for classroom use and then provided me with feedback. Three in particular come to mind. Roger Smitter, formerly of North Central College and now executive director of the National Communication Association, sent a steady stream of material for cases and examples. Thomas Sechrest of St. Edwards University engaged me in dialogue with several groups of his students and commented on this manuscript. James Dittmar of Geneva College invited me to speak to a community audience on the relationship between narrative and leader character.

Bill Essig of Northwest Medical Teams and John Stanley of Messiah College provided insights into ethical diversity and spiritual development for the first edition, and their insights contributed to this version as well. Kristina Hanson, Mark Reed, and Dana Miller supplied material for new chapter end scenarios.

Editor Al Bruckner picked up where editor Marquita Flemming left off, acting as an advocate for this project at Sage. For that I am grateful. Finally, I want to once again thank my wife Mary, who is a steady source of encouragement.

Part I

The Shadow Side of Leadership

SOURCE: DOONESBURY © 2002 G. B. Trudeau. Reprinted with permission of UNIVERSAL
PRESS SYNDICATE. All rights reserved.

Introduction

Fallen Heroes

In the introduction to the first edition of this text, I noted that the heroic leader was alive and well in popular culture. Not any more. The image of the leader as hero has been shattered by one ethical scandal after another. Wherever we turn—military, politics, medicine, education, religion—we find fallen heroes. Nowhere is this more apparent than in business. Just a few years ago, the business section of the local Barnes & Noble or Borders bookstore told glowing stories of dynamic leaders who rescued their corporations from financial ruin. Now the same bookshelves are filled with volumes describing the downfall of these same leaders and their companies.

Fallen heroes pay a high price for their ethical failures. Nearly all sacrifice their positions of leadership as well as their reputations. Many face civil lawsuits, criminal charges, and jail time. The costs can be even greater for followers:

- Thousands of employees lost their jobs as well as their retirement savings when Enron and WorldCom filed for bankruptcy.
- Investors lost billions when accounting scandals caused the stock market to plunge. They lost millions more when brokerages and mutual funds gave them bad advice and overcharged them.
- Hundreds of children suffered sexual abuse at the hands of Catholic clergy. Victims' lawsuits could bankrupt some dioceses.
- Seven Columbia space shuttle astronauts died when NASA officials ignored safety concerns.
- Female cadets at the Air Force Academy dropped out when top officials mishandled their sexual assault complaints.
- Public confidence in the American and British governments dropped due to allegations that the Bush and Blair administrations overstated the risk posed by Saddam Hussein to justify the invasion of Iraq.

The misery caused by immoral leaders drives home an important point: ethics is at the heart of leadership.[1] When we assume the benefits of leadership, we also assume ethical burdens. I believe that we must make every effort to act in such a way as to benefit rather than damage others, to cast light instead of shadow. Doing so will significantly reduce the likelihood that we will join the future ranks of fallen heroes.

You should find this book helpful if you are a leader or an aspiring leader who (a) acknowledges that there are ethical consequences associated with exercising influence over others and (b) seeks to develop the capacity to make more informed ethical choices and to follow through on decisions. There is no guarantee that after reading the following chapters you will act in a more ethical fashion in every situation. Nor can you be sure that others will reach the same conclusions that you do about what is the best answer to an ethical dilemma. Nevertheless, you can increase your ethical competence. This book is dedicated to that end.

Whatever the specific context, leaders face similar kinds of ethical choices. For that reason, I draw examples from a wide variety of settings—business, coaching, education, government, nonprofit organizations, the military. Most are based on actual events, but I don't hesitate to draw from fictional sources as well. Literature and drama can give us rich insights into reality. Cases play an important role in this edition, as they did in the first. There are two cases at the end of each chapter, with the exception of Chapter 7. Look for these in addition to the cases included in the chapters. Once again, you'll find a feature entitled "Leadership Ethics at the Movies." Each of these short summaries introduces a feature film that brings important concepts "to life." Analyzing these DVDs and videos on your own, or better yet in a group, will deepen your understanding of leadership ethics.

Three other features are also found in every chapter. The first, "Self-Assessment" (new to this edition), measures your performance on an important behavior, skill, or concept discussed in the chapter. The second, "Implications and Applications," reviews key ideas and their ramifications for you as a leader. The third, "For Further Exploration, Challenge, and Assessment," encourages you to engage in extended reflection and self-analysis.

Readers of the first edition will note that this version of *Meeting the Ethical Challenges of Leadership* is considerably longer than its predecessor. Additional cases and examples account for some but not all of the new material. In the pages to come, you'll find new and expanded coverage of moral imagination, character, ethical perspectives, decision-making formats, dialogue, healthy ethical organizational climates, globalization, and other topics.

The first two chapters focus on the "dark side" of leadership in the belief that the first step in mastering the ethical challenges of leadership is to recognize their existence. Chapter 1 outlines common shadows cast by leaders: abuse of power and privilege, deception, misplaced and broken loyalties, inconsistency, and irresponsibility. Chapter 2 explores the reasons why leaders cause more harm than good and introduces the ethical capacity model. At the end of the second chapter, we'll pause to preview the remainder of the text. You can read the chapters in any order you wish, but they are designed to build on one another.

Defining Terms

Because this is a book about leadership ethics, we need to clarify what both of these terms mean. *Leadership* is the exercise of influence in a group context.[2] Want to know who the leaders are? Look for the people having the greatest impact on the group or organization. Leaders are change agents engaged in furthering the needs, wants, and goals of leaders and followers alike. They are found wherever humans associate with one another, whether in a social movement, sports team, task force, nonprofit agency, state legislature, military unit, or corporation.

No definition of leadership is complete without distinguishing between leading and following. Generally leaders get the most press. The newfound success of a college football team is a case in point. A head coach gets the lion's share of the credit for changing a losing team into a winner, but the turnaround is really the result of the efforts of many followers. Assistant coaches work with offensive and defensive lines, quarterbacks, and kicking teams; trainers tend to injuries; academic tutors keep players in school; athletic department staff solicit contributions for training facilities; and sports information personnel draw attention to the team's accomplishments.

In truth, leaders and followers function collaboratively, working together toward shared objectives. They are relational partners who play complementary roles.[3] Although leaders exert a greater degree of influence and take more responsibility for the overall direction of the group, followers are more involved in implementing plans and doing the work. During the course of a day or week, we typically shift between leader and follower roles, heading up a project team at work, for example, while taking the position of follower as a student in a night class.

Moving from a follower role to a leadership role brings with it a shift in expectations. Generally, we ask leaders to take more responsibility for the overall direction of the group, whereas followers are more involved in implementing plans and doing the work. Important leader functions include establishing direction, organizing, coordinating activities and resources, motivating, and managing conflicts. Important follower functions include carrying out group and organizational tasks (engineering, social work, teaching, accounting), generating new ideas about how to get jobs done, working as a team member, and providing feedback.[4]

Viewing leadership as a role should put to rest the notion that leaders are born not made. The fact that the vast majority of us will function as leaders if we haven't already done so means that leadership is not limited to those with the proper genetic background, income level, or education. Many ordinary people emerged as leaders during the horrific events of September 11, 2001, for example. Office workers in the World Trade Center calmed victims and bandaged their wounds. They formed human chains to walk down the stairs in the smoke and darkness, assisting those who had difficulty navigating the steps. At the same time these workers were headed down, firefighters of all ranks were rushing up the staircases to help. A paramedic driving near the Pentagon took his bag out of his car, doused burn victims with saline, and got others to drag victims to safety. Passengers on hijacked United Flight 93 rushed the attackers and prevented the plane from striking its intended target.

Leadership should not be confused with position, though leaders often occupy positions of authority. Those designated as leaders, like a disillusioned manager nearing retirement, don't always exert much influence. On the other hand, those without the benefit of a title on the organizational chart can have a significant impact. Lech Walesa was an electrician in a Polish plant. Nonetheless, he went on to lead a revolution that culminated in the overthrow of the nation's communist government.

Human leadership differs in important ways from the pattern of dominance and submission that characterizes animal societies. The dominant female hyena or male chimpanzee establishes rule over the pack or troop through pure physical strength. Each maintains authority until some stronger rival (often seeking mates) comes along. Unlike animals, which seem to be driven largely by instinct, humans consciously choose how they want to influence others. We can use persuasion, rewards, punishments, emotional appeals, rules, and a host of other means to get our way.

Freedom of choice makes ethical considerations an important part of any discussion of leadership. The term *ethics* refers to judgments about whether human behavior is right or wrong. We may be repulsed by the idea that a male lion will kill the offspring of the previous dominant male when he takes control of the pride. Yet we cannot label his actions as unethical because he is impelled by a genetic drive to start his own bloodline. We can and do condemn the actions of leaders who decide to lie, belittle followers, and enrich themselves at the expense of the less fortunate.

Some philosophers distinguish between "ethics," which they define as the systematic study of the principles of right or wrong behavior, and "morals," which they define as specific standards of right and wrong ("Thou shall not steal." "Do unto others as they would do unto you."). Other scholars use these terms interchangeably. I will follow the latter course.

With these preliminaries out of the way, we're now ready to take a closer look at some of the ethical hurdles faced by leaders.

Notes

1. See Ciulla, J. (Ed.). (1998). *Ethics: The heart of leadership.* Westport, CT: Praeger.

2. Bass, B. M. (1990). *Bass and Stogdill's handbook of leadership* (3rd ed.). New York: Free Press.

3. Hollander, E. P. (1992, April). The essential interdependence of leadership and followership. *Current Directions in Psychological Science,* 71–75.

4. Johnson, C. E., & Hackman, M. Z. (1997, November). *Rediscovering the power of followership in the leadership communication text.* Paper presented at the meeting of the National Communication Association, Chicago, IL.

1

The Leader's Light or Shadow

We are not angels, but we may at times be better versions of ourselves.

Historian Erwin Hargrove

What's Ahead

This chapter introduces the metaphor of light and shadow to highlight the ethical challenges of leadership. Leaders have the power to illuminate the lives of followers or to cover them in darkness. They cast shadows when they (a) abuse power, (b) hoard privileges, (c) engage in deceit, (d) act inconsistently, (e) misplace or betray loyalties, and (f) fail to assume responsibilities.

A Dramatic Difference

In an influential essay entitled "Leading From Within," educational writer and consultant Parker Palmer introduced a powerful metaphor to dramatize the distinction between ethical and unethical leadership. According to Palmer, the difference between moral and immoral leaders is as sharp as the contrast between light and darkness, between heaven and hell.

> A leader is a person who has an unusual degree of power to create the conditions under which other people must live and move and have their being, conditions that can either be as illuminating as heaven or as shadowy as hell. A leader must take special responsibility for what is going on inside his or her own self, inside his or her consciousness, lest the act of leadership create more harm than good.[1]

Psychotherapist Carl Jung was the first social scientist to identify the shadow side of the personality. He used the term to refer to the subconscious, which could include both negative (greed, fear, hatred) and positive (creativity, desire for achievement) elements.[2] Unlike Jung and other researchers who use the shadow label to refer to the hidden part of the personality, both good and bad, Palmer equates shadow with destruction. Palmer and Jungian psychologists agree, however, on one point: if we want to manage or master the dark forces inside us, we must first acknowledge that they exist. For this reason, Palmer urges us to pay more attention to the "shadow side" of leadership. Political figures, classroom teachers, parents, clergy, and business executives have the potential to cast as much shadow as light. Refusing to face the dark side of leadership makes abuse more likely. All too often, leaders "do not even know they are making a choice, let alone how to reflect on the process of choosing."[3]

When we function as leaders, we take on a unique set of ethical challenges in addition to a set of expectations and tasks. These dilemmas involve issues of power, privilege, deceit, consistency, loyalty, and responsibility. How we handle the challenges of leadership will determine if we cause more harm than good. Unless we're careful, we're likely to cast one or more of the shadows described in the next section.

The Leader's Shadows

THE SHADOW OF POWER

Power is the foundation for influence attempts. The more power we have, the more likely others will comply with our wishes. Power comes from a variety of sources. The most popular power classification system identifies five power bases.[4] *Coercive power* is based on penalties or punishments like physical force, salary reductions, student suspensions, or embargoes against national enemies. *Reward power* depends on being able to deliver something of value to others, whether tangible (bonuses, health insurance, grades) or intangible (praise, trust, cooperation). *Legitimate power* resides in the position, not the person. Supervisors, judges, police officers, instructors, and parents have the right to control our behavior within certain limits. A boss can require us to carry out certain tasks at work, for example, but in most cases, he or she has no say in what we do in our free time. In contrast to legitimate power, *expert power* is based on the characteristics of the individual, regardless of his or her official position. Knowledge, skills, education, and certification all build expert power. *Referent (role model) power* rests on the admiration one individual has for another. We're more likely to do favors for a supervisor we admire or to buy a product promoted by our favorite sports hero.

Leaders typically draw on more than one power source. The manager who is appointed to lead a task force is granted legitimate power that enables her to reward or punish. Yet in order to be successful, she'll have to demonstrate her knowledge of the topic, skillfully direct the group process, and earn the respect of task force members through hard work and commitment to the group.

There are advantages and disadvantages of using each power type. Coercion, for instance, usually gets quick results but invites retaliation and becomes less effective over time. Researchers report that U.S. workers are more satisfied and productive when their leaders rely on forms of power that are tied to the person (expert and referent) rather than on forms of power that are linked to the position (coercive, reward, and legitimate).[5] Leaders, then, have important decisions to make about the types of power they use and when.

The fact that leadership cannot exist without power makes some Americans uncomfortable. Harvard business professor Rosabeth Moss Kanter goes so far as to declare that power is "America's last dirty word."[6] She believes that for many of us talking about money and sex is easier than discussing power. We admire powerful leaders who act decisively but can be reluctant to admit that we have and use power.

Our refusal to face up to the reality of power can make us more vulnerable to the shadow side of leadership. Cult leader Jim Jones presided over the suicide of 800 followers in the jungles of Guyana. Perhaps this tragedy could have been avoided if cult members and outside observers had challenged Jones's abuse of power.[7] Conversely, ignoring the topic of power prevents the attainment of worthy objectives, leaving followers in darkness. Consider the case of the community activist who wants to build a new shelter for homeless families. He can't help these families unless he skillfully wields power to enlist the support of local groups, overcome resistance of opponents, raise funds, and secure building permits.

I suspect that we treat power as a dirty word because we recognize that power has a corrosive effect on those who possess it. We've seen how Richard Nixon used the power of his office to order illegal acts against his enemies and how special prosecutor Kenneth Starr wielded his authority to coerce witnesses to testify against Bill Clinton. Many of us are uneasy about new powers that have been given to law enforcement officials to fight terrorism (see the Patriot Act case at the end of the chapter).

Even highly moral individuals can be seduced by power. Former Senator Mark Hatfield is widely admired for being the only senator to oppose the Gulf of Tonkin resolution that authorized the war in Vietnam. Yet the Senate later reprimanded him for using his office to secure jobs for his wife.

Unfortunately, abuse of power is an all too common fact of life in modern organizations. In one survey, 90% of those responding reported that they had experienced disrespect from a boss at some time during their working careers.

Twenty percent of the sample said they currently work for an abusive leader. (Complete the Self-Assessment in Box 1.1 to determine if your supervisor is abusive or just tough.) "Brutal" bosses regularly engage in the following behaviors, some of which will be discussed in more detail later in the chapter:[8]

- *Deceit.* Lying and giving false or misleading information
- *Constraint.* Restricting followers' activities outside of work; e.g., telling them who they can befriend, where they can live, with whom they can live, and the civic activities they can participate in
- *Coercion.* Inappropriate or excessive threats for not complying with the leader's directives
- *Selfishness.* Blaming subordinates and making them scapegoats
- *Inequity.* Supplying unequal benefits or punishments based on favoritism or criteria unrelated to the job
- *Cruelty.* Harming subordinates in such illegitimate ways as name-calling or public humiliation
- *Disregard.* Ignoring normal standards of politeness; obvious disregard for what is happening in the lives of followers
- *Deification.* Creating a master-servant relationship in which bosses can do whatever they want because they feel superior

The greater a leader's power, the greater the potential for abuse. This prompted Britain's Lord Acton to observe that "power corrupts and absolute power corrupts absolutely." The long shadow cast by absolute power can be seen in the torture, death, starvation, and imprisonment of millions at the hands of Hitler, Mao, Saddam Hussein, Pol Pot, Stalin, and other despots. Large differences in the relative power of leaders and followers also contribute to abuse. The greater the power differential between a supervisor and a subordinate, the higher the probability that the manager will make demands or threats when friendly, reasonable requests would work just as well and create a more positive emotional climate.[9]

Power deprivation exerts its own brand of corruptive influence. Followers with little power become fixated on what minimal influence they have, becoming cautious, defensive, and critical of others and new ideas. In extreme cases, they may engage in sabotage, such as when one group of fast food employees took out their frustrations by spitting and urinating into the drinks they served customers.

To wield power wisely, leaders have to wrestle with all the issues outlined above. They have to consider what types of power they should use and when and for what purposes. They also have to determine how much power to keep and how much to give away. Finally, leaders must recognize and resist the dangers posed by possessing too much power while making sure that followers aren't corrupted by having too little.

Box 1.1

Self-Assessment

THE BRUTAL BOSS QUESTIONNAIRE

For an assessment of your current experience of abuse by superior(s) and its possible consequences for your health, well-being, and work productivity, complete the questionnaire that follows. Then find your personal rating using the scoring information which is provided on the reverse side.

Rate your boss on the following behaviors and actions. If you agree that a statement categorizes your boss, write a number from 5 to 8, depending on the extent of your agreement. If you disagree with a statement in reference to your boss, write a number from 1 to 4, depending on the extent of your disagreement.

1	2	3	4	5	6	7	8
Strongly Agree						Strongly Disagree	

1. My boss deliberately provides me with false or misleading information. _____

2. My boss treats me unfairly at times for no apparent reason. _____

3. My boss deceives me sometimes. _____

4. My boss deliberately withholds information from me that I need to perform my job. _____

5. My boss criticizes low-quality work from me. _____

6. My boss tells me how I should be spending my time when not at work. _____

7. My boss will "get" me if I don't comply with her or his wishes. _____

8. My boss humiliates me in public. _____

9. My boss calls me unflattering names. _____

10. My boss requires that her or his standards be met before giving a compliment. _____

11. My boss believes that I am generally inferior and blames me whenever something goes wrong. _____

12. My boss acts as if she or he can do as she or he pleases to me, because she or he is the boss. _____

(Continued)

Box 1.1 (*Continued*)

13. My boss treats me like a servant. _____

14. My boss expects me to dress appropriately at all times. _____

15. My boss treats me unjustly. _____

16. My boss steals my good ideas or work products and takes credit for them. _____

17. My boss will make me "pay" if I don't carry out her or his demands. _____

18. My boss displays anger publicly toward me by shouting, cursing, or slamming objects. _____

19. My boss criticizes me on a personal level rather than criticizing my work. _____

20. My boss demands that I give my best effort all the time. _____

21. My boss is tougher on some subordinates because she or he dislikes them regardless of their work. _____

22. My boss is discourteous toward me. _____

23. My boss is dishonest with me. _____

24. My boss shows no regard for my opinions. _____

25. My boss is deliberately rude to me. _____

26. My boss lies to me. _____

27. My boss misleads me for her or his own benefit. _____

28. My boss insists that I work hard. _____

29. My boss places blame for her or his failures on me. _____

30. My boss openly degrades and personally attacks me. _____

31. My boss mistreats me because of my lifestyle. _____

32. My boss demands that I constantly do high-quality work. _____

33. My boss reprimands me in front of others. _____

34. My boss deliberately makes me feel inferior. _____

35. My boss is not honest with the people who rank beneath her or him. _____

36. My boss threatens me in order to get what she or he wants. _____

Box 1.1 *(Continued)*

SCORING

Total your responses to the following questions:

#5: _____

#10: _____

#14: _____

#20: _____

#28: _____

#32: _____

TOUGH BOSS TOTAL: _____

Now total your response to the remaining thirty questions.

BAD BOSS TOTAL: _____

KEY

Tough boss total	+	Bad boss total	=	Assessment of boss
Between 36 and 48		Less than 90		Tough, but not abusive
Less than 36		Less than 90		Not particularly tough
Between 36 and 48		Between 90 and 195		Tough, with instances of abuse. Adverse effects on work and well-being may very well occur.
Any		Greater than 195		Abusive. Deteriorating mental and physical health and lowered productivity are associated with this level of mistreatment.

SOURCE: Hornstein, H. (1996). *Brutal bosses and their prey.* New York: Riverhead Books, pp. 150–152. Used by permission.

THE SHADOW OF PRIVILEGE

Leaders almost always enjoy greater privileges than followers do. The greater the leader's power, generally, the greater the rewards he or she receives. Consider the perks enjoyed by corporate CEOs, for example. Top business executives in the United States are the highest paid in the world, with the wealthiest among them receiving yearly compensation packages (salaries plus stock options) averaging $274 million.[10] They also eat in private dining rooms and travel around in chauffeured limousines. Here are some particularly notable examples of CEO excess:[11]

- Former Tyco CEO Dennis Kozlowski spent millions on paintings to decorate his $18 million Manhattan apartment, paying for some of this art with money from a company program developed to help employees buy Tyco stock. He then tried to avoid paying New York sales tax on his purchases. Kozlowski also collected such knickknacks as a $6,300 sewing basket and a $15,000 dog umbrella.
- Imprisoned ImClone founder Dr. Sam Waksal owned a 7,000-square-foot loft in SoHo and a place in upstate New York. He, too, had an eye for expensive art, purchasing works by de Kooning, Rothko, and Picasso for $20 million.
- John Rigas of Adelphia stole from the cable company's coffers and gave the money to family members.
- WorldCom founder Bernie Ebbers left the bankrupt company with a guaranteed $1.5 million pension and use of the corporate jet. He can enjoy his golden years (if he's not imprisoned) in his 17,000-square-foot house.
- General Electric's Jack Welch's original retirement package (which has been scaled back after public protest) included a Central Park apartment, lifetime use of the company jet, country club memberships, maid service, tickets to the opera and to New York Knicks' home games, and furniture.
- Mattel forgave a $3 million loan to failed CEO Jill Barad, and Kmart wrote off a $5 million loan to ousted chief executive Chuck Conaway.

The link between power and privilege means that abuse of one generally leads to the abuse of the other. Leaders who hoard power are likely to hoard wealth and status as well. Focused on their own desires, they neglect the needs of followers. Some of the same business executives who wouldn't hesitate to spend thousands on themselves make sure that their employees have to account for every penny. Former CBS executive Laurence Tisch once insisted that a company photographer finish every exposure on a roll of film before taking it out of his camera. Ted Turner returned letters without postmarks to the company mailroom and made the clerks cut off and reuse the stamps.[12]

Leader excess is not a new phenomenon. Ancient Chinese philosophers criticized rulers who lived in splendor while their subjects lived in poverty. Old Testament prophets railed against the political and social elites of the nations of Israel and Judah, condemning them for hoarding wealth, feasting while the poor went hungry, and using the courts to drive the lower classes from their land.

The passage of time hasn't lessened the problem but made it worse. According to the United Nations, the richest 225 people in the world have a net worth that is equal to the annual income of the poorest 2.5 *billion* people. The poorest of the poor literally live in a hell on earth, deprived of such basic necessities as food, shelter, clean water, and health care. The AIDS epidemic is fueled in large part by poverty. Only 4% of AIDS sufferers receive proper treatment, and most of these individuals live in industrialized countries. There is little money available in the developing world for prevention efforts or AIDS medicines. As a result, 2.2 million Africans died of AIDS in 1 year. Sixty-eight million people worldwide are expected to succumb to the disease over the next two decades.[13]

Most of us would agree that (a) leaders deserve more rewards because they assume greater risks and responsibilities, and (b) some leaders get more than they deserve. Beyond this point, however, our opinions are likely to diverge. Americans are divided over such questions as the following: How many additional privileges should leaders have? What should be the relative difference in pay and benefits between workers and top management? How do we close the large gap between the world's haves and have nots? We'll never reach complete agreement on these issues, but the fact remains: privilege is a significant ethical burden associated with leadership. Leaders must give questions of privilege the same careful consideration as questions of power. The shadow cast by the abuse of privilege can be as long and dark as that cast by the misuse of power.

THE SHADOW OF DECEIT

Leaders have more access to information than do others in an organization. They are more likely to participate in the decision-making processes, network with managers in other units, have access to personnel files, and formulate long-term plans. Knowledge is a mixed blessing. Leaders must be in the information loop in order to carry out their tasks, but possessing knowledge makes life more complicated. Do they reveal that they are "in the know?" When should they release information and to whom? How much do they tell? Is it ever right for them to lie?

No wonder leaders are tempted to think ignorance is bliss! If all of these challenges weren't enough, leaders face the very real temptation to lie or hide the truth to protect themselves. Tobacco executives, for instance, swore before Congress that smoking was safe even though they had sponsored research that said otherwise. Bill Clinton tried to salvage his image and his presidency by proclaiming "I did not have sexual relations with that woman" (Monica Lewinsky).

The issues surrounding access to information are broader than deciding whether to lie or to tell the truth. Ethicist Sissela Bok in her book *Lying: Moral Choice in Public and Private Life* defines lies as messages designed to make other people believe what we ourselves don't believe.[14] Although leaders often decide between lying and truth telling, they are just as likely to be faced with questions related to the release of information. Take the case of a middle manager who has learned about an upcoming merger that will mean layoffs. Her superiors have asked her to keep this information to herself for a couple of weeks until the deal is completed. In the interim, employees may make financial commitments (home and car purchases) that they would postpone if they knew that major changes were in the works. Should she voluntarily share information about the merger despite her orders? What happens when a member of her department asks her to confirm or deny the rumor that the company is about to merge? (Case Study 1.1 describes a particularly troubling example of how one group of leaders kept vital data to themselves.)

Privacy issues raise additional ethical concerns. Customers of US Bank were outraged to find out that the firm had sold their personal financial information to other companies. E-commerce firms routinely track the activity of Internet surfers, collecting and selling information that will allow marketers to better target their advertisements. Telephone companies can use information gathered from customers to sell additional services to these same subscribers without their knowledge. Hundreds of thousands of video cameras track our movements at ATMs, parking lots, stores, and other public places. Videotapes made for security purposes have shown up on Web sites.[15]

In sum, leaders cast shadows not only when they lie but also when they engage in deceptive practices. Deceitful leaders

- deny having knowledge that is in their possession

- withhold information that followers need

- use information solely for personal benefit

- violate the privacy rights of followers

- release information to the wrong people

- put followers in ethical binds by preventing them from releasing information that others have a legitimate right to know

CASE STUDY 1.1

Keeping It to Themselves:
Personal Injury Lawyers and Firestone Tires

Sometimes concealing information can have deadly consequences. In 1996, a group of personal injury lawyers in Texas noticed that there were problems with Firestone ATX tires mounted on Ford Explorer sport utility vehicles. They hired a leading traffic investigator, Sean Kane, who confirmed their suspicions. The tires separated when they got hot, causing rollovers.

Kane and the attorneys kept their findings to themselves. They didn't file safety complaint forms with the National Highway Traffic Safety Administration (NHTSA) that likely would have prompted government investigations. The lawyers didn't alert NHTSA in part because they didn't trust the agency. Judges had dismissed earlier lawsuits involving tires and SUVs because NHTSA failed to find defects in the products. Attorneys also didn't think that there were enough crashes involving ATX tires to trigger a product recall. Most important, filing safety notices would reduce their chances of winning in court. Evidence that goes into the public record makes it easier for automakers to defend themselves. Personal injury lawyers typically work on a contingency basis, collecting a portion of a settlement. Defeat means that neither victims nor attorneys receive any money.

Kane did make an effort in 1998 to publicize the ATX problem without going directly to federal officials. He notified reporters at several television news-magazines about the defect but none ran the story. In the meantime, the crashes and deaths mounted. One hundred ninety out of the 203 reported ATX tire-related deaths occurred between 1996 (when the trial lawyers first noticed the problem) and 2000, the year that NHTSA opened its investigation and millions of the defective tires were recalled. Ford got wind of problems by 1999, but its safety engineers were misled by the fact that there were very few complaints about the tires in the national database.

The trial lawyers and their consultant did not break any laws by keeping their safety concerns to themselves. They were under no legal obligation to reveal what they knew. Further, they were fulfilling their primary duty: serving the interests of their clients. The fact remains, however, that lives could have been saved had they come forward. Ricardo Martinez was administrator of the NHTSA between 1994 and 1999. He says he would have immediately ordered an investigation if he had been alerted to the tire's problems. A trauma doctor, Martinez draws this comparison between his role as a physician and the choices of the lawyers in this case:

> It's outrageous—I can't say that enough. If I saw something was killing my patients and I didn't say anything because that would reduce the demand for my services, I would be putting my benefit over the benefit of my patients and the public, and that would clearly be unethical.

DISCUSSION PROBES

1. Was the decision of personal injury lawyers to keep ATX tire problems to themselves "outrageous" and unethical? Why? Why not?

2. Evaluate the role of safety consultant Kane. What was his obligation to the attorneys? to the general public? Did he do enough by alerting reporters, but not the government, to potential problems?

3. Should attorneys be required to alert federal agencies about potential public safety problems?

4. What criteria should attorneys use to decide when the interests of the community outweigh their duties to their clients?

REFERENCE

Bradsher, K. (2001, June 24). Firestone tire flaw unreported for 4 years. *The Oregonian,* p. 3M.

Patterns of deception, whether they take the form of outright lies or hiding or distorting information, destroy the trust that binds leaders and followers together. Consider the popularity of conspiracy theories, for example. Many citizens are convinced that the Air Force is hiding the fact that aliens landed in Roswell, New Mexico. They also believe that law enforcement officials are deliberately ignoring evidence that John F. Kennedy and Martin Luther King were the victims of elaborate assassination plots. These theories may seem illogical, but they flourish, in part, because government leaders have created a shadow atmosphere through deceit. It wasn't until after the First Gulf War that we learned that our "smart bombs" weren't really so smart and missed their targets. The president and other cabinet officials apparently overstated the danger posed by Saddam Hussein in order to rally support for the Second Gulf War.

Leaders must also consider ethical issues related to the image they hope to project to followers. In order to earn their positions and to achieve their objectives, leaders carefully manage the impressions they make on others. Impression management can be compared to a performance on a stage.[16] Leader-actors carefully manage everything from the setting to their words and nonverbal behaviors in order to have the desired effect on their follower audiences. Presidential staffers, for example, makes sure that the chief executive is framed by visual images (Mt. Rushmore, the American flag, the deck of an aircraft carrier) that reinforce his messages as well as his presidential standing. Like politicians, leaders in charge of such high-risk activities as mountain climbing or white-water kayaking also work hard to project the desired impressions. In order to appear confident and competent, they stand up straight, look

---

Box 1.2

Leadership Ethics at the Movies:
Saving Private Ryan

Key Cast Members: Tom Hanks, Matt Damon, Tom Sizemore, Edward Burns, Jeremy Davies

Synopsis: After landing on the beaches of Normandy, an Army captain (Tom Hanks) is asked to lead seven men on a mission to find and return a private who parachuted behind German lines. All three of the private's brothers have been killed in battle, and Army Chief of Staff George Marshall wants to spare the private's mother any additional grief. The company loses two of its members while locating Private Ryan (Matt Damon), who does not want to be rescued. The rescue party and the remnants of Ryan's paratroop unit then combine forces to hold a strategic bridge. This film is likely to increase your appreciation for those who fought in World War II.

Rating: R, for some of the most intense, graphic war sequences ever filmed and for profanity

Themes: conflicting duties, loyalty, sacrifice, obedience, the horrors of war, courage under fire, morality on the battlefield, impression management

---

followers in the eye, use an authoritative tone of voice, talk about their wealth of experience, and calm the fears of the group.

Impression management is integral to effective leadership because followers have images of ideal leaders called prototypes.[17] We expect that the mountain climbing guide will be confident (otherwise we would cancel the trip!), that the small-group leader will be active in group discussions, that the military leader will stay calm under fire. The closer the individual is to the ideal, the more likely it is that we will select that person as leader and accept her or his influence. Nonetheless, a number of students find impression management ethically troubling. They value integrity and see role-playing as insincere because the leader may have to disguise his or her true feelings in order to be successful. In the film *Saving Private Ryan,* described in Box 1.2, the army captain played by Tom Hanks appears calm and collected when leading his squad of soldiers. This facade crumbles when he is alone. His hands shake, and at one point he breaks out in uncontrollable sobs. Is the captain morally justified in hiding his true emotional state from his followers? Some in my classes think he is not.

One final note on impression management: even if you believe that leaders are justified in masking their feelings to project the desired image, there is no doubt that impression management can be used to reach immoral ends. Many demagogues, like Huey Long and George Wallace, have used public speaking performances to rally audiences to destructive causes, for instance. When considering the morality of impression management, we need to consider its end products. Ethical impression managers meet group wants and needs, not just the leaders'. They spur followers toward highly moral ends. Unethical impression managers produce the opposite effects, subverting group wishes and lowering purpose and aspiration.

THE SHADOW OF INCONSISTENCY

Leaders deal with a variety of constituencies, each with its own set of abilities, needs, and interests. In addition, they like some followers better than others. The leader-member exchange theory (LMX) is based on the notion that leaders develop closer relationships with one group of followers.[18] Members of the "in-group" become advisers, assistants, and lieutenants. High levels of trust, mutual influence, and support characterize their exchanges with the leader. Members of the "out-group" are expected to carry out the basic requirements of their jobs. Their communication with the leader is not as trusting and supportive. Not surprisingly, members of in-groups are more satisfied and productive than members of out-groups. For that reason, LMX theorists have begun to explore ways that leaders can develop close relationships with all of their followers.

Situational variables also complicate leader-follower interactions. Guidelines that work in ordinary times may break down under stressful conditions. A professor may state in her syllabus that five absences will result in flunking a class, for instance. However, she may have to loosen her standard if a flu epidemic strikes the campus.

Diverse followers, varying levels of relationships, and elements of the situation make consistency an ethical burden of leadership. Should all followers be treated equally even if some are more skilled and committed or closer to us than others? When should we bend the rules and for whom? Shadows arise when leaders appear to act arbitrarily and unfairly when faced with questions like these, as in the case of a resident assistant who enforces dormitory rules for some students but ignores infractions committed by friends. Of course, determining whether a leader is casting light or shadow may depend on where you stand as a follower. When Michael Jordan played for the Chicago Bulls, Coach Phil Jackson allowed him more freedom than other players. Jordan was comfortable with this arrangement, but his teammates weren't as enthusiastic.

Issues of inconsistency can also arise in a leader's relationships with those outside the immediate group or organization. Until recent reforms, for example, Merrill Lynch and other investment banks provided important clients with benefits denied ordinary investors. Investment banks manage the stock offerings of companies going public for the first time. Bankers gave executives doing business with their firms the opportunity to buy initial public offering (IPO) shares. During the stock market boom of the 90s, IPO stocks often increased dramatically in value in a matter of hours or days, creating a financial windfall for these privileged insiders.[19]

Misgivings about the current system of financing political elections stems from the fact that large donors can "buy" access to elected officials and influence their votes. Laws often favor those who have contributed the most, as in the case of the nation's electric utilities. Utility contributions ($18.9 million during the 2000 presidential campaign alone) were rewarded with legislation and policies loosening federal restrictions on their operations. Critics charge that deregulation allowed Southern, Texas El Paso, Reliant, Entergy, and other energy giants to dominate power generation and transmission in Britain, Argentina, Brazil, Pakistan, and other nations.[20]

THE SHADOW OF MISPLACED AND BROKEN LOYALTIES

Leaders must weigh a host of loyalties or duties when making choices. In addition to their duties to employees and stockholders, they must consider their obligations to their families, local communities, professions, larger society, and the environment. Noteworthy leaders put the needs of the larger community above selfish interests. The Ben & Jerry's Corporation, for example, receives praise for its "capitalism with a conscience." The firm supports Vermont dairy farmers, promotes peace, and helps the homeless, among other causes. In contrast, those who appear to put their interests first are worthy of condemnation. Doctors at The Ohio State University Medical Center were harshly criticized for putting the needs of their hospital and the medical profession ahead of the public's in the case of Michael Swango. Swango, a doctor, stands accused of killing 60 patients. Nurses accused Swango of poisoning patients when he was an internist at The Ohio State University Medical Center. Yet faculty put their loyalty to their young colleague and the hospital above the needs of the sick. They believed Swango instead of the nurses (who were of lower status) and protected the image of the hospital by undermining any criminal investigation. Administrators appeared more interested in fending off potential lawsuits than in finding out the truth. As a result of these misplaced loyalties, Swango received his medical license, and he allegedly continued his career as a killer.[21]

Loyalties can be broken as well as misplaced. If anything, we heap more scorn on those who betray our trust than on those who misplace their loyalties. Many of history's villains are traitors—Judas Iscariot, Benedict Arnold, Vidkin Quisling (he sold out his fellow Norwegians to the Nazis), and Tokyo Rose, a U.S. citizen who broadcast to American troops on behalf of the Japanese in

World War II. Enron CEO Ken Lay provides a contemporary example of a leader who violated the trust of followers (see the Casting Shadows at Enron Chapter End Case). Lay betrayed employees by assuring them that the firm was in good shape even as it was headed toward collapse.

Mergers and acquisitions are common forms of corporate betrayal. Executives of the new conglomerate typically assure consumers that they will benefit from the merger. Quality and service, they claim, will improve, not suffer. Employees are told that the best elements of their current companies will be maintained. Sadly, these promises are broken more often than not. Quality and service decline as the new firm cuts costs to pay for its expansion. Important corporate values like family support and social responsibility are lost and benefits slashed.

As egregious as these corporate examples of betrayal appear, they pale in comparison to cases of Catholic priests who sexually abused children in their care. As you'll see in Chapter 4, clergy in Boston, Portland, New Mexico, and elsewhere used their positions as respected spiritual authorities to gain access to young parishioners for sexual gratification. Bishops and cardinals failed to stop the abusers. In far too many cases, they let offending priests continue to minister to and have contact with children. Often church officials transferred pedophiles without warning their new congregations about these priests' troubled pasts.

The fact that I've placed the loyalty shadow after such concerns as power and privilege should not diminish its importance. Philosopher George Fletcher argues that we define ourselves through our loyalties to families, sports franchises, companies, and other groups and organizations.[22] Political strategist James Carville points out that the significance of loyalty is reflected in the central role it plays in drama. "Take apart any great story," he claims, "and there's loyalty at its heart."[23] As evidence of this fact, he points to Shakespeare's *Romeo and Juliet, The Godfather* trilogy, the HBO series *The Sopranos,* and even episodes of *The Andy Griffith Show* (Carville doesn't claim to have excellent taste).

You may think that Carville overstates his case, but the fact remains: loyalty is a significant burden placed on leaders. In fact, well-placed loyalty can make a significant moral statement. Such was the case with Pee Wee Reese. The Brooklyn Dodger never wavered in his loyalty to Jackie Robinson, the first black player in the major leagues. In front of one especially hostile crowd in Cincinnati, Reese put his arm around Robinson's shoulders in a display of support.[24]

Pay particular attention to the shadow of loyalty as you analyze the feature films highlighted in each chapter. In most of these movies, leaders struggle with where to place their loyalties and how to honor the trust that others have placed in them.

THE SHADOW OF IRRESPONSIBILITY

Earlier we noted that the breadth of responsibility is one of the factors distinguishing between the leader and follower roles. Followers are largely responsible for their own actions or, in the case of a self-directed work team, for their peers. This is not the case for leaders. They are held accountable for the performance of their entire department or unit. However, determining the extent of a leader's responsibility is far from easy. Can we blame a college coach for the misdeeds of team members during the off season or for the excesses of the university's athletic booster club? Are Nike executives responsible for the actions of their overseas contractors who force workers to work in sweatshops? Do employers "owe" followers a minimum wage level, a certain degree of job security, and safe working conditions? If military officers are punished for "following orders," should their supervisors receive the same or harsher penalties? Rabbis and pastors encourage members of their congregations to build strong marriages. Should they lose their jobs when they have affairs?

Leaders act irresponsibly when they (a) fail to take reasonable efforts to prevent followers' misdeeds, (b) ignore or deny ethical problems, (c) don't shoulder responsibility for the consequences of their directives, (d) deny their duties to followers, or (e) hold followers to higher standards than themselves. We don't hold coaches responsible for everything their players do. Nonetheless, we want them to encourage their athletes to obey the law and to punish any misbehavior. Most of us expect Nike to make every effort to treat its overseas labor force fairly, believing that the company owes its workers (even the ones employed by subcontractors) decent wages and working conditions. We generally believe that officers giving orders are as culpable as those carrying them out and have little tolerance for religious figures and others who violate their own ethical standards. For that reason, former Secretary of Education William Bennett, the author of *The Book of Virtues,* came under attack for advocating moderation and other character traits at the same time that he was unable to control his gambling habit.

Many corporate scandals demonstrate what can happen when boards of directors fail to live up to their responsibilities. Far too many boards were rubber stamps. Made up largely of friends of the CEO and those doing business with the firm, they were quick to approve executive pay increases and other management proposals. Some directors appeared only interested in collecting their fees and made little effort to understand the company's operations or finances. Other board members were well intentioned but lacked expertise. Now federal regulations require that the chair of the audit committee be a financial expert. The compensation, audit, and nominating committees must be made up of individuals who have no financial ties to the organization. These requirements should help prevent future abuses, but only if directors take their responsibilities seriously.

These, then, are some the common shadows cast by leaders faced with the ethical challenges of leadership. Identifying these shadows raises an important question: *Why is it, when faced with the same ethical challenges, that some leaders cast light and others cast shadow?* In the next chapter, we'll explore the forces that contribute to the shadow side of leadership.

Implications and Applications

- The contrast between ethical and unethical leadership is as dramatic as the contrast between light and darkness. Take care lest you cast more shadow than light.
- Certain ethical challenges or dilemmas are inherent in the leadership role. If you choose to become a leader, recognize that you accept ethical burdens along with new tasks, expectations, and rewards.
- Power may not be a dirty word, but it can have a corrosive effect on values and behavior. You must determine how much power to accumulate, what forms of power to use, and how much power to give to followers.
- Abuse of privilege is the evil twin of power. If you abuse power, you'll generally overlook the needs of followers as you take advantage of the perks that come with your position.
- Access to information will complicate your life. In addition to deciding whether or not to tell the truth, you'll have to determine when to reveal what you know and to whom, how to gather and use information, and so on.
- Creating the desired impression is critical to effective leadership. However, impression management increases the danger of sacrificing integrity and sincerity for image.
- A certain degree of inconsistency is probably inevitable in leadership roles, but you'll cast shadows if you are seen as acting arbitrarily and unfairly.
- As a leader, you'll have to balance your needs and the needs of your small group or organization with loyalties or duties to broader communities. Expect condemnation if you put narrow, selfish concerns ahead of those of society as a whole.
- Leadership brings a broader range of responsibility, but determining the limits of accountability may be difficult. You'll cast a shadow if you fail to make a reasonable attempt to prevent abuse or to shoulder the blame, deny that you have a duty to followers, or hold others to a higher ethical standard than you are willing to follow.

For Further Exploration, Challenge, and Self-Assessment

1. Create an ethics journal. In it describe the ethical dilemmas you have encountered as a leader and follower, how you resolved them, how you felt about the outcomes, and what you learned that will transfer to future ethical decisions. You may also want to include your observations about the moral choices made by public figures. Make periodic entries as you continue to read this text.

2. How does powerlessness corrupt? What are some of the symptoms of powerlessness?

3. What factors do you consider when determining the extent of your loyalty to an individual, group, or organization?

4. In a group, determine if and when impression management is ethical. Keep a record of your deliberations, including the issues you discuss, disagreements and differences between members, and your final conclusions. Report your findings to the rest of the class. If you are unable to reach consensus, describe the elements that still divide you.

5. Evaluate the work of a corporate or nonprofit board of directors. Is the board made up largely of outside members? Are directors qualified? Does the board fulfill its leadership responsibilities? Write up your findings.

6. Which shadow are you most likely to cast as a leader? Why? What can you do to cast light instead? Can you think of any other ethical shadows cast by leaders?

7. Look for examples of unethical leadership behavior in the news and classify them according to the six shadows. What patterns do you note?

CASE STUDY 1.2

Chapter End Case: Casting Shadows at Enron

During the 1990s, Enron was one of the fastest growing, most admired companies in the United States. From its humble origins as a regional natural gas supplier, the Houston firm grew to become the seventh largest company on the *Fortune 500*. In 2000, the company employed 21,000 people, and its stock hit an all-time high of $90 per share.

Enron appeared regularly on lists of the nation's best companies, receiving accolades for its innovative climate. The firm focused on energy transportation, trading, and financing and developed new ways to market nontraditional commodities like broadband width. Founder and CEO Kenneth Lay was profiled in a number of business magazines, gave generously to local charities, and golfed regularly with Presidents Clinton and Bush.

Rising stock values and revenues were the glue that held the company together. To keep debt (which would lower the price of the stock by lowering earnings) off the books, Chief Financial Officer Andrew Fastow created special purpose entities (SPEs). These limited partnerships with outside investors enable firms to share risks while hiding deficits. Although SPEs are legal and used in many industries, Enron's partnerships didn't have enough outside investors. In essence, the company was insuring itself. Employees who managed these investments made millions while acting against the best interests of the firm.

In 2001, losses in overseas projects and a major subsidiary caused a financial meltdown. Enron's stock price dropped, and the company was unable to back its guarantees. Financial analysts and journalists who had previously sung the company's praises began to question Enron's financial statements. In the midst of the unfolding disaster, Chairman Lay repeatedly assured employees that the stock was solid. At one point he declared, "Our performance has never been stronger; our business model has never been more robust; our growth has never been more certain."[25] At the same time that he was making these optimistic pronouncements, Lay and other officials were calling Bush cabinet members to ask them to intervene on the firm's behalf. Arthur Andersen auditors then forced the company to restate earnings and the Securities and Exchange Commission (SEC) began to investigate.

Enron filed for bankruptcy in December 2001, and in January 2002, Lay resigned. Both Fastow and his deputy pled guilty for their roles in creating and managing the illegal partnerships. Enron energy traders also entered guilty pleas for manipulating electricity markets.

Greed, pride, lack of internal controls, pressure to make quarterly earnings projections, and other factors all played a role in Enron's collapse. However, most of the blame must go to the firm's executives, who failed to meet each of the challenges of leadership described in the chapter. Leaders at Enron cast shadows by the following:

Abuse of power. Both Lay and Jeffrey Skilling (Lay's short-term replacement) wielded power ruthlessly. The position of vice-chair was known as the "ejector seat" because so many occupants were removed from the position when they took issue with Lay. Skilling frequently intimidated subordinates.

Excess privilege. Excess typified top management at Enron. Lay told a friend, "I don't want to be rich, I want to be world-class rich."[26] At another point he joked that he had given wife Linda a $2 million decorating budget for a new home in Houston that she promptly exceeded. Lay and other executives were able to unload their shares even as employees' 401K accounts (largely made up of Enron stock) were wiped out.

Deceit. Enron officials manipulated information to protect their interests and to deceive the public, although the extent of their deception is still to be determined. Both executives and board members claim that they weren't aware of the company's off-the-books partnerships and shaky financial standing. However, both Skilling and Lay were warned that the firm's accounting tactics were suspect, and the Senate Permanent Subcommittee on Investigations concluded, "Much that was wrong with Enron was known to the board."[27]

Inconsistent treatment of internal and external constituencies. Five hundred Enron officials received "retention bonuses" totaling $55 million after the firm filed for bankruptcy. At the same time, layed off workers received only a fraction of the severance pay they had been promised. Outsiders also received inconsistent treatment. The company was generous with its friends. As the top contributor to the Bush campaign, Enron used this leverage to nominate friendly candidates to serve on the SEC and the Federal Energy Regulatory Commission (FERC). Company representatives also helped set federal energy policy that deregulated additional energy markets for Enron's benefit. In contrast, critics of the company could expect retribution. Investment bankers who expressed the least bit of doubt about Enron lost underwriting business from the firm. Stock analysts who were critical lost their jobs.

Misplaced and broken loyalties. Enron officials put loyalty to themselves above loyalty to everyone else with a stake in the company's fate—stockholders, business partners, ratepayers, local communities, and foreign governments. They also abused the trust of those who worked for them. Employees felt betrayed, in addition to losing their jobs and retirement savings,

Irresponsibility. Enron's leaders acted irresponsibly by failing to take needed action, failing to exercise proper oversight, and failing to shoulder responsibility for the ethical miscues of their organization. CEO Lay downplayed warnings of financial improprieties and some board members didn't understand the company's finances or operations. Too often managers left employees to their own devices, encouraging them to achieve financial goals by any means possible. Neither CEO stepped forward to accept blame for what happened after the firm's collapse. Lay invoked Fifth Amendment privileges against self-incrimination; Skilling claimed ignorance.

DISCUSSION PROBES

1. Which attitudes and behaviors of Enron's leaders do you find most offensive? Why?

2. Did one shadow caster play a more important role than the others in causing the collapse of Enron? If so, which one and why?

3. How much responsibility should the board of directors assume for what happened at Enron?

4. What similarities do you see between what happened at Enron and at other well-known companies accused of ethical wrongdoing?

5. What can be done to prevent future Enrons?

6. What leadership lessons do you draw from this case?

REFERENCES

Case adapted from the following:

Johnson, C. (2002, November). *Enron's ethical collapse: Lessons from the top*. Paper delivered at the meeting of the National Communication Association, New Orleans, LA.
Johnson, C. (2003). Enron's ethical collapse: Lessons for leadership educators. *Journal of Leadership Education, 2*. Retrieved February 7, 2004, from www.fhsu.edu/jole/issues/archive_index.html.

CASE STUDY 1.3

Chapter End Case: The Patriot Act: Abuse of Power?

After the World Trade Center bombings of September 11, 2001, Congress swiftly passed the USA Patriot Act by an overwhelming margin. The legislation (set to expire in 2005) gives more power to law enforcement officials to fight terrorism. Under the law,

1. Investigators can examine book and computer records at libraries and bookstores. They must get a search warrant, but these proceedings are overseen by the Foreign Intelligence Surveillance Court, which operates in secret. Libraries cannot notify patrons that their records are being monitored.

2. The FBI can seek "any tangible things" from businesses when conducting terrorism investigations. These might include documents, records, and computer data. Once again, those who supply information are forbidden from revealing that a request has been made. There is no way to know who has been targeted for investigation.

3. Colleges and universities must enter information about all foreign students, faculty, and researchers into a national data system. Students from "enemy" countries cannot work at high-security sites.

4. Aid of any kind, even humanitarian assistance, cannot be provided to groups that the U.S. government considers terrorist organizations.

5. Illegal immigrants can be more easily detained and held for deportation.

6. Justice Department officials can conduct secret searches of homes and offices under the "sneak and peek" provision of the act.

7. Law enforcement and intelligence agencies are permitted to share much more information with each other than they could before 9/11.

The Patriot Act has become the center of controversy, even though it passed with little debate. Both liberal (American Civil Liberties Union, American Library Association) and conservative (Rutherford Institute, Free Congress Foundation) groups argue that the bill gives too much power to law enforcement at the expense of civil liberties. A number of local and state governments have passed resolutions condemning sections of the act; some libraries are immediately destroying patron records. Congress has so far turned back attempts to make the Patriot Act permanent and to extend its powers in Patriot Act II. In fact, selected provisions of the current law may be repealed. A federal judge has ruled that a section of the act that prohibits giving expert advice or assistance to foreign terrorist organizations violates free speech rights.

Attorney General Ashcroft argues that the bill has been an effective weapon against terrorism and that critics are overreacting: "The Patriot Act simply does not allow federal law enforcement free or unfettered access to local libraries, bookstores or other businesses."[28] He asserts that only a few warrants for library information have been issued and that, in the past, grand juries could subpoena such records without the involvement of a judge. Further, the use of wiretaps is a "time-tested, law enforcement-honored, court-sanctioned and understood technique which is now being extended into the arena of terror."[29]

Critics are unmoved by Ashcroft's claims. They note that Justice Department leaders have refused to reveal just how many warrants have been issued and to whom, claiming that this information is classified. Representative James Sensenbrenner, Jr., chair of the House Judiciary Committee, declared through an aide that the life of the Patriot Act would continue only "over his dead body."[30]

DISCUSSION PROBES

1. How do you feel about the possibility that the FBI and other law enforcement officials could examine your personal records without your knowledge?

2. What kind of restrictions should be put on foreign students, faculty, and researchers studying and working in the United States?

3. Are critics overreacting to the Patriot Act as Ashcroft and others have claimed?

4. Does the Patriot Act put too much power in the hands of law enforcement officials?

5. Should it be revoked or should it be extended?

6. Under what circumstances should security needs take precedence over civil liberties?

REFERENCES

Bravin, J. (2004, January 17). Judge deals blow to the Patriot Act. *The Wall Street Journal*, p. A6.

Clymer, A. (2003, June 20). Threats and responses: Domestic security. *The New York Times*, p. A12.

Eggen, D. (2003, July 31). Seizure of business records is challenged; ACLU and Arab American groups file lawsuit over element of USA Patriot Act. *The Washington Post*, p. A2.

Guy, S. (2003, July 30). Scientists raise concerns about impact of Patriot Act. *Chicago Sun-Times* I-zine scene, p. 68.

Lichtblau, E. (2003, May 9). Aftereffects: Surveillance; GOP makes deal in Senate to widen anti-terror power. *The New York Times*, p. A1.

Lichtblau, E. (2003, July 31). Threats and responses; Civil liberties; Suit challenges constitutionality of powers in antiterrorism law. *The New York Times*, p. A17.

Neives, E. (2003, April 21). Local officials rise up to defy the Patriot Act. *The Washington Post*, p. A1.

Sanchez, R. (2003, April 10). Librarians make some noise over Patriot Act. *The Washington Post*, p. A20.

Sarasohn, D. (2003, August 3). Refocusing on our rights. *The Oregonian*, pp. E1, E2.

Schmidt, S. (2003, June 6). Ashcroft wants stronger Patriot Act; Expanded death penalty and bond changes sought. *The Washington Post*, p. A11.

Notes

1. Palmer, P. (1996). Leading from within. In L. C. Spears (Ed.), *Insights on leadership: Service, stewardship, spirit, and servant-leadership* (pp. 197–208). New York: Wiley, p. 200.

2. Jung, C. B. (1933). *Modern man in search of a soul.* New York: Harcourt Press.

3. Palmer (1996), Leading from within, p. 200.

4. French, R. P., & Raven, B. (1959). The bases of social power. In D. Cartwright (Ed.), *Studies in social power* (pp. 150–167). Ann Arbor: University of Michigan, Institute for Social Research.

5. Hackman, M. Z., & Johnson, C. E. (2004). *Leadership: A communication perspective* (4th ed.). Prospect Heights, IL: Waveland Press, ch. 5.

6. Kanter, R. M. (1979, July-August). Power failure in management circuits. *Harvard Business Review, 57,* 65–75.

7. Pfeffer, J. (1992, Winter). Understanding power in organizations. *California Management Review,* 29–50.

8. Hornstein, H. A. (1996). *Brutal bosses and their prey.* New York: Riverhead Books.

9. Kipnis, D., Schmidt, S., Swafflin-Smith, C., & Wilkinson, I. (1984, Winter). Patterns of managerial influence: Shotgun managers, tacticians, and bystanders. *Organizational Dynamics,* 58–67.

10. Colvin, G. (2001, June 25). The great CEO pay heist. *Fortune,* 64–70.

11. Huffington, A. (2003). *Pigs at the trough: How corporate greed and political corruption are undermining America.* New York: Crown.

12. Bing, S. (2000). *What would Machiavelli do? The ends justify the meanness.* New York: HarperBusiness.

13. Income disparity statistic taken from *Money* (2000, March), p. 30. Data about the AIDS epidemic taken from Sternberg, S. (2002, July 2). AIDS will claim 68 million more in 20 years, U. N. says. *USA Today,* p. 10D.

14. Bok, S. (1979). *Lying: Moral choice in public and private life.* New York: Vintage Books.

15. Goodman, E. (2002, October 6). Freeze-frame nation. *The Oregonian,* p. C3.

16. Goffman, E. (1959). *The presentation of self in everyday life.* Garden City, NY: Doubleday.

17. Hall, R. J., & Lord, R. G. (1998). Multi-level information processing explanations of followers' leadership perceptions. In F. Dansereau & F. J. Yammarino (Eds.), *Leadership: The multiple-level approaches* (Vol. 2, pp. 159–190). Stamford, CT: JAI; Lord, R. G., & Mahar, K. J. (1991). *Leadership and information processing: Linking perceptions and performance.* Boston, MA: Unwin Hyman.

18. For more information on LMX theory, see Graen, G. B., & Cashman, J. F. (1975). A role-making model of leadership in formal organizations. In J. G. Hunt & L. L. Larson (Eds.), *Leadership frontiers* (pp. 143–65). Kent, OH: Kent State University Press.

Graen, G. B., & Scandura, T. (1987). Toward a psychology of dyadic organizing. *Research in Organizational Behavior, 9,* 175–208.

Graen, G. B., & Uhl-Bien, M. (1998). Relationship-based approach to leadership. Development of leader-member exchange (LMX) theory of leadership over 25 years: Applying a multi-level multi-domain perspective. In F. Dansereau & F. J. Yammarino (Eds.), *Leadership: The multiple-level approaches* (pp. 103–158). Stamford, CT: JAI.

Vecchio, R. P. (1982). A further test of leadership effects due to between-group variation and in-group variation. *Journal of Applied Psychology, 67,* 200–208.

19. Time to outlaw sweetheart IPOs. (2003, May 16). *Rocky Mountain News,* p. 46A.

20. Palast, G. (2003). *The best democracy money can buy* (rev. Am. ed.). New York: Plume, chs. 2, 3.

21. The terrifying story of Dr. Swango is told in Stewart, J. B. (1999). *Blind eye: How the medical establishment let a doctor get away with murder.* New York: Simon & Schuster.

22. Fletcher, G. (1993). *Loyalty: An essay on the morality of relationships.* New York: Oxford University Press.

23. Carville, J. (2000). *Stickin': The case for loyalty.* New York: Simon & Schuster, p. 183.

24. Rampersad, A. (1997). *Jackie Robinson.* New York: Knopf.

25. Cruver, B. (2002). *Anatomy of greed: The unshredded truth from an Enron insider.* New York: Carroll and Graf, p. 92.

26. Cruver (2002), *Anatomy of greed,* p. 23.

27. Associated Press (2002, July 7). Report: Enron board aided collapse. Retrieved August 8, 2002, from www.msncbc.com/news/777112.asp

28. Clymer, A., (2003, June 20). Threats and responses: Domestic security. *The New York Times,* p. 12.

29. Clymer (2003, June 20), Threats and responses, p. 12.

30. Lichtblau, E. (2003, May 9). Aftereffects: Surveillance. GOP makes deal in Senate to widen antiterror power, *The New York Times,* p. A1.

2

Shadow Casters

In the deeps are the violence and terror of which psychology has warned us. But if you ride these monsters down, if you drop with them farther over the world's rim, you find what our sciences can not locate or name, the substrate, the ocean or matrix or ether which buoys the rest, which gives goodness its power for good, and evil its power for evil, the unified field: our complex and inexplicable caring for each other, and for our life together here.

Writer Annie Dillard

What's Ahead

In this chapter, we look at why leaders cast shadow instead of light. Shadow casters include (a) inner motivations or "monsters," (b) faulty decision making caused by errors in thinking, groupthink, organizational pressures to violate personal moral codes, and cultural variables, (c) an inactive or overactive moral imagination, (d) ethical ignorance, and (e) ethical flabbiness that comes from a lack of moral exercise. To address these shadow casters, we need to engage in leadership development aimed at expanding our ethical capacity as leaders. Effective leadership development programs incorporate assessment, challenge, and support, and they broaden our knowledge, skills, perspectives, and motivation.

Only humans seem to be troubled by the question "why?" Unlike other creatures, we analyze past events (particularly the painful ones) to determine their causes. The urge to understand and to account for the ethical failures of leaders has taken on added urgency with the recent spate of corporate scandals. Observers wonder, "Why would bright, talented CEOs steal from their companies, lie to investors, engage in insider trading, use corporate jets to move family furniture, and avoid taxes?" "Why can't multimillionaire executives be satisfied with what they already have?" "Why do they feel they need more?" (See Box 2.1 for one set of answers to these questions.)

Box 2.1

The Warped Minds of Top CEOs

Writers at *USA Today* asked a group of corporate psychologists to describe the internal motivation of greedy top executives like Dennis Kozlowski (Tyco), Jack Welch (General Electric), Gary Winnick (Global Crossing), and John Rigas (Adelphia). The experts concluded that the seemingly insatiable desires of out-of-control CEOs have less to do with money and more to do with the following:

Poor self-image. Many CEOs (i.e., Martha Stewart) have low self-esteem and want to put their humble pasts behind them. They try to make up for their feelings of inadequacy by "building monuments to themselves." Sadly, this strategy never works.

The "I deserve it" myth. Many C-level executives believe that they should get all the credit for their firms' successes. This type of reasoning accounts for Jack Welch's belief that he deserved the lavish retirement package originally granted to him at retirement.

Unchecked fantasies. The desires of most people are controlled by harsh reality. We don't have the money or power to make our dreams come true. Not so with some CEOs. Boards of directors or public opinion didn't rein them in, so they were free to do what they wanted, no matter how outrageous.

Society's blessing. CEOs have gotten the message that they can do whatever they want as long as they produce results. The media has fueled this belief by making business executives heroes with the same status as sports stars.

Competitiveness gone awry. Corporate executives compete with their peers for higher and higher salaries and perks.

Lonesome soldier syndrome. People at the top find it hard to make friends because they fear that others are only attracted by their power. Expensive things then take the place of relationships.

Boredom. Many CEOs at the peak of their careers don't know what to do next. They may invent new challenges that put them in moral jeopardy.

Power corrupts. Executives lose the sense of what is rightfully theirs and what isn't. They become like medieval kings, treating others like peasants and claiming all that they see.

SOURCE: Horovitz, B. (2002, October 11). Scandals grow out of CEOs warped mind-set. *USA Today,* pp. 1B, 2B.

Coming up with an explanation provides a measure of comfort and control. If we can understand *why* something bad has happened (broken relationships, cruelty, betrayal), we may be able to put it behind us and move on. We are also better equipped to prevent something similar from happening again. Such is the case with shadows. Identifying the reasons for our ethical failures (what I'll call "shadow casters") is the first step on the path out of the darkness they create.

As you read about the shadow casters, keep in mind that human behavior is seldom the product of just one factor. Leaders struggling with insecurities, for example, are particularly vulnerable to external pressures. Faulty decision making and inexperience often go hand in hand; we're more prone to make poor moral choices because we haven't had much practice.

Shadow Casters

THE MONSTERS WITHIN

Parker Palmer believes that leaders project shadows out of their inner darkness. That's why he urges leaders to pay special attention to their motivations lest "the act of leadership create more harm than good." Palmer identifies five internal enemies or "monsters" (a term he borrows from the Annie Dillard quote at the beginning of the chapter) living within leaders that produce unethical behavior.[1] I'll include one additional monster to round out the list.

Monster 1: Insecurity. Leaders are frequently deeply insecure people who mask their inner doubts through extroversion and by tying their identity to their roles as leaders. Who they are is inextricably bound to what they do. Leaders project their insecurities on others when they use followers to serve their selfish needs.

Monster 2: Battleground mentality. Leaders frequently use military images when carrying out their tasks, speaking of "wins" and "losses," "allies" and "enemies," and "doing battle" with the competition. For example, IBM chief Lou Gerstner inspired hatred of Microsoft by projecting a picture of Bill Gates on a large screen and telling his managers: "This man wakes up hating you."[2] Acting competitively becomes a self-fulfilling prophecy; competition begets competitive responses in return. This militaristic approach can be counterproductive. More often than not, cooperation is more productive than competition. Instead of pitting departments against each other, for instance, a growing number of companies use cross-functional project teams and task forces to boost productivity.

Monster 3: Functional atheism. Functional atheism refers to a leader's belief that she or he has the ultimate responsibility for everything that happens in a group or organization. "It is the unconscious, unexamined conviction within us that if anything decent is going to happen here, I am the one who needs to make it happen."[3] This shadow destroys both leaders and followers. Symptoms include high stress, broken relationships and families, workaholism, burnout, and mindless activity.

Monster 4: Fear. Fear of chaos drives many leaders to stifle dissent and innovation. They emphasize rules and procedures instead of creativity and consolidate their power instead of sharing it with followers.

Monster 5: Denying death. Our culture as a whole denies the reality of death; and leaders, in particular, don't want to face the fact that projects and programs should die if they're no longer useful. Leaders also deny death through their fear of negative evaluation and public failure. Those who fail should be given an opportunity to learn from their mistakes, not be punished. Only a few executives display the wisdom of IBM founder Thomas Watson. A young executive entered his office after making a $10 million blunder and began the conversation by saying, "I guess you want my resignation." Watson answered: "You can't be serious. We've just spent $10 million educating you!"[4]

Monster 6: Evil. There are lots of other demons lurking in leaders and followers alike—greed, jealousy, envy, rage—but I want to single out evil for special consideration. Palmer doesn't specifically mention evil as an internal monster, but it is hard to ignore the fact that some individuals seem driven by a force more powerful than anxiety or fear. Teenage insecurities and a desire to vanquish their enemies sparked the murderous rampage of Dylan Klebold and Eric Harris at Columbine High. However, these factors don't totally explain how these privileged, suburban children became heartless killers. Evil may help us answer the question "why?" when we're confronted with monstrous shadows like those cast by the Columbine shooters or the Chechen terrorists who killed Russian school children.

Faulty Decision Making

Identifying inner monsters is a good first step in explaining the shadow side of leadership. Yet well-meaning, well-adjusted leaders can also cast shadows, as in the decision to storm the Branch Davidian compound in Waco, Texas, in 1993. Instead of waiting for the cult members to peacefully surrender, FBI agents and other law enforcement officers launched a tank and tear gas attack. Eighty cult members, including some of the children that officials were trying to protect, died when cult leader David Koresh and his followers decided to take their own lives rather than be captured. The failed mission fanned antigovernment sentiment. Timothy McVeigh bombed the federal building in Oklahoma City on the second anniversary of the Davidian disaster.[5]

Blame for many ethical miscues can be placed on the way in which ethical decisions are made. Moral reasoning, although focused on issues of right and wrong, shares much in common with other forms of decision making. Making a wise ethical choice involves many of the same steps as making other important decisions—identifying the issue, gathering information, deciding on criteria, weighing options, and so on. A breakdown anywhere along the way can derail the process.

Decision-making experts David Messick and Max Bazerman speculate that many unethical business decisions aren't the product of greed or callousness but stem instead from widespread weaknesses in how people process information and make decisions. In particular, executives have faulty theories (a) about how the world operates, (b) about other people, and (c) about themselves.[6]

Theories about how the world operates. These assumptions have to do with determining the consequences of choices, judging risk, and identifying causes. Executives generally fail to take into account all the implications of their decisions (see Box 2.2). They overlook low-probability events, fail to consider all the affected parties, think they can hide their unethical behavior from the public, and downplay long-range consequences. In determining risk, decision makers generally fail to acknowledge that many events happen by chance or are out of their control. America's involvement in Vietnam, for example, was predicated on the mistaken assumption that the United States could successfully impose its will in the region. Other times, leaders and followers mislabel risks, thus minimizing the dangers. For instance, a new drug seems more desirable when it is described as working half of the time rather than as failing half of the time.

The perception of causes is the most important of all our theories about the world because determining responsibility is the first step to assigning blame or praise. In the United States, we're quick to criticize the person when larger systems are at fault. Consider the Sears automotive repair scandal, for example. Investigators discovered that Sears automotive technicians, who were paid commissions based on the number and cost of the repairs they ordered, charged customers for unnecessary work. Although the mechanics should be held accountable for their actions, the commission system was also at fault. Executives should be blamed for creating a program that rewarded dishonesty. Messick and Bazerman also point out that we're more likely to blame someone else for acting immorally than for failing to act. We condemn the executive who steals. However, we are less critical of the executive who doesn't disclose the fact that another manager is incompetent.

Box 2.2

Decision-Making Biases

Theories of the World

- ignoring low-probability events even when they could have serious consequences later
- limiting the search for stakeholders and thus overlooking the needs of important groups
- ignoring the possibility that the public will find out about an action
- discounting the future by putting immediate needs ahead of long-term goals
- underestimating the impact of a decision on a collective group (industry, city, profession, etc.)
- acting as if the world is certain instead of unpredictable
- failure to acknowledge and confront risk
- framing risk differently than followers
- blaming people when larger systems are at fault
- excusing those who fail to act when they should

Theories About Other People

- believing that our group is normal and ordinary (good) whereas others are strange and inferior (bad)
- giving special consideration and aid to members of the "in-group"
- judging and evaluating according to group membership (stereotyping)

Theories About Ourselves

- rating ourselves more highly than other people
- underestimating the likelihood that negative things will happen to us, like divorce, illness, accidents, and addictions
- believing that we can control random events
- overestimating our contributions and the contributions of departments and organizations
- being overconfident, which prevents us from learning more about a situation
- concluding that the normal rules and obligations don't apply to us

---

SOURCES: Box reprinted from Hackman, M. Z., & Johnson, C. E. (2004). *Leadership: A communication perspective* (4th ed.). Prospect Heights, IL: Waveland Press. Reprinted by permission.

Messick, D. M., & Bazerman, M. H. (1996, Winter). Ethical leadership and the psychology of decision making. *Sloan Management Review,* 9–23.

Theories about other people. These are "our organized beliefs about how 'we' differ from 'they'" (competitors, suppliers, managers, employees, ethnic groups). Such beliefs, which we may not be aware of, influence how we treat other people. Ethnocentrism and stereotyping are particularly damaging. *Ethnocentrism* is the tendency to think that we are better than they, that our way of doing things is superior to theirs. We then seek out (socialize with, hire) others who look and act like us. Military leaders often fall into the trap of ethnocentrism when they underestimate the ability of the enemy to resist hardships. For example, commanders have no trouble believing that their own citizens will survive repeated bombings but don't think that civilian populations in other nations can do the same. Such was the case in World War II. The British thought that bombing Berlin would break the spirit of the Germans, forgetting that earlier German air raids on London had failed to drive Britain out of the war. Similar reasoning fed into the decision to storm the Branch Davidian compound. FBI officers underestimated the commitment of Koresh and his followers to their cause. They thought that Koresh was afraid of physical harm and would surrender rather than risk injury. Instead, he led his followers in a mass suicide.[7]

Stereotypes, our beliefs about other groups of people, are closely related to ethnocentrism. These theories (women are weaker than men, Asians have technical but not managerial skills, the mentally challenged can't do productive work) can produce a host of unethical outcomes, including sexual and racial discrimination.

Theories about ourselves. The last group of theories concerns self-perceptions. Leaders need to have a degree of confidence to make tough decisions, but their self-images are often seriously distorted. Executives tend to think they (and their organizations) are superior, are immune to disasters, and can control events. No matter how fair they want to be, leaders tend to favor themselves when making decisions. Top-level managers argue that they deserve larger offices, more money, or stock options because their divisions contribute more to the success of the organization. Overconfidence is also a problem for decision makers because it seduces them into thinking that they have all the information they need, so they fail to learn more. Even when they do seek additional data, they're likely to interpret new information according to their existing biases.

Messick and Bazerman emphasize that unrealistic self-perceptions of all types put leaders at ethical risk. Executives may claim that they have a "right" to steal company property because they are vital to the success of the corporation. Over time they may come to believe that they aren't subject to the same rules as everyone else or that they'll never get caught.

The loftier a leader's position, the greater the chances that he or she will overestimate his or her abilities. Powerful leaders are particularly prone to think they are godlike. They develop what Harvard psychologist Robert Sternberg calls a sense of omniscience (being all-knowing), a sense of omnipotence (being all-powerful), and a sense of invulnerability (being safe from all harm).[8] Top leaders can mistakenly conclude they know everything because they have access to many different sources of information and followers look to them for answers. They believe that they can do whatever they want because they have so much power. Surrounded by an entourage of subservient staff members, these same officials are convinced that they will be protected from the consequences of their actions. Former President Clinton's affair with Monica Lewinsky demonstrates the impact of these delusions. Caught up in the power of his position, Clinton didn't expect to be found out or to face negative repercussions from his actions.

Contextual Pressures

Faulty individual beliefs aren't the only factors contributing to breakdowns in the ethical decision-making process. Group, organizational, and cultural forces are at work as well. Conformity is a problem for many small groups. Members put a higher priority on cohesion than on coming up with a well-reasoned choice. They pressure dissenters, shield themselves from negative feedback, keep silent when they disagree, and so on.[9] Members of shadowy groups engage in unhealthy communication patterns that generate negative emotions while undermining the reasoning process. Some organizations are also shadow lands. Car dealerships, for instance, are known for their deceptive practices, and computer retailers are rapidly earning the same reputation. Obviously, working in such environments makes moral behavior much more difficult, but no organization is immune from ethical failure. Top managers at some organizations may fire employees who talk about ethical issues so that they can claim ignorance if followers do act unethically. This "don't ask, don't tell" atmosphere forces workers to make ethical choices on their own without the benefit of interaction. They seldom challenge the questionable decisions of others and assume that everyone supports the immoral acts.

Organizational communication scholars Charles Conrad and Marshall Scott Poole also identify a number of less obvious, "hidden" organizational pressures that derail the ethical decision-making process.[10] Division of labor allows low-level employees to claim that they just follow orders and upper level employees to claim that they only set broad policies and, therefore, can't be held accountable for the illegal acts of their subordinates. When tasks are broken down in small segments, workers may not even know that they are engaged in an improper activity. The secretary who shreds documents, for example, may not realize that the papers are wanted in a civil or criminal investigation.

Socialization is yet another hidden pressure that can encourage employees to violate their personal codes. Organizations use orientation seminars and other means to help new hires identify with the group (see the Arthur Andersen case at the end of Chapter 9). Loyalty to the organization is essential. However, the socialization process may blind members to the consequences of their actions. This may have happened at Microsoft. A federal judge ruled that the company used unfair tactics in order to monopolize software and Web browser markets. Many Microsoft executives and employees refused to acknowledge any wrongdoing. Instead, they claimed that the court's ruling was just the latest in a series of unfair attacks against the company. In addition, the pressures of organizational, ethical decision making also create a kind of "ethical segregation." Leaders and followers may have strong personal moral codes that regulate their personal lives but act much less ethically while at work.

Cultural differences, like group and organizational forces, can also encourage leaders to abandon their personal codes of conduct. A corporate manager from the United States may be personally opposed to bribery. Her company's ethics code forbids such payments and so does federal law. She may, nonetheless, bribe customs and government officials in her adopted country if (a) such payments are an integral part of the national culture, and (b) appear to be the only way to achieve her company's goals.

Inactive or Overactive Moral Imagination

According to many ethicists, moral imagination—being sensitive to moral issues and options—is the key to ethical behavior.[11] In the next chapter, for example, you'll read how awareness of possible ethical problems is the first step in moral judgment and action. University of Virginia professor Patricia Werhane offers an extended definition of moral imagination. Those with moral imagination are sensitive to ethical dilemmas, she argues, but can also detach themselves from the immediate situation in order to see the bigger picture. They recognize their typical ways of thinking and set aside these normal operating rules to come up with creative solutions that are "novel, economically viable, and morally justifiable."[12]

Werhane cites Merck CEO Roy Vagelos (profiled at the end Chapter 3) as one example of a leader with a vivid moral imagination. He proceeded with the development of the drug Mectizan (which treats river blindness) even though the product didn't fit the company's criteria that every drug should generate $20 million in profits. When relief agencies didn't step forward to fund and distribute the drug, Merck developed its own distribution system in poor nations. In contrast, NASA engineer Roger Boisjoly recognized the ethical problem of launching the *Challenger* shuttle in cold weather in 1985 but failed to generate a creative strategy for preventing the launch. He stopped objecting and deferred to management (normal operating procedure). Boisjoly made no effort to go outside the chain of command to express his concerns to the agency director or to the press. As a result, the *Challenger* exploded on liftoff, killing all seven aboard. (See Chapter 8 for a description of the causes of the recent *Columbia* shuttle disaster.)

Leaders fail to exercise moral imagination in large part because they are victims of their typical mental models or scripts. Scripts are mental shortcuts that enable decision makers to process data rapidly in order to make quick choices. We function easily in class, for instance, because we have well-developed scripts about how class periods are structured, what roles professors and students play, and so forth. Unfortunately, our scripts can leave out the ethical dimension of a situation. Consider the case of Ford Motor's failure to recall and repair the gas tanks on Pintos manufactured between 1970 and 1976. Gas tanks on these subcompacts were located behind the rear axle and ruptured during low-speed, rear-end collisions. Fuel ignited by sparks would then engulf the car in flames. Fixing the problem would have only cost $11 per vehicle, but Ford refused to act. The firm believed that all small cars were inherently unsafe and that customers weren't interested in safety. Further, Ford managers conducted a cost-benefit analysis and determined that the costs in human life were less than the costs to repair the problem.

The National Highway Traffic Safety Administration (NHTSA) finally forced Ford to recall the Pinto in 1978. By that time the damage had been done. The company lost a major lawsuit brought by a burn victim. In a trial involving the deaths of three Indiana teens in a rear-end crash, Ford became the first major corporation to face criminal, not civil, charges for manufacturing faulty products. The automaker was later acquitted, but its image was severely tarnished.

Business professor Dennis Gioia, who served as Ford's recall coordinator from 1973 to 1975, blames moral blindness for the company's failure to act.[13] Ethical considerations weren't part of the safety committee's script. The group made decisions about recalls based on the number of incidents and cost-benefit analyses. Because there were only a few reports of gas tank explosions and the expense of fixing the tank didn't seem justified, members decided not to act. At no point did Gioia and his colleagues question the morality of putting a dollar value on human life and of allowing customers to die in order to save the company money.

Werhane cautions that moral imagination can also become overactive when leaders and followers focus on creativity at the expense of ethical common sense. For example, managers and employees at personal computer disk manufacturer MiniScribe tried to meet impossible sales goals in the 1980s by double shipping to customers, making up accounts, altering auditors' reports, and at one point, shipping bricks in disk drive cartons. These were highly

---

Box 2.3

Leadership Ethics at the Movies: *Insomnia*

Key Cast Members: Al Pacino, Robin Williams, Hilary Swank, Martin Donovan.

Synopsis: Veteran police LAPD detective Will Dormer (Pacino) and his colleague Hap Echohart (Donovan) are under investigation for shaking down drug dealers and planting false evidence. The duo travels to a small town in Alaska to take charge of a murder case while distancing themselves from the scandals in Los Angeles. Dormer shoots Echohart (who has agreed to cooperate with Internal Affairs), either accidentally or on purpose. He then tries to pin the blame on the murder suspect—local author Walter Finch (Williams). Wracked by guilt and tormented by the midnight sun, Dormer finds it impossible to sleep. At the same time, he must outwit Finch who knows his terrible secret. Swank plays an earnest police rookie faced with a choice between lying to protect Dormer's reputation or telling the truth and maintaining her integrity.

Rating: R for language and violence

Themes: inner demons, moral choices, ends vs. means, deceit, loyalty, character

---

creative but highly immoral responses to an ethical dilemma. (For another example of a group that put innovation above ethics, read the DARPA Chapter End Case.) Audi had to recall its 5000 series German automobile when drivers and the media claimed that the vehicle suffered from an acceleration problem. As it turned out, deaths that were believed linked to a mechanical defect were really the result of drivers accidentally putting their foot on the accelerator instead of on the brake. Hyperactive moral imagination created a false scenario that cost Audi 80% of its market share.

Ethical Deficiencies

Leaders may unintentionally cast shadows because they lack the necessary knowledge, skills, and experience. Not understanding how to go about making ethical decisions can be an issue; so can ignorance of ethical perspectives or frameworks that can be applied to ethical dilemmas. Every year in my introductory communication class, I ask students to read and respond to the hypothetical Multiplied Abused Children Case (Case Study 2.1). Groups of students generally reach a consensus about whether Hanson was justified in exaggerating his statistics in order to raise money for this most worthy cause. When I ask them about the standards they used to reach their conclusions, however, they generally give me a blank look. Some teams make their decision based on personal feelings ("We don't like to be lied to no matter how good the cause."). Other groups employ a widely used ethical principle ("Lying is always wrong." "It's okay to lie if more people are helped than hurt.") in their deliberations but don't realize that they've done so.

It's possible to blunder into good ethical choices, but it's far more likely that we'll make wise decisions when we are guided by some widely used ethical principles and standards. These ethical theories help us define the problem, highlight important elements of the situation, force us to think systematically, encourage us to view the problem from a variety of perspectives, and strengthen our resolve to act responsibly.

CASE STUDY 2.1

The Multiplied Abused Children

Save The Kids is a nonprofit group that pushes for tougher laws against those who sexually abuse children. Currently Save The Kids is in its biggest lobbying effort ever in an attempt to get the state legislature to pass a law that requires convicted sex offenders to register their whereabouts with local police departments. The organization's founder, Steve Hanson, is convinced that such a law can significantly reduce the number of child abuse cases in the state. Unfortunately, contributions aren't keeping up with expenses, and Save The Kids may have to drastically reduce its lobbying efforts just as the sex offender registration bill comes before the legislature. Chances are that this law will only pass if Save The Kids keeps up its lobbying campaign. Mr. Hanson is now raising money for Save The Kids through a series of speeches. To encourage contributions, Hanson knowingly exaggerates both the number of convicted sex offenders in the state as well as the number of children who are abused every year.

DISCUSSION PROBES

1. Do you agree with Hanson's decision to exaggerate in order to raise money for Save The Kids? Why or why not?

2. Does the amount of exaggeration make a difference in your evaluation of Hanson's action? What if he decides to only slightly exaggerate? What if he greatly inflates the figures?

3. Does the fact that Hanson intentionally lied make a difference in how you evaluate his decision? What if he exaggerated because he didn't check his facts carefully?

4. How do you determine whether or not someone is justified in lying? What standards do you use to determine whether or not you should tell the truth?

Making and implementing ethical decisions takes both critical thinking and communication skills. We must be able to articulate our reasoning, convince other leaders of the wisdom of our position, and work with others to put the choice into place. A manager who wants to eliminate discriminatory hiring practices, for instance, will have to listen effectively, gather information, analyze and formulate arguments, appeal to moral principles, and build relationships. Failure to develop these skills will doom his reform effort.

Ethicist Rushworth Kidder, in a book with the intriguing title *How Good People Make Tough Choices,* encourages readers to develop their ethical fitness by putting their ethical commitments to work in real-life settings.[14] Kidder's exhortation implies that many of us are ethically unfit or flabby. Faulty decision making, ethical ignorance, and underdeveloped skills surely contribute to this condition, but lack of practice plays a role as well. Studying ethical theories and discussing ethical cases are essential to any ethical fitness program. Reasoning and communication skills can be sharpened during class. Ultimately, however, we need the firsthand experience that comes from tackling real-life leadership dilemmas.

Stepping Out of the Shadows: Expanding Our Ethical Capacity

Taking on the role of leader is a "stretching" experience. We must acquire additional skills to tackle broader responsibilities (see our discussion of the difference between leading and following in Chapter 1) and master a new set of ethical dilemmas. This requires continuous leadership development. Researchers at the Center for Creative Leadership (CCL) define leadership development as "the expansion of a person's capacity to be effective in leadership roles and processes."[15] Leadership development programs assume (a) that individuals can expand their leadership competence, and (b) that the skills and knowledge they acquire will make them more effective in a wide variety of leadership situations, ranging from business and professional organizations to neighborhood groups, clubs, and churches.

The CCL researchers report that individuals develop a number of capacities in leadership development programs, including heightened self-confidence, greater creativity, and a broader, systematic point of view. We can and should expand our ethical capacity as well. Business ethicist Lynn Sharp Paine describes moral thinking as "an essential capability" for organizational managers.[16] She contrasts *moral reasoning,* which is concerned with ethical principles and the consequences of choices, with *strategic* or results-based thinking, which focuses on reaching objectives like increased revenue, finding new distributors, or manufacturing products. Although distinct, these two strands of reasoning intertwine. Managers making strategic choices ought to consider important moral principles and weigh potential ethical consequences or outcomes. If they don't, their organizations lose the right to operate in modern society. Conversely, managers must be good strategic thinkers in order to make wise moral decisions. They must understand how their groups operate, for example, in order to implement their ethical choices.

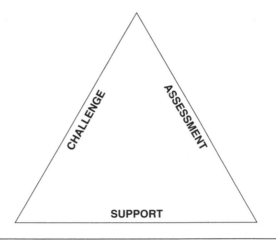

Figure 2.1   Developmental Components

The same elements that go into developing other leadership competencies also go into building our ethical effectiveness. The three most important components of the leadership development process, according to the CCL researchers, are assessment, challenge, and support (see Figure 2.1).

Successful developmental programs provide plenty of feedback that lets participants know how they are doing and how others are responding to their leadership strategies. Assessment data provokes self-evaluation ("What am I doing well?" "How do I need to improve?") and provides information that helps answer these questions. Simply put, a leader learns to identify gaps between current performance and where he or she needs to be. The most powerful leadership experiences also challenge people. As long as individuals don't feel the need to change, they won't. Difficult experiences force leaders outside their comfort zones and give them the opportunity to practice new skills. To make the most of feedback and challenges, leaders need support. Supportive comments ("I appreciate the effort you're making to become a better listener." "I've got confidence that you can handle this new assignment.") sustain the leader during the struggle to improve. The most common source of support is other people (family, coworkers, bosses), but developing leaders can also draw on organizational and learning resources. Supportive organizations believe in continuous learning (more on this in Chapter 9), help individuals develop growth plans, provide funds for training, reward progress, and so on. Learning resources include mentors, experts, conferences, books, Web sites, tapes, and DVDs.

All three elements—assessment, challenge, and support—should be part of your plan to increase your ethical capacity. You need feedback about how well you handle ethical dilemmas, how others perceive your character, and how your decisions affect followers. You need the challenges and practice that come from moving into new leadership positions. Seek out opportunities to influence others by engaging in service projects, chairing committees, teaching children, or taking on a supervisory role. You also need the support of others to maximize your development. Talk with colleagues about ethical choices at work, draw on the insights of important thinkers, and find groups that will support your efforts to change.

Feedback, challenge, and support are incorporated into the design of this book. To encourage assessment, I ask you to reflect on and evaluate your own experiences and to get feedback from others. A self-assessment instrument is included in every chapter of this edition (see Box 2.4) along with additional self-analysis activities at the end of every chapter. To highlight challenge, I introduce a number of cases and encourage you to explore ideas further. To provide support, I gather and organize concepts from a variety of sources, identify additional resources, tell the stories of leaders, and encourage you to work with others (friends, small group members, classmates) to increase your ethical competence. Make this text one part of a larger, ongoing program to develop your ethical capacity and other leadership abilities.

The remaining chapters are based on the foundation laid in these first two. Now that we have identified the leader's shadows and their causes, we're ready to expand our ethical capacity to better master them. Ethical capacity, according to the Center for Creative Leadership, consists of knowledge, skills, perspectives, and motivations. You need to increase your understanding, sharpen your skills, broaden your worldview, and strengthen your motivation to become more ethically competent. (A model of this process is found in Figure 2.2.) Expect to learn new terminology along with key principles, decision-making formats, and important elements of the ethical context. This information will be drawn from a number of different fields of study—philosophy, communication, theology, psychology, political science, organizational behavior—because we need insights from many different disciplines if we're to step out of the shadows. You can anticipate reading about and then practicing a variety of skills, ranging from information gathering to listening and conflict management. Some material will encourage you to challenge your assumptions and to develop new perspectives on ethical problems. You'll also find that motivation is a central concern of this book. I'll touch on the "why" of ethics when discussing such topics as character, altruism, communitarianism, and servant leadership.

Part II, Looking Inward, focuses on the inner dimension of leadership. Chapter 3 examines the role of character development in overcoming our internal enemies, and Chapter 4 explores the nature of evil, forgiveness, and spirituality. Part III, Ethical Standards and Strategies, addresses our ethical deficiencies by describing ethical theories and techniques that can be applied

Box 2.4

Self-Assessment

ETHICAL SELF-AWARENESS INSTRUMENT

The following survey is designed to provide you with feedback about your ethical self-understanding. Respond to each of the following items on a scale of 1 (strongly disagree) to 5 (strongly agree). The higher your total score (maximum 60), the more aware you think you are of your ethical strengths and weaknesses, motivations, personal mission, values, and self-confidence. Pay particular attention to lower-ranked items. You may want to address these thoughts, feelings, and behaviors in your development plan in question 6, For Further Exploration, Challenge, and Self-Assessment, at the end of the chapter.

1. _____ I can tell other people what is most important to me.

2. _____ I periodically think about my priorities in life.

3. _____ I spend quite a bit of time thinking about ethical issues and problems.

4. _____ As I grow older, I sense more ethical problems in the world.

5. _____ I am confident in my ability to make good moral decisions.

6. _____ I have written a personal mission statement.

7. _____ Once I decide what to do, I generally follow through on my ethical choice.

8. _____ The subject of ethics frequently comes up when I talk with my friends, fellow students, and coworkers.

9. _____ I do the right thing no matter what the consequences.

10. _____ I can defend my ethical choices when challenged by others.

11. _____ I have a clear sense of what I want to accomplish in life.

12. _____ Others think of me as someone with high moral standards.

_____ Total

to ethical problem solving. Chapters 5 and 6 survey a wide range of perspectives, both general and leader-focused, which can help us set moral priorities. Chapter 7 then describes systems or formats that we can use to make better ethical choices. Part IV, Shaping Ethical Contexts, looks at ways that leaders can

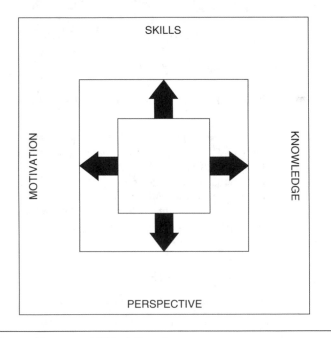

Figure 2.2   Elements of Ethical Capacity

shed light in a variety of situations. Chapter 8 examines ethical group decision making; Chapter 9 describes the creation of ethical organizational climates; and Chapter 10 highlights the challenges of ethical diversity.

The ultimate goal of developing ethical capacity is to cast light rather than shadow. However, measuring your progress toward this goal is more difficult than, say, determining whether or not you are mastering the principles of accounting or learning computer skills. There is no one widely accepted ethics exam to tell you how you stack up against other leaders. Further, ethical development, like other aspects of leadership development, never ends. We never reach a point at which we can say that we have reached full ethical capacity, that we have "arrived" as moral leaders. We can always develop further.

Marking our progress may be difficult for the reasons described above, but it is not impossible. You'll know that you are becoming more ethically competent if you note the following milestones.[17]

- *Greater self-awareness.* Feedback and personal reflection (particularly on the inner dimension of leadership) will deepen your self-understanding. You'll become more aware of your strengths, weaknesses, and motivations. You should develop a clearer grasp of your personal mission and your values. At the same time, you will likely become more aware of the purposes, values, and moral blind spots you share in common with others in your group or organization.

- *Greater self-confidence.* Participants in leadership development programs often rate self-confidence as the most important outcome of their experiences. They become more self-assured as they master new, difficult situations and are more willing to take on greater leadership challenges. Expect the same benefit from mastering ethical dilemmas. As you resolve moral problems, you should gain the confidence you need to shoulder the heavier ethical burdens that come with greater responsibilities.
- *Stronger character.* Character consists of displaying admirable qualities in a variety of settings. (More on this in the next chapter.) You can mark your progress by noting if you consistently demonstrate positive traits no matter in what context you find yourself.
- *Healthy moral imagination.* Expanding your ethical capacity will make you aware of a wider array of ethical problems. You'll become more sensitive to the presence of ethical dilemmas and issues. In addition, you'll break out of your normal patterns of thinking to develop creative solutions that are grounded in moral principles.
- *Sounder moral reasoning.* Rejecting faulty assumptions, building arguments, gathering information, and taking a systematic approach to problem solving are all part of reasoned ethical decision making. You should be able to offer a well-thought, thorough defense of the conclusions you reach. Sound moral reasoning, as noted earlier, employs widely used ethical standards and principles while anticipating the likely consequences of choices.
- *Greater resistance to outside pressures.* Resisting group, organizational, and cultural pressures to set aside your personal convictions is an important sign of growth.
- *Better follow-through.* There is a gap between believing and doing. Holding the right values and making reasoned choices is not enough; you must follow through by implementing your choices. Acting on what you think and believe is a significant indication that you're making ethical progress.
- *Healthier ethical climate.* Progress comes from reshaping the ethical environment in addition to resisting it. Expanding ethical capacity means working to change the climate of your small group, organization, and community.

Now that we've identified the key components of a successful leadership development program, defined ethical capacity, and identified some visible outcomes of ethical growth, we're ready to end the chapter by putting these elements together with the comprehensive model of ethical development found in Figure 2.3.

Implications and Applications

- Unethical/immoral behavior is the product of a number of factors, both internal and external. All of these elements must be addressed if you want to cast light rather than shadow.
- "Good" leaders can and do make bad ethical decisions. Honorable intentions alone won't save you from casting shadows.

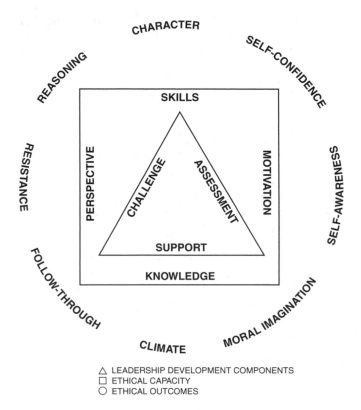

Figure 2.3   Ethical Capacity Development Model

- Beware of faulty assumptions about how the world operates, other people, and yourself. These can lead to underestimating risks and overestimating your abilities and your value to your organization.
- Never put cohesion first when making important group decisions.
- Your organization, no matter how high-minded, may undermine your personal moral code.
- Exercise your moral imagination (be sensitive to ethical issues, step outside your normal way of thinking, come up with creative solutions). However, don't let your imagination become overactive, causing you to substitute creativity for sound reasoning and evidence.
- When it comes to ethics, ignorance is dangerous. Learning about ethical standards and principles will likely help you make wiser ethical choices.
- Experience is vital. Put what you're learning to use in solving real-life ethical dilemmas.
- Leadership development (expansion of your capacity to be effective in leadership roles and processes) provides a useful framework for understanding ethical growth. You develop your ethical capacity (which is made up of knowledge,

skills, perspectives, and motivations) in the same way that you develop your other leadership capacities—through assessment, challenge, and support.
- Ethical development is a lifelong process. You're making progress if you demonstrate one or more of the following: (a) greater self-awareness and self-confidence, (b) strong, consistent character, (c) healthy moral imagination, (d) sound moral reasoning, (e) resistance to pressures to compromise personal standards, (f) better follow-through on choices, and (g) creation of a healthier ethical climate.

For Further Exploration, Challenge, and Self-Assessment

1. What monsters would you add to the list provided in the chapter?

2. Analyze a time when you cast a shadow as a leader or as a follower. Which of the shadow casters led to your unethical behavior?

3. Does your employer pressure you to abandon your personal moral code of ethics? If so, how? What can you do to resist the pressure?

4. Describe a time when you exercised or failed to exercise moral imagination.

5. Can you think of any other signs of ethical progress beyond those named in the chapter?

6. Create a plan for expanding your ethical capacity that incorporates assessment, challenge, and support.

CASE STUDY 2.2

Chapter End Case: Betting on Terrorism

The Defense Advance Research Projects Agency, or DARPA, is probably the most creative agency in the federal government. Founded at the beginning of the Cold War, the agency organizes and funds innovative research projects designed to strengthen the military and promote science and technology. The group is credited with the development of the Internet, global positioning, stealth fighters, and unmanned combat aircraft. It is currently investigating new stimulants to keep soldiers awake for a week, computers that correct users' mistakes, land-based combat robots, and bombs that can hit moving targets.

At times, the creativity of DARPA scientists and engineers outweighs their moral good sense. The agency was criticized for proposing the Total Information Awareness system, a gigantic computer database that would have collected and analyzed data on all Americans. However, DARPA leaders came under the most fire for the Policy Analysis Market. This innocent-sounding program was designed to encourage traders to "bet" on the likelihood of acts of terrorism or assassinations in the Middle East. For example, participants could buy future contracts on the likelihood of a biological weapons attack on Israel and the assassination of Palestinian leader Yasser Arafat. Developers of the program believed that this terrorist futures market would provide more accurate predictions than more traditional intelligence-gathering methods.

Ethics was apparently not part of the script that DARPA officials followed when designing the Policy Analysis Market. Their ethical insensitivity drew attacks from senators of both parties (once they realized that the program was not a hoax). Democratic Minority Leader Tom Daschle called the terrorist futures market a "plan to trade in death." Senator Barbara Boxer (D-California) commented that she thought there is something very sick about it and that the careers of whoever thought that up should be ended. She pointed out that terrorists, knowing they were planning an attack, could have bet on the attack and collected a lot of money. Republican Majority Leader Bill Frist of Tennessee couldn't conceive of any reason why the U.S. government should be involved in a project of this nature.

The Senate called for immediate hearings on the program and eliminated its funding. Yet the agency itself continues to enjoy congressional support. Only one top DARPA official, John Poindexter, was forced to resign as a result of the scheme, and some economists continue to defend the idea of using the marketplace to anticipate future crises.

DISCUSSION PROBES

1. Do you see any merit at all in the idea of a terrorism futures market?

2. Was DARPA punished severely enough for its decision to fund the terrorism futures project?

3. What should DARPA do to ensure that ethical considerations are part of the script that members follow when designing future programs?

4. What suggestions would you make to DARPA to foster a healthy moral imagination? Would you make the same suggestions to other groups and organizations?

5. What leadership lessons do you draw from this case?

REFERENCES

Foley, J. (2003, May 19). Data debate—Security or privacy? *Information Week.* Retrieved August 12, 2003, from LexisNexis (www.lexisnexis.com/search/).

Guggenheim, K. (2003, July 29). Pentagon's threat-bet program to be canceled under fire from all sides. *Associated Press.* Retrieved August 12, 2003, from LexisNexis (www.lexisnexis.com/search/).

Guggenheim, K. (2003, July 30). GOP senators said they had few clues about terror market plans. *Associated Press,* retrieved August 12, 2003, from LexisNexis (www.lexisnexis.com/search/).

Pimentel, B. (2003, May 26). Blazing the trail for tech; Defense agency has a long history of exploring wild and risky ideas. *San Francisco Chronicle,* p. B1.

CASE STUDY 2.3

Chapter End Case:
The Ethical Saga of Salomon, Inc.

Some companies can't seem to stay out of ethical trouble. Firestone, for example, was forced to merge with Bridgestone of Japan due in part to financial losses caused by the recall of defective 500 series tires. Years later, Bridgestone/Firestone was embroiled in another scandal, this time involving ATX tires mounted on Ford Explorers (see Chapter 1). Salomon, Inc. is another company with a troubled history. The firm survived one serious scandal only to succumb to the next.

In the 1980s, giant brokerage house Salomon, Inc. was one of the most influential players in the financial world. *BusinessWeek* magazine proclaimed CEO John Gutfreund "king of Wall Street." Salomon's ethical troubles began in the firm's government securities division. When the U.S. government issues treasury bonds to finance the national debt, it relies on a select group of dealers, including Salomon, to acquire and then resell the bonds to other dealers and private individuals. This arrangement worked well for many years until Salomon's government securities trader, Paul Mozer, began to corner a large share of the market. Concerned that Salomon's growing influence would reduce income from bond sales, the Treasury Department passed a regulation (called the "Mozer Law") preventing any one brokerage and its customers from bidding on more than 35% of the total bonds available at a given auction.

Mozer protested this "rash decision" by the Treasury Department and, in February 1991, circumvented the new rule. He exceeded the 35% regulation by entering a bid from Salomon and one in the name of a customer (without that firm's knowledge or consent). Mozer later confessed to his boss, John Meriwether, but claimed that this was his first and only offense. Gutfreund and other company executives took no action against Mozer. On May 22, he once again submitted an illegal bid in the name of a customer. The firm investigated and found that Mozer had made a series of illegal bids, not just one, dating back to the previous December. On August 8, some 3 months after first hearing of Mozer's criminal behavior, Gutfreund finally revealed this information to the Treasury Department. Treasury then threatened to suspend Salomon's trading privileges. Soon Gutfreund resigned, and investor Warren Buffet assumed his role on a temporary basis. Buffet appointed himself chief legal compliance officer, ordered all Salomon officers to report every legal and moral violation (except parking tickets) directly to him, and spent hours answering the questions of federal investigators and the press.

Greed and jealousy motivated Mozer. He was paid based on his performance and was jealous of competing traders at other firms who received bigger bonuses. However, it is harder to explain the inaction of Mozer's superiors, particular CEO Gutfreund. Why did he fail to punish the rogue trader (who had antagonized government officials), and why did he wait 3 months before reporting to the Treasury Department? The executive's style may account for part of his hesitation. Gutfreund admitted that he was an "indecisive" manager. He depended heavily on the firm's "stars" (like Mozer) to produce profits. When the stars violated the rules, he was reluctant to rein them in.

Corporate culture also played a role in the scandal. Stock and bond trading is a high-stakes, high-risk business. Gutfreund sanctioned this "bet the company" atmosphere. His formula for success was to wake up every day "ready to bite the ass off a bear." Gutfreund once challenged John Meriwether to a game of liar's poker for $1 million. Meriwether responded by raising the stakes to $10 million. In liar's poker, two or more players hold a dollar bill against their chests. They make statements, some true and some false, about the serial numbers on the bills they hold. The winner is the person who correctly challenges the false claims of the other players. Gutfreund and Meriwether never played their winner-take-all game; however, their reckless example helped create a go-for-broke atmosphere that was to cost the company dearly.

Warren Buffet's single-minded devotion to restoring the firm's ethical image kept it from collapse, but the fallout, nevertheless, was severe. In addition to paying millions of dollars of fines, the company lost three quarters of its stock underwriting business, was prevented from making $4 billion in bond trades, and saw its stock value plummet. Trader Mozer spent 4 months in jail, Gutfreund lost his pension and stock options, and several executives received limited or lifetime bans from the securities market. Salomon largely regained its financial health but was acquired by the Travelers Group insurance company in 1997. A year later Travelers merged with Citicorp, and Salomon Smith Barney began to operate as the investment banking/brokerage arm of the new conglomerate.

Salomon's next ethical crisis came at the beginning of the new millennium. Salomon, Merrill Lynch, and other Wall Street firms were fined $1.4 billion for lying to investors. In some cases, brokers recommended stocks to clients that in private they referred to as "dogs" and "junk." Some of the most serious charges were leveled against Salomon's Jack Grubman who, like Mozer a decade earlier, was a company "star." Grubman was perhaps the top telecom research analyst in the world. His recommendations could make or break a phone company's stock price, and he was paid handsomely for his efforts, earning $20 million a year.

After the telecom industry crashed in 2000, New York Attorney General Eliot Spitzer, the SEC, and investor groups began to question the objectivity of Grubman's advice. Grubman was an informal adviser to WorldCom and continued to tout its stock until it was too late for investors to bail out before the firm filed for bankruptcy. Salomon investment bankers also brought pressure to bear on Grubman. The company made huge profits handling the stock offerings of public firms like WorldCom. Potential clients were much more likely to give their business to Salomon if they received a favorable rating from the firm. This pressure apparently played a part in Grubman's decision to issue a "buy" rating for AT&T Wireless stock and Winstar Communications.

Grubman accepted a lifetime ban from the securities industry in 2003 and paid a $15 million fine. State and federal investigators have broadened their probes to determine if Salomon managers were at fault for failing to properly supervise the superanalyst and if they sacrificed the interests of investors for banking fees. New federal guidelines have been instituted that clearly separate research and investment banking functions. The once proud Salomon name has been retired from Wall Street and renamed Citicorp Global Markets.

DISCUSSION PROBES

1. Why do some firms continue to experience one scandal after another?

2. What shadow casters contributed to the ethical problems of Salomon, Inc.? Was any factor more important than the others? Why?

3. Should financial services companies be prevented from offering both research advice and investment banking services?

4. How can corporate image be restored after scandals like those faced by Salomon?

5. What advice would you offer leaders supervising employee superstars like Mozer and Grubman?

6. What steps can firms, particularly ones in high-pressure, high-stakes environments, take to prevent ethical abuses?

7. What leadership lessons do you draw from this case?

REFERENCES

Etzel, B. (2002, July 1). WorldCom's wrong number. *Investment Dealers' Digest*, 9–12.
Guyon, J. (2002, October 14). The king and I. *Fortune* (Europe), 38.
Julavits, R. (2003, March 28). NASD's Grubman probe going up the ladder. *American Banker*, 20.
Lewis, M. (1989). *Liar's Poker*. New York: Norton.
Loomis, C. J., & Kahn, J. (1999, January 11). Citigroup: Scenes from a merger. *Fortune*, 76–83.
Sweeping up the street. (2003, May 12). *BusinessWeek*, 114.
Timmons, H., Cohn, L., McNamee, M., & Rossant, J. (2002, August 5). CITI's sleepless nights. *BusinessWeek*, 42–43.
Useem, M. (1998). *The leadership moment*. New York: Times Business, ch. 7.

Notes

1. Palmer, P. (1996). Leading from within. In L. C. Spears (Ed.), *Insights on leadership: Service, stewardship, spirit and servant-leadership* (pp. 197–208). New York: Wiley.

2. Bing, S. (2000). *What would Machiavelli do? The ends justify the meanness.* New York: HarperBusiness.

3. Palmer (1996), Leading from within, p. 205.

4. Garvin, D. A. (1993, July-August). Building a learning organization. *Harvard Business Review,* 78–91.

5. Milloy, R. E. (2000, June 21). 2 Sides give 2 versions of facts in Waco suit. *The New York Times,* p. A14; Johnston, D. (1995, April 25). Terror in Oklahoma: The overview. *The New York Times,* p. A1.

6. Messick, D. M., & Bazerman, M. H. (1996, Winter). Ethical leadership and the psychology of decision making. *Sloan Management Review,* 9–23.

7. Verhovek, S. H. (1993, April 22). Death in Waco: F.B.I. saw the ego in Koresh, but not a willingness to die. *The New York Times,* p. A1.

8. Sternberg R. J. (2002). Smart people are not stupid, but they sure can be foolish. In R. Sternberg (Ed.), *Why smart people can be so stupid* (pp. 232–242). New Haven, CT: Yale University Press.

9. Janis, I. (1971, November). Groupthink: The problems of conformity. *Psychology Today,* 271–279; Janis, I. (1982). *Groupthink* (2nd ed.). Boston, MA: Houghton Mifflin; Janis, I. (1989). *Crucial decisions: Leadership in policymaking and crisis management.* New York: Free Press; Janis, I., & Mann, L. (1977). *Decision making.* New York: Free Press.

10. Conrad, C., & Poole, M. S. (1998). *Strategic organizational communication: Into the twenty-first century* (4th ed.). Fort Worth, TX: Harcourt Brace, ch. 12; See also, for example, Guroian, V. (1996, Fall). Awakening the moral imagination. *Intercollegiate Review, 32,* 3–13.

11. Johnson, M. (1993). *Moral imagination.* Chicago: University of Chicago Press; Kekes, J. (1991). Moral imagination, freedom, and the humanities. *American Philosophical Quarterly, 28*(2), 101–111; Tivnan, E. (1995). *The moral imagination.* New York: Routledge, Chapman, and Hall.

12. Werhane, P. (1999). *Moral imagination and management decision-making.* New York: Oxford University Press, p. 93.

13. Gioia, D. A. (1992). Pinto fires and personal ethics: A script analysis of missed opportunities. *Journal of Business Ethics, 11,* 379–389.

14. Kidder, R. M. (1995). *How good people make tough choices: Resolving the dilemmas of ethical living.* New York: Fireside.

15. McCauley, C. D., Moxley, R. S., & Van Velsor, E. (Eds.). (1998). *The Center for Creative Leadership handbook of leadership development.* San Francisco: Jossey-Bass, p. 4.

16. Paine, L. S. (1996). Moral thinking in management: An essential capability. *Business Ethics Quarterly, 6,* 477–492.

17. Johnson, C., & Hackman, M. Z. (2002, November). *Assessing ethical competence.* Paper presented at the meeting of the National Communication Association, Atlanta, GA.

Part II

Looking Inward

3

The Leader's Character

Leadership always comes down to a question of character.

Management expert Warren Bennis

What we crave is not dignity as an end in itself, but the participation in a struggle that is dignifying.

Philosopher Stanley Hauerwas

What's Ahead

This chapter addresses the inner dimension of leadership ethics. To shed light rather than shadow, we need to develop strong, ethical character made up of positive traits or virtues. We promote character development through understanding the components of moral action, telling and living collective stories, paying attention to role models, learning from hardship, establishing effective habits, determining a clear sense of direction, and examining our values.

Elements of Character

In football, the best defense is often a good offense. When faced with high scoring opponents, coaches often design offensive game plans that run as much time as possible off the clock. If they're successful, they can rest their defensive players while keeping their opponent's offensive unit on the sidelines. Building strong, ethical character takes a similar proactive approach to dealing with our inner monsters or demons. To keep from projecting our fears on others, we need to go on the offensive, replacing or managing our insecurities through the development of positive leadership traits or qualities called virtues. Interest in virtue ethics dates from at least as far back as Plato, Aristotle, and Confucius. The premise of virtue ethics is simple: good people (those of high moral character) make good moral choices. Despite its longevity, this approach has not always been popular among scholars. Only in recent years have modern philosophers turned back to it in significant numbers.[1]

Character plays an important role in leadership. Former CEOs Jeffrey Skilling (Enron), Sam Waksal (Imclone), and Martha Stewart (Martha Stewart Living Omnimedia) cast shadows due to greed, arrogance, dishonesty, ruthlessness, and other character failings. Their lack of virtue stands in sharp contrast to the leaders of great companies described in the book *Good to Great.* Jim Collins and his team of researchers identified 11 firms that sustained outstanding performance over 15 years (cumulative stock returns 6.9 times the general market average). Collins specifically told his investigators to downplay the role of top executives at these firms so they wouldn't fall into the trap of giving CEOs too much credit. But they couldn't. Team members soon discovered that leaders of great companies like Circuit City, Kimberly-Clark, and Fannie Mae combine humility with a strong will. All of these CEOs (called Level 5 leaders) downplay their roles in their companies' success, giving accolades to others. In fact, they are uncomfortable talking about themselves. For example, Darwin Smith of Kimberly-Clark told researchers "I never stopped trying to be qualified for the job." Others were quick to say, "There are a lot of people in this company who could do my job better than I do."[2]

Level 5 leaders also live modestly. Ken Iverson of Nucor is typical of the sample. He gets his dogs from the pound and lives in a small house that has a carport instead of a garage. However, when it comes to the collective success of their companies, Iverson and his fellow leaders set high standards and persevere in the face of difficult circumstances. They don't hesitate to make tough choices like removing family members from the business or take major risks like abandoning profitable product lines. (Refer to Box 3.1 for a summary of the two sides or virtues of Level 5 leadership.)

Proponents of virtue ethics start with the end in mind. They develop a description or portrait of the ideal person (in this case a leader) and identify the admirable qualities or tendencies that make up the character of this ethical role model. They then suggest ways that others can acquire these virtues.

There seems to be widespread agreement about the qualities of model leaders. To determine if this is the case, take a blank sheet of paper and divide it into two columns. In the first column, list the qualities or characteristics you associate with a model political leader. In the second column, list the traits of an ideal business leader. Now compare your two lists. There may be minor variations between them, but chances are the similarities far outweigh the differences. Americans tell researchers that they want elected officials to act with

---

Box 3.1

The Virtues of Level 5 Leadership

Summary: The Two Sides of Level 5 Leadership

Professional Will	Personal Humility
Creates superb results, a clear catalyst in the transition from good to great.	Demonstrates a compelling modesty, shunning public adulation; never boastful.
Demonstrates an unwavering resolve to do whatever must be done to produce the best long-term results, no matter how difficult.	Acts with quiet, calm determination; relies principally on inspired standards, not inspiring charisma, to motivate.
Sets the standard of building an enduring great company; will settle for nothing less.	Channels ambition into the company, not the self; sets up successors for even greater success in the next generation.
Looks in the mirror, not out the window, to apportion responsibility for poor results, never blaming other people, external factors, or bad luck.	Looks out the window, not in the mirror, to apportion credit for the success of the company—to other people, external factors, and good luck.

SOURCE: Collins, J. (2001). *Good to great: Why some companies make the leap . . . and others don't.* New York: Harper Business, p. 38. Used by permission.

integrity, restrain their impulses, respect others, rally followers, exercise good judgment, and persist in the face of adversity.[3] These qualities are remarkably similar to what we want in our business leaders. Fifteen thousand managers from Europe, the United States, and Australia report that they most admire superiors who are honest, forward looking, inspiring, and competent.[4]

There are three important features of virtues. First, virtues are interwoven into the inner life of leaders. They are not easily developed or discarded but persist over time. Second, virtues shape both the way leaders see and behave. Being virtuous makes them sensitive to ethical issues and encourages them to act morally. Third, virtues operate independently of the situation. A virtue may be expressed differently depending on the context (what's prudent in one situation may not be in the next). Yet a virtuous leader will not abandon his or her principles to please followers or demonstrate courage only when supported by peers.[5]

Aristotle and Plato identified the primary virtues as prudence (discernment, discretion), justice (righteousness, integrity), courage (strength in the face of adversity), and self-restraint (temperance). When the Christians came along, they added faith, hope, and love. Other virtues, such as empathy, compassion, generosity, hospitality, modesty, and civility, were derived from the original seven. The number of virtues has multiplied in modern times. One recent list, for example, identifies 45 positive character traits, including such qualities as resourcefulness, liveliness, magnanimity, and decency.

Coming up with a single, universal list of virtues is not as important as blending a set of desirable qualities together to form a strong, ethical character. This is far from easy, of course. At times, our personal demons will overcome even our best efforts to keep them at bay. We're likely to make progress in some areas while lagging in others. We may be persistent yet tactless, compassionate yet humorless, honest yet impatient. No wonder some prominent leaders reflect both moral strength and weakness. Martin Luther King showed great courage and persistence in leading the civil rights movement but engaged in extramarital relationships. FDR was revered by many of his contemporaries but had a long-standing affair with Lucy Mercer. In fact, Mercer (not Eleanor Roosevelt) was present when he died.

The poor personal behavior of political leaders has sparked debate about personal and public morality. One camp argues that the two cannot be separated. Another camp makes a clear distinction between the public and private arena. According to this second group, we can be disgusted by the private behavior of a politician like Bill Clinton but vote for him anyway based on his performance in office.

I suspect that the truth lies somewhere between these extremes. We should expect contradictions in the character of leaders, not be surprised by them. Private lapses don't always lead to lapses in public judgment. On the other hand, it seems artificial to compartmentalize private and public ethics. Private tendencies can and do cross over into public decisions. FDR tried to deceive the public as well as his wife and family. He proposed expanding the number of Supreme Court justices from nine to fifteen, claiming that the justices were old and overworked. In reality, he was angry with the court for overturning many New Deal programs and wanted to appoint new justices that would support him. Roosevelt's dishonest attempt to pack the Supreme Court cost him a good deal of his popularity. In a similar fashion, Bill Clinton's moral weaknesses overshadowed many of his political accomplishments.

Fostering character is a lifelong process requiring sustained emotional, mental, and even physical effort. In the remainder of this chapter, I'll introduce a variety of factors that encourage the development of leadership virtues. These include understanding the components of moral action, the identification of role models, telling and living out shared stories, learning from hardship, cultivation of habits, creating a personal mission statement, and clarifying values.

Character Building

COMPONENTS OF MORAL ACTION

James Rest of the University of Minnesota identifies four thought processes or components that lead to ethical behavior.[6] Component 1 is *moral sensitivity*. We first need to recognize that an ethical problem exists. In addition, we must identify possible courses of action and determine the consequences of each strategy. Component 2 is *moral judgment or reasoning*, deciding which course of action is the right one to follow. Component 3 is *moral motivation*. The desire to follow moral principles generally conflicts with other values like security, social acceptance, or wealth. Ethical behavior will only result if moral considerations take precedence over competing values. Component 4 is *moral action*, the implementation stage of the model. Being motivated is not enough. Opposition, distractions, fatigue, and other factors make it tough to follow through. Overcoming these obstacles takes persistence and determination, a positive, optimistic attitude ("I can and will succeed"), and interpersonal skills. Turn to the Battling Blindness Chapter End Case for one example of a leader and organization that followed through on a significant ethical decision.

Rest presents the four processes in a logical sequence but notes that they don't always occur in this order in real life. For example, what we define as immoral (Component 2) will influence our sensitivity to moral issues (Component 1). Further, we're likely to be strong in some components and weak in others. Some individuals are sensitive to the slightest hint of impropriety. Others have to be told that a potential ethical problem exists.

Ethical breakdowns occur when one or more of the components malfunction. We can demonstrate moral sensitivity and judgment but not carry through if (a) other values become more important than moral values, and (b) we lack the necessary willpower and skills. Consider the case of the supervisor who wants to tell the truth but hesitates to confront a marginal employee about his poor performance. Her commitment to honesty may be subverted by her desire to avoid conflict and her inability to manage confrontations. As a result, she practices a form of deception by keeping unpleasant truths to herself.

Business ethics educators Charles Powers and David Vogel offer an alternative model of moral judgement.[7] They identify six factors or elements that underlie ethical decision making and follow-through. The first is *moral imagination,* the recognition that even routine choices and relationships have an ethical dimension. The second is *moral identification and ordering,* which as the name suggests, refers to the ability to identify important issues, determine priorities, and sort out competing values. The third factor is *moral evaluation,* or using analytical skills to evaluate options. The fourth element is *tolerating moral disagreement and ambiguity,* which arises when managers disagree about values and courses of action. The fifth is the ability to *integrate managerial competence with moral competence.* This integration involves anticipating possible ethical dilemmas, leading others in ethical decision making, and making sure any decision becomes part of an organization's systems and procedures. The sixth and final element is a sense of *moral obligation,* which serves as a motivating force to engage in moral judgment and to implement decisions.

Identifying your strengths and weaknesses is the first step in character formation. Both models can help you determine where you should focus your efforts. You may lack moral sensitivity or have a hard time evaluating options and tolerating disagreement. Or perhaps you lack the desire to do the right thing and want to further develop virtues, such as persistence, courage, optimism, and determination, which will enable you to implement your moral choices. With your goals in mind, you can seek out leaders who demonstrate these qualities.

FINDING ROLE MODELS

Some attempts to promote character development are as blatant as displaying lists of the virtues in prominent places. On visits to the Midwest, for example, I saw "virtue banners" hanging from the fence of an elementary school playground in a small Iowa town as well as from the lobby ceiling in an inner-city Chicago high school. Deliberate moralizing (telling children how to behave) is less effective with older students, however. Character appears to be more "caught than taught." More often than not, we learn what it means to be virtuous by observing and imitating exemplary leaders. That makes role models crucial to developing high moral character.[8] Three such role models were selected as *Time* magazine's 2002 Persons of the Year. FBI agent Coleen Rowley testified before Congress about the agency's failure to take a terrorist warning seriously before 9/11. Cynthia Cooper, an auditor at WorldCom, blew the whistle on shady accounting practices to the company board's audit committee. Enron Vice President of Development Sherron Watkins warned CEO Kenneth Lay of "an elaborate accounting hoax" that could mean disaster for the company.[9]

CASE STUDY 3.1

The Hero as Optimist: Explorer Ernest Shackleton

The early twentieth century has been called the Heroic Age of Polar Exploration. Teams of adventurers from Norway and Great Britain competed to see who would be first to reach the south pole. Antarctic expeditions faced temperatures as low as -100 degrees Fahrenheit and gale force winds up to 200 miles an hour. Britain's Captain Robert Scott tried unsuccessfully to claim Antarctica for the crown in 1901. Ernest Shackleton, who had accompanied Scott on his first journey, came within 100 miles of the pole in 1909 but had to turn back to save his party. Scott and his companions died during their second expedition launched in 1911. Norwegian Roald Amundsen, who set out at the same time as Scott, succeeded in reaching the southernmost point on earth in January 1912.

Undeterred by Amundsen's success, Shackleton decided to launch "one last great Polar journey" aimed at crossing the entire Antarctic continent. This adventure has been chronicled in a number of recent books and films. Author and museum curator Caroline Alexander provides one of the most detailed accounts in her book entitled *The Endurance: Shackleton's Legendary Antarctic Expedition*. Shackleton and his crew of 27 men set sail on their wooden sailing ship—the *Endurance*—in August 1914, just days before World War I broke out. Soon the last great polar journey turned into one of the world's most incredible tales of survival.

The *Endurance* was trapped by pack ice at the end of January, stranding the party. When the ice melted the following October (springtime in the Southern Hemisphere), it crushed and sank the ship. The crew relocated to ice floes. At the end of April, 15 months after being marooned, the group abandoned camp on the shrinking ice packs and made it to an uninhabited island in three small dories.

Shackleton and five companions then set out in one of the small boats (only 22 feet long) to reach the nearest whaling station on South Georgia Island 800 miles away. This voyage would later be ranked as one of the greatest sea journeys of all time. The odds were against the small party from the beginning. They were traveling in the dead of winter on one of the roughest oceans in the world. Darkness made navigation nearly impossible, and they survived a severe storm, one that sank a much bigger tanker sailing at the same time in the same waters. The crew overcame these hurdles and, frostbitten and soaked to the skin, reached South Georgia Island. Yet even then, their suffering was far from over. Shackleton and two colleagues had to cross a series of ridges and glaciers before reaching the whaling camp. Alexander describes how the survivors looked when they finally reached help.

> At three in the afternoon, they arrived at the outskirts of Stromness Station. They had traveled for thirty-six hours without rest. Their bearded faces were black with blubber smoke, and their matted hair, clotted with salt, hung almost to their shoulders. Their

filthy clothes were in tatters. . . . Close to the station they encountered the first humans outside their own party they had set eyes on in nearly eighteen months—two small children, who ran from them in fright. (p. 164)

It would be another 4 months before Shackleton could reach the rest of his crew stranded on the first island. Amazingly, not one member of the party died during the whole 22-month ordeal.

Many qualities made Shackleton an effective leader. He had great strength and physical stature that enabled him to endure extreme conditions and to deal with rebellious followers. He understood the skills and limitations of each expedition member and made the most of each person's abilities. Shackleton was both accessible and firm. He mixed easily with his men but, at the same time, enforced discipline in a fair, evenhanded manner. Whatever the setting, he quickly established a routine and made every effort to maintain the group's morale, planning songfests, lectures, dog races, and other activities for his men.

Alexander suggests that Shackleton's character was the key to his success. In 1909, Shackleton could have been the first to reach the south pole, but he turned back to save the life of his companions. As the supply of food dwindled, he made expedition member Frank Wild (who would join him on the *Endurance* voyage) eat one of his (Shackleton's) daily rations of four biscuits. Shackleton continued to demonstrate concern and compassion for the needs of his followers on his trans-Antarctic voyage. When the most unpopular crew member was laid up with a bad back, the commander let him use his own cabin and brought him tea. He made sure that those of lower rank got the warmest clothes and sleeping bags. During the perilous trip to South Georgia Island, Shackleton kept an eye out for those who were growing weak but never embarrassed anyone by singling him out for special help. If one sailor appeared on the verge of collapse, he made sure that everyone got warm milk or food. Shackleton himself valued optimism above all other virtues. "Optimism," he said, "is true moral courage." Relentless optimism kept him going during the hard times, and he had little patience for those who were anxious about the future.

Alexander sums up the essential quality of Ernest Shackleton's leadership this way:

> At the core of Shackleton's gift for leadership in crisis was an adamantine conviction that quite ordinary individuals were capable of heroic feats if the circumstances required; the weak and the strong could and *must* survive together. The mystique that Shackleton acquired as a leader may partly be attributed to the fact that he elicited from his men strength and endurance they had never imagined they possessed; he ennobled them. (p. 194)

DISCUSSION PROBES

1. What is the relationship between optimism and courage? Can we be optimistic without courage? Can we be courageous without being optimistic?

2. Generate a list of the virtues demonstrated by Shackleton on the *Endurance* voyage.

3. Do dangerous situations like polar exploration put a premium on some aspects of character that would be less important in other, more routine contexts?

4. Who are our true, modern-day heroes? What character qualities do they possess?

5. What leadership lessons can we draw from the life of Ernest Shackleton?

REFERENCES

Alexander, C. (1999). *The Endurance: Shackleton's legendary Antarctic expedition*. New York: Knopf (also available as a PBS Nova documentary film).
For more information on Shackleton and his expedition, see Morrell, M., Capparell, S., & Shackleton, A. (2001). *Shackleton's Way: Leadership lessons from the great Antarctic explorer*. New York: Viking Press.
Perkins, D. N. T. (2000). *Leading at the edge*. New York: AMACOM.
Shackleton, E. (1998). *South: A memoir of the* Endurance *voyage*. New York: Carroll & Graf.

Government ethics expert David Hart argues that it is important to distinguish between different types of moral examples or exemplars.[10] Dramatic acts, like rescuing a child from danger, capture our attention. However, if we're to develop worthy character, we need examples of those who demonstrate virtue on a daily basis. Hart distinguishes between *moral episodes* and *moral processes*. Moral episodes are made up of *moral crises* and *moral confrontations*. Moral crises are dangerous, and Hart calls those who respond to them "moral heroes." Oskar Schindler, a German industrialist, was one such hero. He risked his life and fortune to save 1,000 Jewish workers during World War II. Moral confrontations aren't dangerous, but they do involve risk and call for "moral champions." Marie Ragghianti emerged as a moral champion when, as chair of the parole board in Tennessee, she discovered that the governor and his cronies were selling pardons and reported their illegal activities to the FBI. (Another moral champion is profiled in Box 3.2, Leadership Ethics at the Movies: *Erin Brockovich*.)

Moral processes consist of *moral projects* and *moral work*. Moral projects are designed to improve ethical behavior during a limited amount of time and require "moral leaders." A moral leader sets out to reduce corruption in government, for example, or to improve the working conditions of migrant farm workers. Moral work, in contrast to a moral project, does not have a beginning or end but is ongoing. The "moral worker" strives for ethical consistency throughout life. This moral exemplar might be the motor vehicle employee who tries to be courteous to everyone who comes to the DMV office or the neighbor who volunteers to coach youth soccer.

Hart argues that the moral worker is the most important category of moral exemplar. He points out that most of life is lived in the daily valleys, not on the heroic mountain peaks. Because character is developed over time through a series of moral choices and actions, we need examples of those who live consistent moral lives. Those who engage in moral work are better able to handle moral crises. Andre and Magda Trocme, for instance, committed themselves to a life of service and nonviolence as pastors in the French village of La Chambon. When the German occupiers arrived, the Trocmes didn't hesitate to protect the lives of Jewish children and encouraged their congregation to do the same. This small community became an island of refuge to those threatened by the Holocaust.[11]

TELLING AND LIVING COLLECTIVE STORIES

Character building never takes place in a vacuum. Virtues are more likely to take root when nurtured by families, schools, governments, and religious bodies. These collectives impart values and encourage self-discipline, caring, and other virtues through the telling of narratives or stories. Shared narratives both explain and persuade. They provide a framework for understanding the world and, at the same time, challenge us to act in specified ways. For example, one of the most remarkable features of the American political system is the orderly transition of power between presidents.[12] George Washington set this precedent by voluntarily stepping down as the country's first leader. His story, told in classrooms, books, and films, helps explain why the current electoral system functions smoothly. Further, modern presidents and presidential candidates follow Washington's example, as in the case of the 2000 election. Al Gore garnered more popular votes than George W. Bush but stepped aside, after losing a court battle, to let his opponent take office.

Character growth comes from "living up" to the roles we play in the story. According to virtue ethicist Alasdair MacIntyre: "I can only answer the question 'What am I to do?' if I can answer the prior question, 'Of what story or stories do I find myself a part?' "[13] Worthy narratives call out the best in us, encouraging us to suppress our inner demons and to cast light instead of shadow. Religious stories can play a particularly important role in developing character. In a study of 23 moral exemplars, Anne Colby and William Damon found that religious faith, as well as a faith in a greater good or power, kept these moral models working for the good of others despite hardship.[14]

In the introduction to this text, I argued that we could learn about leadership ethics from fictional characters as well as from real-life ones. Ethics professor C. David Lisman offers several reasons why the ethical models contained in literature can provide a moral education that helps us to nurture our virtues.[15] Lisman focuses on literature, but his observations also apply to other forms of fiction (films, plays, television shows). Fiction, in Lisman's estimation, helps us understand our possibilities and limits. We can try to deny the reality

---

Box 3.2

Leadership Ethics at the Movies: *Erin Brockovich*

Cast: Julia Roberts, Albert Finney, Aaron Eckhart

Synopsis: Erin Brockovich (Julia Roberts) makes a most unlikely moral champion. The real-life, twice-divorced mother of three talks her way into a job with the legal firm that failed to win her personal injury lawsuit. She dresses like a streetwalker, alienates her coworkers, and sasses her boss (played by Albert Finney). Brockovich seems destined for failure until she stumbles on a case involving Pacific Gas and Electric and residents of Hinkley, California. PG&E has been leaking a toxic chemical into the local water supply while assuring citizens that all is well. Residents have been coming down with a variety of cancers and other ailments. Brockovich unmasks the corporate cover-up, convinces her boss to take the case, and rallies townspeople to join a class action suit. Thanks to the dedication and persistence of this "mom on a mission," PG&E settles the case for over $300 million.

Rating: R for profanity, sexual references, and Brockovich's revealing wardrobe

Themes: mission, courage, persistence, compassion, the making of a leader

---

of death, the fact that we're aging, and that there are factors outside of our control. However, novels and short stories force us to confront these issues.

Literature explores many common human themes like (a) freedom of choice, (b) moral responsibility, (c) conflict between individual and society, (d) conflict between individual conscience and society's rules, and (e) self-understanding. Fiction writers help us escape our old ways of thinking and acting. Their best works expand our emotional capacity, enabling us to better respond to the needs of others. They also provide us with an opportunity to practice moral reflection and judgment by evaluating the actions of important characters.[16] In sum, almost any story about leaders, whether real or fictional, can teach us something about ethical and unethical behavior. Moral exemplars can be found in novels, television series, and feature films as well as in news stories, biographies, documentaries, and historical records.

HARDSHIP

Hardship and suffering also play a role in developing character. The leaders we admire the most are often those who have endured the greatest hardships. Nelson Mandela, Vaclav Havel, and Alexander Solzhenitsyn served extended prison terms, for instance, and English parliamentarian William Wilberforce worked for 46 years to bring about the elimination of slavery in the British Empire.

Perhaps no other American leader has faced as much hardship as did Abraham Lincoln. He was defeated in several elections before winning the presidency. Because of death threats, he had to slip into Washington, D.C., to take office. He presided over the slaughter of many of his countrymen and women, lost a beloved son, and was ridiculed by Northerners (some in his cabinet) and Southerners alike. All these trials, however, seemed to deepen both his commitment to the Union and his spirituality. His second inaugural address is considered to be one of the finest political and theological statements ever produced by a public official.

Trainers at the Center for Creative Leadership (CCL) have identified hardship as one of the factors contributing to leadership development. Leaders develop the fastest when they encounter situations that stretch or challenge them. Hardships, along with novelty, difficult goals, and conflict, challenge individuals. CCL staffer Russ Mosley believes that hardships differ from other challenging experiences because they're unplanned, are experienced in an intensely personal way, and involve loss:

> At the core of any hardship experience is a sense of loss: of credibility, a sense of control, self-efficacy, a former identity. . . . The loss provokes confrontation with self, and in dealing with loss and the pain accompanying it, learning results.
>
> This sense of loss causes people who usually live in an external world to turn inward. What did I do wrong? Do I not measure up? What could I have done differently? Could I have done anything to prevent it?[17]

Research conducted by the CCL reveals that leaders experience five common categories of hardship events. Each type of hardship can drive home important lessons.

1. *Business mistakes and failures.* Examples of this type of hardship event include losing an important client, failed products and programs, broken relationships, and bankruptcies. These experiences help leaders build stronger working relationships, recognize their limitations, and profit from their mistakes.

2. *Career setbacks.* Missed promotions, unsatisfying jobs, demotions, and firings make up this hardship category. Leaders faced with these events lose (a) control over their careers, (b) their sense of self-efficacy or competence, and (c) their professional identity. Career setbacks function as "wake-up calls," providing feedback about weaknesses. They encourage leaders to take more responsibility for managing their careers and to identify the type of work that is most meaningful to them.

3. *Personal trauma.* CCL investigators were surprised to find that many hardships unrelated to the job teach lasting leadership lessons. Examples of personal

trauma include divorce, cancer, death, and difficult children. These experiences, which are a natural part of life, drive home the point that leaders (who are used to being in charge) can't control the world around them. As a result, they may strike a better balance between work and home responsibilities, develop coping strategies, and persist in the face of adversity.

4. *Problem employees.* Troubled workers include those who steal, defraud, can't perform, or perform well only part of the time. In dealing with problem employees, leaders may learn how important it is to hold followers to consistently high standards. They may become more skilled at confronting subordinates.

5. *Downsizing.* Downsizing has much in common with career setbacks, but in this type of hardship, leaders lose their jobs through no fault of their own. Downsizing can help leaders develop coping skills and force them to take stock of their lives and careers. Those carrying out the layoffs can also learn from the experience by gaining a deeper understanding of how their organizations operate and by developing greater empathy for the feelings of followers.

Being exposed to a hardship is no guarantee that you'll learn from the experience. Some ambitious leaders, for instance, never get over being passed over for a promotion and become embittered and cynical. Benefiting from adversity takes what Warren Bennis and Robert Thomas call "adaptive capacity." Bennis and Thomas compared leaders who came of age during the period from 1945 to 1954, whom they called Geezers, and those who came of age during the period from 1991 to 2000, whom they called Geeks.[18] They found that, regardless of generation, effective leaders come through crucible moments that have a profound impact on their development. These intense experiences include failures, like losing an election, but also encompass more positive events, like climbing a mountain or finding a mentor. Participants in their sample experienced just as many crises as everyone else but were able to learn important principles and skills from their struggles. This knowledge enabled them to move on to more complex challenges.

Successful Geeks and Geezers see hard times as positive high points of their lives. Less successful leaders, in contrast, are defeated and discouraged by similar events. To put it another way, effective leaders tell a different story than their ineffective counterparts. They identify hardships as stepping-stones, not as insurmountable obstacles. We, too, can enlarge our adaptive capacity by paying close attention to our personal narratives, defining difficult moments in our lives as learning opportunities rather than as permanent obstacles.

HABITS

No one has done more to popularize virtue or character ethics than business consultant Stephen Covey. Not only is he the author of the best-selling book *The Seven Habits of Highly Effective People* (1989), but thousands of businesses, nonprofit groups, and government agencies have participated in workshops offered by the Covey Leadership Center.[19] Covey argues that effectiveness is based on such character principles as integrity, fairness, service, excellence, and growth. The habits are the tools that enable leaders and followers to develop these characteristics. Covey defines a habit as a combination of knowledge (what to do and why to do it), skill (how to do it), and motivation (wanting to do it). Leadership development is an "inside-out" process that starts within the leader and then moves outward to affect others. There are seven habits of effective/ethical leaders:

Habit 1. Be proactive. Proactive leaders realize that they can choose how they respond to events. When faced with a career setback, they try to grow from the experience instead of feeling victimized by it. Proactive individuals also take the initiative by opting to attack problems instead of accepting defeat. Their language reflects their willingness to accept rather than to avoid responsibility. A proactive leader makes such statements as "Let's examine our options," and "I can create a strategic plan." A reactive leader makes comments like "The organization won't go along with that idea," "I'm too old to change," and "That's just who I am."

Habit 2. Begin with the end in mind. This habit is based on the notion that "all things are created twice." First we get a mental picture of what we want to accomplish, and then we follow through on our plans. If we're unhappy with the current direction of our lives, we can generate new mental images and goals, a process Covey calls "rescripting." Creating personal and organizational mission statements is one way to identify the results we want and thus control the type of life we create. (I'll talk more about how to create a mission statement in the next section.) Covey urges leaders to center their lives on inner principles like fairness and human dignity rather than on such external factors as family, money, friends, or work.

Habit 3. Put first things first. A leader's time should be organized around priorities. Too many leaders spend their days coping with emergencies, mistakenly believing that urgent means important. Meetings, deadlines, and interruptions place immediate demands on their time, but other less-pressing activities, like relationship building and planning, are more important in the long run. Effective leaders carve out time for significant activities by identifying their most important roles, selecting their goals, creating schedules that enable them to reach their objectives, and modifying these plans when necessary. They also know how to delegate tasks and have the courage to say "no" to requests that don't fit their priorities.

Habit 4. Think win/win. Those with a win/win perspective take a cooperative approach to communication, convinced that the best solution benefits both parties. The win/win habit is based on these dimensions: (a) character (integrity, maturity, and a belief that the needs of everyone can be met); (b) trusting relationships committed to mutual benefit; (c) performance or partnership agreements that spell out conditions and responsibilities; (d) organizational systems that fairly distribute rewards; and (e) principled negotiation processes in which both sides generate possible solutions and then select the one that works best.

Habit 5. Seek first to understand, then to be understood. Ethical leaders put aside their personal concerns to engage in empathetic listening. They seek to understand, not to evaluate, advise, or interpret. Empathetic listening is an excellent way to build a trusting relationship. Covey uses the metaphor of the emotional bank account to illustrate how trust develops. Principled leaders make deposits in the emotional bank account by showing kindness and courtesy, keeping commitments, paying attention to small details, and seeking to understand. These strong relational reserves help prevent misunderstandings and make it easier to resolve any problems that do arise.

Habit 6. Synergize. Synergy creates a solution that is greater than the sum of its parts and uses right brain thinking to generate a third, previously undiscovered alternative. Synergistic, creative solutions are generated in trusting relationships (those with high emotional bank accounts) in which participants value their differences.

Habit 7. Sharpen the saw. Sharpening the saw refers to continual renewal of the physical, mental, social-emotional, and spiritual dimensions of the self. Healthy leaders care for their bodies through exercise, good nutrition, and stress management. They encourage their mental development by reading good literature and by writing thoughtful letters and journal entries. They create meaningful relationships with others and nurture their inner or spiritual values through study or meditation and time in nature. Continual renewal, combined with the use of the first six habits, creates an upward spiral of character improvement.

MISSION STATEMENTS

Developing a mission statement is the best way to keep the end or destination in mind. Leaders who cast light have a clear sense of what they hope to accomplish and seek to achieve worthwhile goals. For example, Abraham Lincoln was out to preserve the Union, Nelson Mandela wanted to abolish apartheid, and Mother Teresa devoted her whole life to reducing suffering.

Author and organizational consultant Laurie Beth Jones believes that useful mission statements are short (no more than a sentence long), easily understood

and communicated, and committed to memory.[20] Developing a personal
mission statement, according to Jones, begins with personal assessment. Take a
close look at how your family has influenced your values and interests. Identify
your strengths and determine what makes you unique (what Jones calls your
"unique selling point"). Once you've isolated your gifts and unique features,
examine your motivation. What situations make you excited or angry? Chances
are your mission will be related to those factors that arouse your passion or
enthusiasm (teaching, writing, coaching, or selling, for example).

Jones outlines a three-part formula for constructing a mission statement.
Start with the phrase, "My mission is to . . ." and record three action verbs that
best describe you (i.e., accomplish, build, finance, give, discuss). Next, plug in
a principle, value, or purpose that you could commit the rest of your life to
(joy, service, faith, creativity, justice). Finish by identifying the group or cause
that most excites you (real estate, design, sports, women's issues). Your final
statement ought to inspire you and should direct all your activities, both on
and off the job.

Leadership consultant Juana Bordas offers an alternative method or path
for discovering personal leadership purpose based on Native American culture.
Native Americans discovered their life purposes while on vision quests. Vision
cairns guided members of some tribes. These stone piles served both as direc-
tional markers and as a reminder that others had passed this way before.
Bordas identifies nine cairns or markers for creating personal purpose.[21]

Cairn 1: Call your purpose; listen for guidance. All of us have to be silent in order to
listen to our intuition. Periodically you will need to withdraw from the noise of
everyday life and reflect on such questions as "What am I meant to do?" and "How
can I best serve?"

Cairn 2: Find a sacred place. A sacred place is a quiet place of reflection. It can be officially designated as sacred (a church or meditation garden, for example) or merely
be a spot that encourages contemplation, such as a stream, park, or favorite chair.

Cairn 3: See time as continuous; begin with the child and move with the present. Our
past has a great impact on where we'll head in the future. Patterns of behavior are
likely to continue. Bordas suggests that you should examine the impact of your
(a) family composition, (b) gender, (c) geography, (d) cultural background, and
(e) generational influences. A meaningful purpose will be anchored in the past but
will remain responsive to current conditions like diversity, globalization, and technological change.

Cairn 4: Identify special skills and talents; accept imperfections. Take inventory by
examining your major activities and jobs and evaluating your strengths. For example, how are your people skills? technical knowledge? communication abilities?

Consider how you might further develop your aptitudes and abilities. Also take stock of your significant failures. What did they teach you about your limitations? What did you learn from them?

Cairn 5: Trust your intuition. Sometimes we need to act on our hunches and emotions. You may decide to turn down a job that doesn't "feel right," for instance, in order to accept a position that seems to be a better "fit."

Cairn 6: Open the door when opportunity knocks. Be ready to respond to opportunities that are out of your control, like a new job assignment or a request to speak or write. Ask yourself if this possibility will better prepare you for leadership or fit in with what you're trying to do in life.

Cairn 7: Find your passion and make it happen. Passion energizes us for leadership and gives us stamina. Discover your passion by imagining the following scenarios: If you won the lottery, what would you still do? How would you spend your final 6 months on earth? What would sustain you for 100 more years?

Cairn 8: Write your life story; imagine a great leader. Turn your life into a story that combines elements of reality and fantasy. Imagine yourself as an effective leader and carry your story out into the future. What challenges did you overcome? What dreams did you fulfill? How did you reach your final destination?

Cairn 9: Honor your legacy, one step at a time. Your purpose is not static but will evolve and expand over time. If you're a new leader, you're likely to exert limited influence. That influence will expand as you develop your knowledge and skills. You may manage only a couple of individuals now, but in a few years, you may be responsible for an entire department or division.

VALUES

If a mission statement identifies our final destination, then our values serve as a moral compass to guide us on our journey. Values provide a frame of reference, helping us to set priorities and to determine right or wrong. There are all sorts of values. For example, I value fuel economy (I like spending less on gas), so I drive a small, fuel-efficient pickup truck. However, ethical decision making is primarily concerned with identifying and implementing moral values. Moral values are directly related to judgments about what's appropriate or inappropriate behavior. I value honesty, for instance, so I choose not to lie. I value privacy, so I condemn Internet retailers who gather personal information about me without my permission.

There are two ways to identify or clarify the values you hold. You can generate a list from scratch or rate a list of values supplied by someone else. If brainstorming a list of important values seems a daunting task, you might try the following exercise developed by James Kousez and Barry Posner. The credo memo asks you to spell out the important values that underlie your philosophy of leadership.

> Imagine that your organization has afforded you the chance to take a six-month sabbatical, all expenses paid. You will be going to a beautiful island where the average temperature is about eighty degrees Fahrenheit during the day. The sun shines in a brilliant sky, with a few wisps of clouds. A gentle breeze cools the island down in the evening, and a light rain clears the air. You wake up in the morning to the smell of tropical flowers.
>
> You may not take any work along on this sabbatical. And you will not be permitted to communicate to anyone at your office or plant—not by letter, phone, fax, e-mail, or other means. There will be just you, a few good books, some music, and your family or a friend.
>
> But before you depart, those with whom you work need to know something. They need to know the principles that you believe should guide their actions in your absence. They need to understand the values and beliefs that you think should steer their decision making and action taking.[22]
>
> You are permitted no long reports, however. Just a one-page memorandum. If given this opportunity, what would you write on your one-page credo memo? Take out one piece of paper and write that memo.

Examples of values that have been included in credo memos include "operate as a team," "listen to one another," "celebrate successes," "seize the initiative," "trust your judgment," and "strive for excellence." These values can be further clarified by engaging in dialogue with coworkers. Many discussions in organizations (i.e., how to select subcontractors, when to fire someone, how to balance the needs of various stakeholders) have an underlying values component. Listen for the principles that shape your opinions and the opinions of others.

Working with a list of values can also be useful. Psychologist Gordon Allport identified six major value-types. Individuals can be categorized based on how they organize their lives around each of the following value sets.[23] Prototypes are examples of occupations that fit best into a given value orientation.

1. *Theoretical.* Theoretical individuals are intellectuals who seek to discover the truth and pride themselves on being objective and rational. Prototypes: research scientists, engineers.

2. *Economic.* Usefulness is the most important criteria for those driven by economic values. They are interested in production, marketing, economics, and accumulating wealth. Prototype: small business owners.

3. *Aesthetic.* Aesthetic thinkers value form and harmony. They enjoy each event as it unfolds, judging the experience based on its symmetry or harmony. Prototypes: artists, architects.

4. *Social.* Love of others is the highest value for social leaders and followers. These "people persons" view others as ends, not means, and are kind and unselfish. Prototype: social workers.

5. *Political.* Power drives political individuals. They want to accumulate and exercise power and enjoy the recognition that comes from being in positions of influence. Prototypes: senators, governors.

6. *Religious.* Religious thinkers seek unity through understanding and relating to the cosmos as a whole. Prototypes: pastors, rabbis, Moslem clerics.

Identifying your primary values orientation is a good way to avoid situations that could cause you ethical discomfort. If you have an economic bent, you will want a job (often in a business setting) in which you solve real-life problems. On the other hand, if you love people, you may be uncomfortable working for a business that puts profits first.

Milton Rokeach developed the most widely used value system.[24] He divided moral values into two subcategories. *Instrumental values* are a means to an end. Diligence and patience are valuable, for example, because they enable us to reach difficult goals like completing a degree program or remodeling a house. *Terminal values* generally reflect our lifelong aspirations, like becoming wise, experiencing happiness, or living comfortably. They stand by themselves. Rokeach's list of instrumental and terminal values is found in the self-assessment in Box 3.3. Take a moment and rank the items on both lists.

Comparing our responses with other individuals and groups opens the way for additional dialogue about priorities. We may discover that we don't fit in as well as we would like with the rest of the group and decide to leave or work for change. (More on the importance of shared organizational values in Chapter 9.) Researchers can also use a list of values to determine if different classes of people have different priorities and how values change over time. University of Tennessee management professor William Judge[25] compared the values of CEOs with those of a cross section of the U.S. population from the 1960s. His results are reported in Box 3.4.

Some well-meaning writers and consultants make values the end-all of ethical decision making. They assume that groups will prosper if they develop a set of lofty, mutually shared values. However, as we saw earlier, having worthy values doesn't mean that individuals, groups, or organizations will live by these principles. Other factors—time pressures, faulty assumptions, corrupt systems—undermine their influence. Values, although critical, have to be translated into action. Further, our greatest struggles come from choosing between two good values. Many corporate leaders value both customer service and product quality, but what do they do when reaching one of these goals means sacrificing the other? Pushing to get a product shipped to satisfy a customer may force the manufacturing division into cutting corners in order to meet the deadline. Resolving dilemmas like these takes more than values

Box 3.3

Self-Assessment

INSTRUMENTAL AND TERMINAL VALUES

Instructions

Rank the values on each list from 1 (most important) to 18 (least important) to you. Rate the instrumental values first and then rank order the terminal values. You will end up with two lists. A low ranking doesn't mean that a value is insignificant; it means only that the item is less important to you than other, more highly rated values.

Terminal Values

Freedom (independence, free choice)
Self-respect (self-esteem)

A sense of accomplishment (lasting contribution)
Mature love (sexual and spiritual intimacy)
An exciting life (activity)
A comfortable life (prosperity)
Family security (taking care of loved ones)
True friendship (close companionship)
Social recognition (respect, admiration)
Wisdom (an understanding of life)

Happiness (contentedness)
Inner harmony (freedom from inner conflict)
Equality (brotherhood, equal opportunity for all)
A world at peace (free of war and conflict)
A world of beauty (beauty of nature and art)
Pleasure (an enjoyable, leisurely life)
National security (protection from attack)
Salvation (saved, eternal life)

Instrumental Values

Loving (affection, tenderness)
Independent (self-reliant, self-sufficient)
Capable (competent, effective)

Broad-minded (open-minded)

Intellectual (intelligent, reflective)
Honest (sincere, truthful)
Responsible (dependable, reliable)

Ambitious (hardworking, aspiring)
Imaginative (daring, creative)
Helpful (working for the welfare of others)
Forgiving (willing to pardon others)
Self-controlled (restrained, self-disciplined)
Logical (consistent, rational)

Courageous (standing up for your own beliefs)
Cheerful (lighthearted, joyful)

Polite (courteous, well-mannered)
Obedient (dutiful, respectful)

Clean (neat, tidy)

SOURCE: Reprinted with the permission of The Free Press, a division of Simon & Schuster, Inc., from *The nature of human values* (p. 28), by Milton Rokeach. Copyright © 1973 by The Free Press.

Box 3.4

Comparing Terminal Values

William Judge surveyed 91 CEOs (all males, average age 54) using Rokeach's values survey. He found that the executives, representing 57 industries, had a significantly different set of terminal values than a sample of adult Americans from the 1960s (see the chart below). The instrumental values of the management executives, however, were virtually identical to the broader sample. The only difference? The CEOs rated courage more highly than other U.S. residents.

Comparison of CEOs' Terminal Values With American Adults' Terminal Values.

Terminal Value	CEOs' Composite Rank (N = 91)	Adult Americans' Rank[a] (N = 1,409)
Sense of accomplishment	1	10
Family security	2	12
Self-respect	3	5
Salvation	4	8
Happiness	5	4
Wisdom	6	6
Freedom	7	3
An exciting life	8	18
A comfortable life	9	9
Mature love	10	14
True friendship	11	11
Inner harmony	12	13
A world at peace	13	1
National security	14	2
Social recognition	15	16
Equality	16	7
A world of beauty	17	15
Pleasure	18	17

SOURCE: Judge, W. A. (1999). *The leader's shadow.* Thousand Oaks, CA: Sage, p. 68. Used by permission.
a. Based on a national sample of American adults during the mid-1960s (Rokeach, 1973).

clarification; we also need some standards for determining ethical priorities. With that in mind, I'll identify ethical decision-making principles in Chapters 5 and 6. But first we need to confront one final inner monster—evil—in Chapter 4.

Implications and Applications

- Your inner fears and insecurities can't be eliminated, but they can be managed through development of positive qualities or virtues (integrity, perseverance, courage) that make up a moral character.
- Character is integral to effective leadership, often making the difference between success and failure.
- Strive for consistency, but don't be surprised by contradictions in your character or in the character of others. Become more tolerant of yourself and other leaders.
- Moral action is the product of such factors as moral imagination, sensitivity, judgment, motivation, obligation, evaluation, tolerating disagreement, and implementation. Use these components to pinpoint your ethical strengths and weaknesses.
- Never underestimate the power of a good example. Be on the lookout for real and fictional ethical role models.
- Shared narratives nurture character development, encouraging you to live up to the role you play in the collective story.
- Hardships are an inevitable part of life and leadership. The sense of loss associated with these events can provide important feedback, spur self-inspection, encourage the development of coping strategies, force you to reorder your priorities, and nurture your compassion. However, to benefit from them, you must see challenges as learning opportunities that prepare you for future leadership responsibilities.
- Adopting habits can speed the development of character. Seek to be proactive, begin with the end in mind, organize around priorities, strive for cooperation, listen for understanding, develop synergistic solutions, and engage in continual self-renewal.
- Having an ultimate destination will encourage you to stay on your ethical track. Develop a personal mission statement that reflects your strengths and passions. Use your values as a moral compass to keep you from losing your way.

For Further Exploration, Challenge, and Self-Assessment

1. Can the private and public morals of leaders be separated? Try to reach a consensus on this question in a group.
2. Brainstorm a list of moral exemplars. What does it take to qualify for your list? How would you classify these role models according to the types described in the chapter?
3. Reflect on the ways that a particular shared narrative has shaped your worldview and behavior. Write up your conclusions.
4. Create your own list of hardships common to leaders. How does it compare with the one provided by the Center for Creative Leadership? What hardships have you faced and what have you learned from them?

5. Examine the role that hardship has played in the life of a prominent leader. Summarize your findings in an oral presentation and/or research paper.
6. Interview a leader that you admire. Determine his or her crucible moment and capacity to learn from that experience.
7. Rate yourself on each of the seven habits of effective people and develop a plan for addressing your weaknesses. Explore the habits further through reading and training seminars.
8. Develop a personal mission statement using the guidelines provided by Jones and/or Bordas.
9. How do your instrumental and terminal values compare with those reported in Box 3.3? Are you comfortable with your rankings? Why or why not?
10. Complete the credo memo exercise from the subsection on Values if you haven't already done so. Encourage others in your work group organization to do the same and compare your statements. Use this as an opportunity to dialogue about values.

CASE STUDY 3.2

Chapter End Case: "Chainsaw"
Al Dunlap and "Mensch" Aaron Feuerstein

During the 1990s, Al Dunlap may have been the most admired and the most hated CEO in America. Dunlap earned the name "Chainsaw" for aggressively cutting costs at troubled companies. He didn't shy away from tough decisions but would close plants, lay off employees, and sell assets in order to improve the bottom line. At the Lily-Tulip disposable cup and plate company, for example, he cut 20% of the staff and half the management team along with 40% of the firm's suppliers. At Scott Paper, Dunlap laid off over 11,000 workers, deferred maintenance costs, slashed the research budget, and eliminated donations to charity. These cost reductions drove the stock price up 225% and made Scott Paper an attractive takeover candidate. When Kimberly-Clark bought the firm in 1995, Dunlap pocketed $100 million through the sale of his stock options. Dunlap then moved to the Sunbeam Corporation in 1996 and started another round of cutbacks. He hoped to once again reap millions by boosting the company's stock value and then selling out.

The media and Wall Street investors loved Al Dunlap. He was readily available to the press and his forthright style made him a good interview. Chainsaw became the "poster child" of shareholder capitalism. Shareholder capitalists believe that publicly held corporations serve the interests of only one group—stockholders. Other constituencies like customers, employees, and local communities don't matter. According to Dunlap, "Stakeholders are total rubbish. It's the shareholders who own the company" (Byrne, 1999, pp. xiv–xv). He made investors, particularly the large investors who sat on the boards of Scott and Sunbeam, lots of money.

Company insiders had an entirely different opinion of Dunlap. Those who lost their jobs despised him, and those who survived the cuts viewed him as a tyrant. Remaining employees had to work long hours to reach impossible production and sales goals. *BusinessWeek* writer and author John Byrne offers this description of life under Dunlap:

> Working on the front lines of a company run by Albert Dunlap was like being at war. The pressure was brutal, the hours exhausting, and the casualties high. Dunlap and his consultants had imposed such unrealistic goals on the company that virtually everyone understood he was engaged in a short-term exercise to pretty up the business for a quick sale.
>
> By sheer brutality, he began putting excruciating pressure on those who reported to him, who in turn passed that intimidation down the line. It went beyond the ordinary pressure to do well in a corporation. People were told, explicitly and implicitly, that either they hit the number or another person would be found to do it for them. Their livelihood hung on making numbers that were not makeable.

> At Sunbeam Dunlap created a culture of misery, an environment of moral ambiguity, indifferent to everything except the stock price. He did not lead by intellect or by vision, but by fear and intimidation.[26]

Dunlap's dream of selling Sunbeam and cashing in began to collapse when the firm's stock price went too high to interest corporate buyers. Shortly thereafter, the firm began falling short of its income projections. The company inflated 1997 sales figures by convincing dealers to sign up for merchandise that was then stored in Sunbeam warehouses. This maneuver allowed the corporation to count these "sales" as immediate income before customers had even paid for the products. By 1998, large accounts like Wal-Mart and Costco were glutted with inventory and this accounting trick no longer worked. Sunbeam couldn't reverse the slide because Dunlap had fired essential employees, eliminated profitable plants and product lines, and alienated vendors. Share prices then dropped dramatically, and Dunlap was forced out. Following his ouster, the company defaulted on a major loan payment, and the Securities and Exchange Commission began to audit the company's books.

Chainsaw Al had few of the virtues we associate with high moral character. To his credit, he was decisive, hardworking, and loyal to a few business associates and subordinates. However, he was also bullying, angry, abusive (to family members as well as employees), egotistical, sensitive to the slightest criticism, vengeful, inconsistent, uncaring, and cowardly (he rarely fired anyone himself).

Working for Al could be hell on earth. Why, then, was he so successful, and why did people continue to work for him? As I noted earlier, he appeared to get results (at least in the short term) and got lots of favorable attention in the press. If he hadn't fallen short of earnings projections, he probably would still be at Sunbeam despite his shabby treatment of employees and other stakeholder groups. High-level executives continued to work for Sunbeam in hopes of getting rich and out of fear. They would make millions from their stock options if the company succeeded and were afraid to stand up to the boss. Said one vice president who had often considered quitting: "But it was like being in an abusive relationship. You just didn't know how to get out of it."

Summing up the career of Chainsaw Al, Byrne concludes,

> At Sunbeam, he eluded all the safeguards of a public corporation: a well-meaning board of directors, independent, outside auditors, and an army of honest and talented executives. Every system depends on people, people who will say no even when faced with the threat of losing a job or a business. Dunlap worked so hard at creating fear, dependence, and guilt that no one dared to defy him—until it was too late. It is a lesson no one should ever forget.[27]

During the same period that Al Dunlap was ransacking Sunbeam, Aaron Feuerstein, CEO of textile manufacturer Malden Mills, was setting a very different example. On December 11, 1995, the company's plant in Lawrence, Massachusetts, burned down in one of the largest fires in the state's history. Even while the ashes of the plant were still smoldering, Feuerstein pledged to continue to pay the salaries of his workers. Further, he promised to rebuild in Lawrence rather than go out of business or move operations in order to reduce labor costs.

Feuerstein (69 at the time of the fire) is the latest in his family to run the privately held company that is best known for producing PolarTec fleece. He learned his business principles from his father and uncles. These principles include treating all employees fairly, encouraging loyalty, and being a responsible member of the community. Malden offers wages nearly 20% higher than the industry average, and its unionized workforce has never gone on strike.

CEO Feuerstein's decision to keep paying employees while rebuilding in the same location was based in large part on his values as an orthodox Jew. Feuerstein continually links his choices to Hebrew scripture. In talking about the fire in an interview on *60 Minutes*, he quotes the Jewish proverb: "When all is in moral chaos, this is the time to be a 'mensch.'" *Mensch* is the Yiddish word for a "man with a heart."

The Malden Mill executive exhibits the humility and modest lifestyle of the Level 5 leaders studied by Jim Collins. He could have taken the $300 million insurance settlement and retired, but as he told *60 Minutes* correspondent Morley Safer, he's not interested in moving to Florida to play golf. Mr. and Mrs. Feuerstein's idea of a good time is reading together in front of the fire at their five-room condominium.

Unfortunately, Feuerstein hasn't enjoyed the success of the Level 5 leaders in the Collins study. Malden Mills was forced to declare bankruptcy due to additional debt and reduced market share resulting from the fire. In addition, the U.S. textile industry can't compete with overseas producers. The mensch of Lawrence, Massachusetts, promises to fight on, however. He remains confident in his employees and is cheered by the fact that many consumers want to buy PolarTec from Malden Mills in order to show their support for the company.

DISCUSSION PROBES

1. What responsibility should followers share for the actions of Dunlap? How would you evaluate the character of those who decided to stay and work for him?

2. How much blame do you place on the company directors who hired Dunlap and were supposed to oversee his activities?

3. How can we prevent future Al Dunlaps from taking over companies and other organizations?

4. Was Feuerstein's decision foolish based on the firm's subsequent bankruptcy?

5. Could the CEO of a publicly held company make the same choice as Feuerstein? Why or why not?

6. What factors go into making a "mensch?"

7. What leadership lessons do you glean from the rise and fall of Chainsaw Al and from Feuerstein's example?

REFERENCES

Byrne, J. (1999). *The notorious career of Al Dunlap in the era of profit-at-any-price.* New York: HarperCollins.

Malden Mills [Television series episode]. (2002, March 24). *60 Minutes.* New York: CBS Television.

Seeger, M. W., & Ulmer, R. R. (2001). Virtuous responses to organizational crisis: Aaron Feuerstein and Milt Cole. *Journal of Business Ethics, 31,* 369–376.

Ulmer, R. R., & Seeger, M. W. (2000). Communication ethics and the Malden Mills disaster. In G. L. Peterson (Ed.), *Communicating in organizations* (2nd ed., pp. 191–194). Boston, MA: Allyn & Bacon.

CASE STUDY 3.3

Chapter End Case: Battling Blindness: Merck Does the Right Thing

River blindness is one of the world's most devastating diseases, affecting approximately 20 million people, mostly in West Africa and South America. The illness is spread by blackflies that breed in fast-moving water. These tiny insects pick up the larvae of a parasite by biting a victim and then leave it behind when they bite someone who is not yet infected. The parasites quickly grow to as long as 2 feet and send out millions of microworms that spread throughout the body. Globs of these worms push through the skin, resulting in loss of pigmentation or "leopard" skin. Left untreated, the worms spread to the eyes, causing blindness, and shorten life expectancy by one third.

For decades all attempts to wipe out river blindness failed. Pesticides didn't eliminate the flies because they rapidly complete their reproductive cycle in many different locations. A few drugs had been developed, but they had serious side effects and could only be administered under close supervision. Unable to defeat the disease, residents of some rural communities fled their traditional homes in the fertile valleys for arid high ground.

In 1978, a research scientist at Merck & Company stumbled across a potential cure for river blindness while developing a treatment for parasitic worms that attack pets and livestock. Realizing that the same microbe would probably eliminate similar parasites in humans, he asked his laboratory director, Dr. Roy Vagelos, for permission to develop the drug for human use. Developing the medication would be expensive, requiring years of laboratory work followed by testing in West Africa. Failure would lower the company's return to stockholders and nasty side effects could also expose the company to lawsuits. Even if the drug worked, there was little hope that victims could pay for it since most lived in extreme poverty.

Backed by the company's drug development council (the group that made recommendations as to which drugs to support), Vagelos gave his enthusiastic go-ahead. By 1980, the company was field-testing the product called Mectizan in Ghana, Liberia, Mali, and Senegal. The results were nothing short of miraculous. Taken in pill form once a year, the drug killed the microworms and drove the parasites from the skin (preventing flies from spreading them). Side effects were minimal but relief was immediate and dramatic. The severe itching caused by the microworms eased after just one dose.

Developing the drug was the first step. Next the company faced the challenge of distributing it. The World Health Organization, the U.S. Agency for International Development, and other relief groups were skeptical at first and refused to pay for its manufacture and distribution. Finally in 1987, Vagelos (who had been promoted to CEO 2 years earlier) decided to give the drug away and to ensure its delivery. Later, the same private and public relief organizations that had refused to finance distribution stepped forward to help. In 1995, the World Bank hailed the reduction of river blindness as "one of the most remarkable achievements in the history of development assistance."[28] Children no longer faced the prospect of early death and blindness; communities returned to the riverbanks. The cost to Merck was high, however. Lost income from the drug totaled over $200 million.

Merck has a long tradition of "doing well by doing good." Following World War II, the company donated streptomycin to combat an outbreak of tuberculosis in Japan. It produces a variety of lifesaving drugs like penicillin, streptomycin, and Mevacor, a cholesterol-lowering drug that greatly reduces the risks of heart attack. Company values clearly state that improving the health of customers and patients takes priority over the needs of stockholders. According to George Merck, son of the company founder,

> We try never to forget that medicine is for the people. It is not for the profits. The profits follow, and if we have remembered that, they have never failed to appear. The better we have remembered it, the larger they have been.[29]

Even with the support of the organization's culture, the ultimate fate of Mectizan rested on the shoulders of Vagelos. Senior vice presidents were deadlocked on the issue, fearing that free distribution would undercut sales of other products in developing countries. Vagelos ended the debate, declaring later that "I thought the company couldn't have done otherwise."[30] He didn't even tell his board of directors what he was going to do before his public announcement. Not a single shareholder complained about the company's decision, however.

In the end, Vagelos reminded the corporation of its ultimate purpose—to reduce the suffering of humanity. The company's example encouraged other firms to follow suit. Glaxo gave away a new antimalaria drug. DuPont now donates nylon to filter guinea worm parasites out of drinking water, and American Cyanamid provides a larvacide to kill them.

Roy Vagelos admits that his decision boosted Merck's reputation and made it easier to recruit talented researchers. But he declares that he would have made the same choice even without side benefits. Combating river blindness was the culmination of a life that he had dedicated, first as a professor of medicine and then as a pharmaceutical executive, to meeting the needs of others.

DISCUSSION PROBES

1. Would Vagelos have been criticized had he decided not to develop and distribute the Mectizan?

2. What other firms "do well by doing good?" How can we encourage more firms to do the same?

3. What elements of a climate of integrity were present at Merck?

4. Professor and writer Michael Useem, who profiles both the Merck and Salomon cases, refers to critical decisions as "leadership moments." Leaders must make the right moves at these points or the group or organization will suffer. What leadership moments (decisions) have you faced? What ethical implications did they have?

5. What leadership lessons do you draw from this case?

REFERENCE

Useem, M. (1998). *The leadership moment: Nine stories of triumph and disaster and their lessons for us all.* New York: Times Books.

Notes

1. Johannesen, R. L. (2002). *Ethics in human communication* (5th ed.). Prospect Heights, IL: Waveland Press, ch. 1.

2. Collins, J. (2001). *Good to great.* New York: HarperBusiness, pp. 20, 27.

Collins, J. (2001, January). Level 5 leadership: The triumph of humility and fierce resolve. *Harvard Business Review,* 67–76.

3. Johannesen, R. L. (1991). Virtue ethics, character, and political communication. In R. E. Denton (Ed.), *Ethical dimensions of political communication* (pp. 69–90). New York: Praeger.

4. Kousez, J. M., & Posner, B. Z. (1993). *Credibility: How leaders gain and lose it, why people demand it.* San Francisco: Jossey-Bass.

5. My discussion of virtue ethics draws from a variety of sources, including the following:

Alderman, H. (1997). By virtue of a virtue. In D. Statman (Ed.), *Virtue ethics* (pp. 145–164). Washington, DC: Georgetown University Press.

Hart, D. K. (1994) Administration and the ethics of virtue. In T. C. Cooper (Ed.), *The handbook of administrative ethics* (pp. 107–123). New York: Marcel Dakker.

Luke, J. S. (1994). Character and conduct in the public service. In T. C. Cooper (Ed.), *The handbook of administrative ethics* (pp. 391–412). New York: Marcel Dakker.

Meilander, G. (1986). Virtue in contemporary religious thought. In R. J. Neihaus (Ed.), *Virtue: Public and private* (pp. 7–30). Grand Rapids, MI: Eerdmans.

Solomon, R. (1988). Internal objections to virtue ethics. In P. A. French, T. Uehling, & H. Wettstein (Eds.), *Midwest Studies in Philosophy* (Vol. 18, pp. 428–441). Notre Dame, IN: University of Notre Dame Press.

6. Rest, J. (1986). *Moral development: Advances in research and theory.* New York: Praeger.

Rest, J. R. (1993). Research on moral judgment in college students. In A. Garrod (Ed.), *Approaches to moral development* (pp. 210–211). New York: Teachers College Press.

Rest, J. R. (1994). Background: Theory and research. In J. R. Rest & D. Narvaez (Eds.), *Moral development in the professions: Psychology and applied ethics* (pp. 1–25). Hillsdale, NJ: Erlbaum.

7. Powers, C. W., & Vogel, D. (1980). *Ethics in the education of business managers.* Hastings-on-Hudson, NY: Institute of Society, Ethics and the Life Sciences.

8. MacIntyre, A. (1984). *After virtue: A study in moral theory* (2nd ed.). Notre Dame, IN: University of Notre Dame Press.

Hauerwas, S. (1981). *A community of character.* Notre Dame, IN: University of Notre Dame Press.

9. Lacayo, R., & Ripley, A. (2002, December 30). Persons of the year. *Time,* 30–60.

10. Hart, D. K. (1992). The moral exemplar in an organizational society. In T. L. Cooper & N. D. Wright (Eds.), *Exemplary public administrators: Character and leadership in government* (pp. 9–29). San Francisco: Jossey-Bass.

11. Haillie, P. (1979). *Lest innocent blood be shed: The story of the village of Le Chambon and how goodness happened there.* New York: Harper & Row.

12. Burns, J. M. (2003). *Transforming leadership: A new pursuit of happiness.* New York: Atlantic Monthly Press, ch. 5.

13. MacIntyre (1984), *After virtue,* p. 216.

14. Colby, A., & Damon, W. (1992). *Some do care: Contemporary lives of moral commitment.* New York: Free Press.

15. Lisman, C. D. (1996). *The curricular integration of ethics: Theory and practice.* Westport, CT: Praeger.

16. Lisman's arguments are echoed by Goldberg, M. (1997). Doesn't anybody read the Bible anymo'? In O. F. Williams, *The moral imagination: How literature and films can stimulate ethical reflection in the business world* (pp. 19–32). Notre Dame, IN: University of Notre Dame Press.

17. Moxley, R. S. (1998). Hardships. In C. D. McCauley, R. S. Moxley, & E. Van Velsor (Eds.), *Handbook of leadership development* (pp. 194–213). San Francisco: Jossey-Bass, p. 194.

18. Bennis, W. G., & Thomas, R. J. (2002). *Geeks and geezers: How era, values, and defining moments shape leaders.* Boston, MA: Harvard Business School Press.

19. Covey, S. (1989). *The seven habits of highly effective people.* New York: Simon & Schuster.

20. Jones, L. B. (1996). *The path: Creating your mission statement for work and for life.* New York: Hyperion.

21. Bordas, J. (1995). Becoming a servant-leader: The personal development path. In L. Spears (Ed.), *Reflections on leadership* (pp. 149–160). New York: Wiley.

22. Kousez, & Posner (1993), *Credibility,* pp. 62–63.

23. Allport, G. (1961). *Pattern and growth in personality.* New York: Holt, Rinehart & Winston.

Guth, W. D., & Tagiuri, R. (1965, September-October). Personal values and corporate strategy. *Harvard Business Review,* 123–132.

24. Rokeach, M. (1973). *The nature of human values.* New York: Free Press.

25. Judge, W. (1999). *The leader's shadow: Exploring and developing executive character.* Thousand Oaks, CA: Sage.

26. Byrne, J. (1999). *The notorious career of Al Dunlap in the era of profit-at-any-price.* New York: HarperCollins, pp 153–154.

27. Byrne (1999), *The notorious career of Al Dunlap,* p. 354.

28. Useem, M. (1998). *The leadership moment: Nine stories of triumph and disaster and their lessons for us all.* New York: Times Books, p. 39.

29. Useem (1998), *The leadership moment,* p. 29.

30. Useem (1998), *The leadership moment,* p. 33.

4

Combating Evil

Evil, in whatever intellectual framework, is by definition a monster.

Essayist Lance Morrow

Without forgiveness there is no future.

South African Archbishop Desmond Tutu

What's Ahead

In this chapter, we wrestle with the most dangerous monster of all—evil. Section one surveys some of the forms or faces of evil. Section two examines the role of forgiveness in breaking cycles of evil. Section three probes the relationship between spirituality and leadership, highlighting spiritual development and spiritual disciplines.

The Faces of Evil

The terrorist attacks of September 11, 2001, reintroduced the word evil into the national vocabulary. No other term, it seemed, could adequately describe the death and destruction at Ground Zero and the Pentagon. Ordinary citizens and commentators joined President Bush in condemning the hijackings as evil acts done by evildoers.

The trauma of 9/11 heightened national and international awareness of the existence of evil, an important first step. However, we can't combat evil until we first understand our opponent. Contemporary Western definitions of evil emphasize its destructiveness.[1] Evil inflicts pain and suffering, deprives innocent people of their humanity, and creates feelings of hopelessness and despair. The ultimate product of evil is death. Evil destroys self-esteem, physical and emotional well-being, relationships, communities, and nations.

We can gain some important insights into the nature of evil by looking at the various forms or faces it displays. In this section, I'll introduce six perspectives on evil and then talk about how each approach can help us better deal with this powerful, destructive force.

EVIL AS DREADFUL PLEASURE

University of Maryland political science professor C. Fred Alford defines evil as a combination of dread and pleasure. Alford recruited 60 respondents from a variety of ages and backgrounds to talk about their experiences with evil. He discovered that people experience evil as a deep sense of uneasiness, "the dread of being human, vulnerable, alone in the universe and doomed to die."[2] They do evil when, instead of coming to grips with their inner darkness, they try to get rid of it by making others feel "dreadful." Inflicting this pain is enjoyable. Part of the pleasure comes from being in charge, of being the victimizer instead of the victim.

EVIL AS DECEPTION

Psychiatrist Scott Peck identifies evil as a form of narcissism or self-absorption.[3] Mentally healthy adults submit themselves to something beyond themselves, like God or love or excellence. Submission to a greater power encourages them to obey their consciences. Evil people, on the other hand, refuse to submit and try to control others instead. They consider themselves above reproach and project their shortcomings, attacking anyone who threatens their self-concepts. Evil individuals are consumed with keeping up appearances. Peck calls them "the people of the lie" because they deceive themselves and others in hopes of projecting a righteous image. Peck believes that truly evil people are more likely to live in our neighborhoods than in our jails. They generally hide their true natures and appear to be normal and successful. Inmates, on the other hand, land in prison because they've been morally inconsistent or stupid. (See the Justifying Terror Chapter End Case for a closer look at how evil leaders deceive themselves as well as their followers.)

EVIL AS BUREAUCRACY

The twentieth century was the bloodiest period in history. Over 100 million people died as the direct or indirect result of wars, genocide, and other violence.

According to public administration professors Guy Adams and Danny Balfour, the combination of science and technology made the 1900s so destructive.[4] Scientific and technological developments (tanks, airplanes, chemical warfare, nuclear weapons) made killing highly efficient. At the same time, belief in technological progress encouraged government officials to take a rational approach to problems. The combination of these factors produced *administrative evil.* In administrative evil, ordinary people commit heinous crimes while carrying out their daily tasks. Balfour and Adams argue that the true nature of administrative evil is masked or hidden from participants. Officials are rarely asked to engage in evil; instead they inflict pain and suffering while fulfilling their job responsibilities.

The Holocaust provides the most vivid example of administrative evil in action. Extermination camps would not have been possible without the willing cooperation of thousands of civil servants engaged in such functions as tax collection, municipal government, and running the Social Security system. These duties may seem morally neutral, but in carrying them out, public officials condemned millions to death. Government authorities defined who was undesirable and then seized their assets. Administrators managed the ghettos, built concentration camp latrines, and employed slave labor. Even the railway authority did its part. The Gestapo had to pay for each prisoner shipped by rail to the death camps. Railroad officials billed the SS at third-class passenger rates (one way) for adult prisoners with discounts for children. Guards were charged round-trip fares.

EVIL AS SANCTIONED DESTRUCTION

Social scientists Nevitt Sanford and Craig Comstock believe that widespread evil occurs when victimizers are given permission or sanction to attack groups that have been devalued or dehumanized.[5] Such permission opens the door for such crimes as mass murder and genocide. Sanctions can be overt (a direct statement or order) or disguised (a hint, praise for others engaging in aggressive behavior). Once given, sanctions open the door to oppression because targeted groups no longer enjoy the protections given to the rest of society. American history is filled with examples of devalued peoples. Native Americans were the targeted for extinction; African Americans were routinely lynched for, among other reasons, public entertainment; Chinese laborers were denied citizenship. Recently the entire U.S. population has become the target of dehumanization. Some Moslems consider the United States to be the "Great Satan" populated by infidels. Such reasoning accounts for the spontaneous celebrations that broke out on the streets of some Islamic nations on news of the 9/11 bombings.

EVIL AS A CHOICE

Any discussion of good and evil must consider the role of human choice. Just how much freedom we have is a matter of debate, but a number of scholars have argued that we become good or evil through a series of small, incremental decisions. In other words, we never remain neutral but are moving toward one pole or another. Medieval scholar C. S. Lewis draws on the image of a road to illustrate this point.[6] On a journey, we make a decision about which direction to take every time we come to a fork in the road. We face a similar series of decisions throughout our lives. We can't correct poor decisions by continuing on but must go back to the "fork" and take the other path.

Psychologist Erich Fromm makes the same argument as Lewis. Only those who are very good or very bad have no choice; the rest of us do. However, each choice we make reduces our options.

> Each step in life which increases my self-confidence, my integrity, my courage, my conviction also increases my capacity to choose the desirable alternative, until eventually it becomes more difficult to choose the undesirable rather than the desirable action. On the other hand, each act of surrender and cowardice weakens me, opens the path for more acts of surrender, and eventually freedom is lost. Between the extreme when I can no longer do a wrong act and the other extreme when I have lost my freedom to right action, there are innumerable degrees of freedom of choice. In the practice of life the degree of freedom to choose is different at any given moment. If the degree of freedom to choose the good is great, it needs less effort to choose the good. If it is small, it takes a great effort, help from others, and favorable circumstances.[7]

Fromm uses the story of Israel's exodus from ancient Egypt to illustrate what happens when leaders make a series of evil choices. Moses repeatedly asks Pharaoh to let his people go, but the Egyptian ruler turns down every request. Eventually the king's heart is "hardened," and he and his army are destroyed.

EVIL AS EVOLVING STORY

Essayist Lance Morrow is convinced that evil is an historical fact. "The question is not whether evil exists," he says, "but how it exists, how it works."[8] Evil is part of the human story, past, present, and future. We see how evil works when it is captured in historical narrative. The story of ancient King Herod's slaughter of the innocents gives us insight into the nature of evil, for example. So does the contemporary story of civil war in Sierra Leone. Soldiers on both sides of the Sierra Leone conflict cut off the arms, hands, and feet of babies, children, and adults. To Morrow, evil evolves as history evolves. Every time and place has its unique form of evil. The horrors of the Holocaust were followed by the threat of nuclear extinction, which was followed in turn by the reemergence of violent religious extremism. Evil is also opportunistic. It takes advantage of available resources like hatred, fanaticism, power, fear, cowardice, peer pressure, and the desire for entertainment. The impact of evil, once contained by distance and technological limitations, now extends to the entire world. Globalization and the miniaturization of nuclear and biochemical weapons means that just one individual can wreak as much havoc as infamous world leaders like Caligula and Stalin did in the past.

FACING EVIL

"Your Honor, may I point out to the court that my client pleaded guilty to wrongdoing, but not evildoing."

SOURCE: Reprinted with permission.

Each of the perspectives described above provides insights into how we can come to grips with evil as leaders. The dreadful pleasure approach highlights both the origins of evil and the attraction of doing evil, forcing us to examine our motivations. We need to ask ourselves: Am I projecting my insecurities onto others? Am I punishing a subordinate because of her or his poor performance or because exercising coercive power makes me feel strong? Am I making a legitimate request or merely demonstrating that I have the authority to control another person?

The evil-as-deception viewpoint makes it clear that people aren't always as they seem. Evil individuals appear, on the surface, to be successful and well adjusted. In reality, they exert tremendous energy keeping up appearances. Deceit and defensiveness can serve as warning signs. If we routinely lie to protect our images, refuse constructive feedback, and always blame others, we may be engaged in evil. The same may be true of other leaders and followers who display these behaviors. Peck, like Parker Palmer, believes that to master our inner demons we must first name them. Once we've identified these tendencies, we can then begin to deal with them by examining our will. We should determine if we're willing to submit to a positive force (an ideal, authority) that is greater than we are. Peck urges us to respond to the destructive acts of others with love. Instead of attacking evildoers, we can react with goodness and thereby "absorb" the power of evil.

The administrative evil perspective introduces a new type of evil, one based on technology and logic. Modern evil has greater capacity for destruction, and its face may be masked or hidden from those who participate in it. We need to be aware of how our activities contribute to good or evil. Claiming that we were "just carrying out orders" (as did Nazi war criminal Adolf Eichmann) is no excuse.

The evil-as-sanction approach should alert us to the danger of dehumanizing any segment of the population. Language is one of the evildoers' most powerful tools. It is much easier to persecute others who have been labeled as "nerds," "pigs," "scum," "Moslem extremists," or "tree huggers." We need to challenge and eliminate these labels (whether we use them or someone else does). Also, be alert to disguised sanctions. If you don't respond to racial slurs, for example, you legitimize these behaviors and encourage future attacks.

Evil as a choice puts the ethical burden squarely on our shoulders. Group and organizational pressures may contribute to our wrongdoing. However, we make the decision to participate in evil acts. Further, the choices we make now will limit our options in the future. Every moral decision, no matter how insignificant it seems at the time, has lasting consequences.

The final perspective, evil as evolving story, suggests that evil will always be with us, ready to take advantage of any opportunity. We need to be constantly alert to conditions that allow evil to flourish and recognize that any setting has the potential to be twisted by its influence. (Turn to the Covering Up Evil Chapter End Case for one example of evil operating in a most unlikely place.)

Making a Case for Forgiveness

BREAKING THE CYCLE OF EVIL

Scott Peck is not alone in arguing that loving acts can overcome evil. A growing number of social scientists believe that forgiving instead of retaliating can prevent or break cycles of evil. In a cycle of evil, aggressive acts provoke retaliation followed by more aggression. When these destructive patterns characterize relations between ethnic groups (Turks vs. Armenians, Serbs vs.

Croats), they can continue for hundreds of years. Courageous leaders can end retaliatory cycles through dramatic acts of reconciliation, however. Former Egypt prime minister Anwar Sadat engaged in one such conciliatory gesture when he traveled to Jerusalem to further the peace process with Israel. Pope John Paul II went to the jail cell of his would-be assassin to offer forgiveness. Archbishop Desmond Tutu and Nelson Mandela prevented a bloodbath in South Africa by creating the Truth and Reconciliation Commission. This body, made up of both blacks and whites, investigated crimes committed during the apartheid era and allowed offenders to confess their guilt and ask for pardon.

The concept of forgiving evildoers is controversial. (See Case Study 4.1 for a closer look at some of the issues raised by forgiveness.) Skeptics worry that guilty parties will get off without paying for their crimes, that forgiveness is a sign of weakness, that forgiveness is impossible in some situations, that forgiveness can't be offered until after the offender asks for it, and that no leader has the right to offer forgiveness on behalf of other victims. Each of these concerns is valid. You will have to decide if forgiveness is an appropriate response to evil deeds. However, before you make that determination, I want to describe the forgiveness process and identify some of the benefits that come from extending mercy to others.

CASE STUDY 4.1

To Forgive or Not to Forgive?

Like many other European Jews, Simon Wiesenthal endured unimaginable suffering at the hands of the Nazis. Eighty-nine of his relatives perished in the Holocaust, and Wiesenthal himself spent the war in a concentration camp. Hunger, torture, and death were his constant companions.

One day, a nurse called Wiesenthal away from his work detail, which was removing rubbish from a hospital, to hear the confession of an SS officer named Karl who had been severely wounded by an artillery shell. Blind and near death, Karl told how he had rejected his Catholic upbringing to join the Hitler Youth. Later, he volunteered for the SS. Posted to the Russian front, he participated in a massacre in a small town named Dnepropetrovsk. Jews from the area were crammed into a house that was set on fire. All who tried to escape, including small children, were shot. This incident haunted Karl, and now he wanted to confess his crime to Wiesenthal as a representative of the Jewish race. He begged for forgiveness so that he could die in peace. Wiesenthal pondered the request and then left without saying a word.

Prisoner Wiesenthal had mixed feelings about his decision, asking companions if he had made the right choice. He went to Karl's home after the war ended and met Karl's mother who still believed that her son was a "good boy." In order to protect Karl's reputation, Wiesenthal hid the fact that her son had become a murderer. Later Wiesenthal would become the world's most famous Nazi hunter, bringing over 1,100 war criminals to justice.

Wiesenthal describes his encounter with the SS soldier in a book entitled *The Sunflower*. In the first half of the book, he recounts the story. In the second half, he asks 42 theologians, political leaders, writers, Holocaust survivors, and others what they would have done in his place. They wrestle with such questions as "Must we forgive when asked?" "Can we forgive on behalf of other people?" "Does forgiveness diminish the seriousness of the crime?" "What does forgiveness do to the victim? to the perpetrator?"

As you might imagine, responses to this moral dilemma vary widely. Some respondents argue that forgiveness is a form of "cheap grace' that diminishes the enormity of the crime and the suffering of the victims. Even God can't forgive some atrocities, they argue. Others believe that only the offended can forgive the offenders; no one can offer mercy on their behalf. Still others claim that genuine remorse deserves forgiveness. They believe that mercy in the face of honest repentance is the way to break the cycle of retribution and to help victims regain control over their lives.

What would you have done had you been in Wiesenthal's place? Why?

THE FORGIVENESS PROCESS

There are lots of misconceptions about what it means to forgive another person or group of people. According to Robert Enright, professor of educational psychology and president of the International Forgiveness Institute at the University of Wisconsin, forgiveness is **not** the following:[9]

– Forgetting past wrongs to "move on"

– Excusing or condoning bad, damaging behavior

– Reconciliation or coming together again (forgiveness opens the way to reconciliation, but the other person must change or desire to reconcile)

– Reducing the severity of offenses

– Offering a legal pardon

– Pretending to forgive in order to wield power over another person

– Ignoring the offender

– Dropping our anger and becoming emotionally neutral

Enright and his colleagues define forgiving as "a willingness to abandon one's right to resentment, negative judgment, and indifferent behavior toward one who unjustly injured us, while fostering the undeserved qualities of compassion, generosity, and even love toward him or her."[10] This definition recognizes that (a) the wronged party has been unjustly treated (slandered, betrayed, imprisoned), (b) the offended person willingly chooses forgiveness regardless of the offender's response, (c) forgiving involves emotions, thoughts, and behavior, and (d) forgiveness is a process that takes place over time.

Enright and his colleagues offer a four-stage model to help people forgive. (A list of the psychological factors that go into each stage is found in Box 4.1.) In the first phase—*uncovering*—a victim may initially deny that a problem exists. However, when the individual does acknowledge the hurt, he or she may experience intense feelings of anger, shame, and betrayal. The victim invests a lot of psychic energy in rehashing the offense and comparing his or her condition with that of the offender. Feeling permanently damaged, the individual may believe that life is unfair.

During the second phase—*decision*—the injured party recognizes that he or she is paying a high price for dwelling on the injury, considers the possibility of forgiveness, and commits him or herself to forgiving.

Forgiveness is accomplished in stage three—*work*. The wronged party tries to understand (not condone) the victimizer's background and motivation. He or she may experience empathy and compassion for the offender. Absorbing pain is the key to this stage. The forgiver decides to endure suffering rather

Box 4.1

Psychological Elements of Forgiveness

Psychological Variables That May Be Involved When We Forgive

UNCOVERING PHASE

1. Evaluation of psychological defenses

2. Confrontation of anger; the point is to release, not harbor, the anger

3. Admittance of shame, when this is appropriate

4. Awareness of cathexis

5. Awareness of cognitive rehearsal of the offense

6. Insight that the injured party may be comparing self with the injurer

7. Realization that oneself may be permanently and adversely changed by the injury

8. Insight into a possibly altered "just world" view

DECISION PHASE

9. A change of heart, conversion, new insights that old resolution strategies are not working

10. Willingness to consider forgiveness as an option

11. Commitment to forgive the offender

WORK PHASE

12. Reframing, through role taking, who the wrongdoer is by viewing him or her in context

13. Empathy toward the offender

14. Awareness of compassion, as it emerges, toward the offender

15. Acceptance and absorption of the pain

(Continued)

Box 4.1 *(Continued)*

DEEPENING PHASE

16. Finding meaning for self and others in the suffering
    and in the forgiveness process

17. Realization that self has needed others'
    forgiveness in the past

18. Insight that one is not alone (universality, support)

19. Realization that self may have a new
    purpose in life because of the injury

20. Awareness of decreased negative affect and, perhaps,
    increased positive affect, if this begins to emerge,
    toward the injurer; awareness of internal, emotional release

SOURCE: Enright, R. D., Freedman, S., & Rique, J. (1998). The psychology of interpersonal forgiveness. In R. D. Enright & J. North (Eds.), *Exploring forgiveness.* Madison: University of Wisconsin Press, p. 53. Used by permission.

than pass it on, thereby breaking the cycle of evil. Viewed in this light, forgiveness is a gift of mercy to the wrongdoer. One demonstration of the hard work of forgiveness is found in the Leadership Ethics at the Movies case, *Dead Man Walking,* Box 4.2.

The fourth and final phase—*deepening*—describes the outcomes of forgiving. A forgiver may find deeper meaning in suffering, realize his or her own need for forgiveness, and come to a greater appreciation for support groups (friends, congregations, classmates). In the end, the person offering forgiveness may develop a new purpose in life and find peace.

The four-stage model has been used successfully with a variety of audiences: survivors of incest, inmates, college students deprived of parental love, and elderly women suffering from depression. In each case, forgivers experienced significant healing. Enright emphasizes that personal benefits should be a by-product, not the motivation, for forgiving. Nonetheless, forgiveness can pay significant psychological, physical, and relational dividends.[11] Those who forgive are released from resentments and experience less depression and anxiety. Overall, they enjoy a higher sense of well-being. By releasing their grudges, forgivers experience better physical health. Reducing anger, hostility, and

---

Box 4.2

Leadership Ethics at the Movies: *Dead Man Walking*

Key Cast Members: Susan Sarandon, Sean Penn

Synopsis: Based on the book of the same name, this is the sobering story of Sister Helen Prejean, a nun in Louisiana who becomes the spiritual adviser for an inmate on death row. The condemned man (Penn) has been convicted of the brutal murder and torture of two teenagers. Sister Prejean, played by Sarandon (who won an Oscar for her performance), ministers to Penn and his family at the same time she tries to understand the needs of the victims' parents. Penn finally admits his guilt on the way to his lethal injection. One set of parents appears ready to consider forgiveness, but the other couple remains locked in hate. "Dead man walking" is what the guards call out as they escort an inmate to the death chamber.

Rating: R for strong subject matter

Themes: evil, forgiveness, personal responsibility, spirituality, the death penalty, compassion vs. justice, courage

---

hopelessness lowers the risks of heart attack and high blood pressure while increasing the body's resistance to disease. Acting mercifully toward transgressors also maintains relationships between friends and family members.

The social-scientific study of forgiveness is relatively recent, but results so far are extremely encouraging. Forgiving does appear to absorb or defuse evil. If this is the case, then as leaders we should practice forgiveness when treated unjustly by followers, supervisors, peers, or outsiders. When we give offense ourselves, we will need to apologize and ask for mercy. At times, though, we will need to go further and follow the example of Anwar Sadat and Nelson Mandela by offering forgiveness on behalf of the group in hopes of reconciling with a long-standing enemy.

Donald Shriver uses the metaphor of a cable to explain how warring groups can overcome their mutual hatred and bind together to restore fractured relationships.[12] This cable is made up of four strands. The first strand is *moral truth*. Forgiveness starts with recalling the past and rendering a moral judgment. Both parties need to agree that one or both engaged in behavior that was wrong, unjust, and caused injury. Refusal to admit the truth makes reconciliation impossible. That's why South Africa's Truth and Reconciliation Commission began the process of national healing after apartheid by publicly airing black victims' statements and requests for amnesty by white police officers.

The second strand of the cable is *forbearance*. Forbearance means rejecting revenge in favor of restraint. Moral indignation often fuels new crimes as offended parties take their vengeance. Forbearance breaks this pattern and may soften enemies who expect retaliation.

The third strand is *empathy* for the enemies' humanity. Empathy doesn't excuse wrongs but acknowledges that offender and offended share much in common. This recognition opens the way for both sides to live together in peace. Ulysses S. Grant demonstrated how to combine the judgment of wrong with empathy at Appomattox. When Southern troops surrendered to end the Civil War, Grant wrote the following in his journal. "I felt . . . sad and depressed at the downfall of a foe who had fought so long and valiantly, and had suffered so much for a cause, though that cause was, I believe, one of the worst for which a people ever fought."[13]

The fourth and final strand of the forgiveness cable is *commitment* to restore the broken relationship. Forgivers must be prepared to live and interact with their former enemies. At first, the two parties will likely coexist in a state of mutual toleration. Later, they may fully reconcile, as the United States and Germany have done since the end of World War II.

In sum, I believe that forgiveness is one of a leader's most powerful weapons in the fight against evil. Or, to return to the central metaphor of this text, forgiving is one of the ways that leaders cast light rather than shadow. We must face our inner darkness, particularly our resentments and hostilities, in order to offer genuine forgiveness. By forgiving, we short circuit or break the shadowy, destructive cycles that poison groups, organizations, or societies. Offering forgiveness brightens our lives by reducing our anxiety levels and enhancing our sense of well-being.

Spiritual Resources

SPIRITUALITY AND LEADERSHIP

Coming to grips with evil is hard work. We must always be on the lookout for evil whatever form it takes, continually evaluate our motivations and choices, and make a conscious effort to forgive by reshaping our thoughts, emotions, and behaviors. All the elements we introduced in the last chapter—virtues, habits, hardships, purpose, and values—can equip us for these tasks. A great number of leaders also look to spirituality for help when addressing the shadow side of leadership.

Discussions of spirituality in organizational settings emphasize connection and integration. Based on their interviews with managers and executives, Ian Mitroff and Elizabeth Denton define spirituality as "the basic feeling of being connected with one's complete self, others, and the entire universe." Connection with self means getting in touch with our deepest yearnings and emotions or "heart knowledge."[14] Connection with others is expressed through concern for coworkers, teamwork, respect, and community involvement. Connection with "the entire universe" refers to developing relationships with larger forces like God and nature. It should be noted that religion and spirituality overlap but are not identical. Religious institutions encourage and structure spiritual experiences, but spiritual encounters can occur outside formal religious channels.[15]

If spirituality seems to be a strange topic to discuss in a book about leadership ethics, consider the recent explosion of interest in spirituality in the workplace. There are an estimated 4,000 chaplains who work for private corporations (excluding hospitals, jails, and colleges). Mediation rooms and reflective gardens are part of many company headquarters. Some organizations sponsor groups for spiritual seekers and send employees to business and spirituality workshops. David Whyte, James Autry, Terrence Deal, and Thomas Chappell are a few of the popular writers who focus on spiritual development at work.

In his study of 91 top executives at publicly held companies cited in the last chapter, University of Tennessee management professor William Judge found that "spirituality is central to executive character."[16] Most of the CEOs he surveyed were connected with religious denominations and engaged in regular spiritual activities like prayer. All reported some sort of "trigger event," generally a major setback, which convinced them that they were not in control and deepened their faith in God. Judge's findings are consistent with those of other researchers who report that middle- and upper-level managers are more religious than the population as a whole.

The recent surge of interest in spirituality in the workplace has been fueled, in large part, by the growing importance of organizations. For better or for worse, the organization has replaced other groups (family, church, social groups) as the dominant institution in society. Work takes up increasing amounts of our time and energy. As a result, we tend to develop more friendships with coworkers and fewer with individuals outside the organization. Many of us want a higher return on this investment of time and energy, seeking meaningful tasks and relationships that serve higher purposes. Organizations, in turn, hope to benefit from more connected members. Spirituality has been found to enhance commitment to mission, core values, and ethical standards; foster organizational learning and creativity; improve morale; generate higher productivity; and encourage closer collaboration.[17]

Any organizational discussion of spirituality must be undertaken with great care. Some members will be uncomfortable with the topic and their wishes must be respected. Avoid proselytizing for a particular religious doctrine or attacking the belief systems of followers. Be careful that a focus on shared spiritual values doesn't make your organization "cultish" by suppressing dissent and encouraging conformity and totalitarian leadership. Make every effort to ensure that spirituality doesn't become just another tool that manipulates employees into working harder to improve profits.

SPIRITUAL DEVELOPMENT

It's one thing to acknowledge that spiritual resources can help leaders; figuring out how to develop them is quite another. Fortunately, we don't have to start from scratch. Emory University professor James Fowler provides one description of the process of spiritual development or spiritual formation.[18] Fowler believes that we go through spiritual or faith phases in the same way that we pass through stages of physical and emotional development. Each stage focuses on a particular set of spiritual concerns and poses its own unique set of challenges. Individuals shift or "convert" from one stage to another. When their current worldview doesn't seem to explain events, they abandon it for the next. Chronological age is a necessary precondition for spiritual formation but, in and of itself, doesn't bring spiritual maturity. Spiritual development can stop as physical development continues. Fowler identifies seven stages of spiritual growth:

Primal faith (infancy). Before a child begins to speak, she or he learns to trust in parents and other caregivers.

Intuitive-projective faith (early childhood). Guided by their feelings and imaginations, young children develop images of good and evil powers based on stories and symbols.

Mythic-literal faith (childhood and beyond). Older children develop the ability to think logically and thus bring order to their worlds. They can determine cause and effect, measure time and space, and so forth. They also adopt the beliefs and values of their families.

Synthetic-conventional faith (adolescence and beyond). In this stage the individual builds a unified sense of the self. However, most of the beliefs and values that make up the self-concept or personal story are uncritically borrowed from others, making this an age of conformity.

Individuative-reflective faith (young adulthood and beyond). This is a period of critical reflection during which a person thinks carefully about personal beliefs and values, sees her or his place in the larger system, and internalizes standards. Doubts and questions are common. The individual consciously chooses which beliefs, values, and commitments to hold.

Conjunctive faith (midlife and beyond). People in this stage learn to recognize and live with opposites or paradoxes. Common paradoxes include the need to have both masculine and feminine qualities, the joy of life and the reality of death, and the recognition of personal strengths and weaknesses. Those with conjunctive faith are open to the truths of other traditions while remaining committed to their own beliefs.

Universalizing faith (midlife and beyond). The few who reach this final state show very little concern for themselves. Instead, they commit themselves at great personal cost to serving larger purposes and forces, such as love and nonviolence. The moral exemplars we described in the last chapter would fit into this category, as would Gandhi and Mother Teresa, Martin Luther King, Jr., and German theologian and resistance leader Dietrich Bonhoeffer.

The seven-stage model is the story of how people, in general, develop spiritually. Fowler says we also need to develop our personal stories of spiritual formation within this larger narrative. Our individual stories revolve around our vocation. By vocation Fowler means a sense of calling. This calling should incorporate our careers but extend to all aspects of our lives. A teacher, for example, may exercise her vocation through her job in an elementary school, as a mentor to her grandchildren, and as a volunteer in a local literacy center.

Vocation and the stages of spiritual formation move in tandem. Individuals modify and refine their sense of vocation as they move through the phases of life. Young adults are occupied with identifying their vocations. Middle-aged adults, in contrast, must reevaluate their vocations in light of their experiences, acknowledging that some of their earlier dreams may never be fulfilled. They may experience burnout because they denied their vocations in order to make money or to meet the expectations of other people. Older adults don't have to be as concerned about career success as younger people and can take on new roles and projects. Their example can be an inspiration to those just starting on their vocations or reevaluating their choices.

Fowler has been criticized for developing a theory that promotes Christianity and identifies one stage—universalizing—as superior to the others. Fowler responds to these charges by noting that adherents of all religions seem to follow the same general spiritual path as they seek the same goal. For example, the state of enlightenment, which is the goal of Buddhist spiritual development, appears to be a form of universalizing faith.

The debate over what constitutes the highest level of spiritual growth shouldn't diminish the importance of Fowler's model and others like it.[19] Any spiritual training must take developmental differences into account by addressing the unique needs of various age groups. Spiritual issues at age 20 (critical examination of beliefs, identifying a vocation) will be replaced by other concerns in middle age (balancing contradictions, facing death, reevaluation and deepening of vocation). The developmental approach should also put to rest the mistaken belief that spiritual formation is quick and easy. There may be periods when we find ourselves caught in the transition between levels, disillusioned with the past stage but not yet at home in the next.

Fowler's discussion of spiritual growth enriches our understanding of personal mission and hardship, two concepts introduced in the last chapter. The ultimate goal of vocation is service, not personal success and achievement. As writer Frederick Buechner notes, vocation is "the place where your deep gladness and the world's deep hunger meet."[20] We would do well to incorporate this outward focus in our mission statements. Fowler's research also suggests that spiritual development, like other forms of leadership development, is a by-product of hardship. Failures, setbacks, personal trauma, and downsizing can reveal the inadequacies of our current faith system and move or convert us to another.

Ambition appears to be the greatest barrier to finding and following one's vocation. Often there is a clash between what we want to do and what our culture defines as success. We want to help the disadvantaged, teach, and become active in community affairs, but our cultural script encourages us to pursue other goals like making money, getting promoted, and achieving status. Seminary professor Brian Mahan argues that to follow our vocation we have to "forget ourselves on purpose."[21] First we need to determine what is most meaningful and satisfying to us (see the Self-Assessment in Box 4.3). Then we

---

Box 4.3

Self-Assessment

FINDING YOURSELF BY LOSING YOURSELF

The following exercise can help you identify your call or vocation. Gather a pen and paper, find a quiet location, and then take a few moments to relax. When you're ready, write or draw answers to the following sentence fragment: "I will be happy when . . ." After 5 or 6 minutes, respond to this sentence fragment: "I was so happy when . . ."

According to Brian Mahan, who developed this activity, your responses to the first statement will likely be peaceful ones (relaxing, gazing, strolling, etc.). Your responses to the second statement will probably describe times when you forgot about yourself for a while in some activity. In both cases, you will have set aside social scripts and other preoccupations and focus on what is most meaningful to you. You will have taken a small step toward "forgetting yourself on purpose."

SOURCE: Mahan, B. (2002). *Forgetting ourselves on purpose: Vocation and the ethics of ambition.* San Francisco: Jossey-Bass, pp. 62–65.

have to find out what it is that prevents us from hearing that call by asking, "What is keeping me from living fully for the thing I want to live for?" Finally, we have to deal with those preoccupations, acknowledging that pride and the trappings of success are distractions. Our focus should be on what we find most fulfilling. The end result will be a productive life in which the self is largely forgotten.

SPIRITUAL DISCIPLINES

Practicing spiritual disciplines is one way to promote our spiritual progress. Richard Foster, director of the Renovare spiritual renewal movement, identifies 13 disciplines or practices that have been used for centuries by such spiritual seekers as Augustine, Madame Guyon, Brother Lawrence, George Fox, and Thomas Merton. Foster focuses on their use in the Judeo-Christian tradition, but adherents of other faiths also engage in these practices. Fasting plays an important role in Islam, for instance, and meditation is central to Zen Buddhism. Foster divides the spiritual disciplines into three categories: inward, outward, and corporate.[22]

INWARD DISCIPLINES

The first group of disciplines encourages us to explore the inner dimension of spirituality. They tend to be "invisible" because they are practiced in private.

1. *The discipline of meditation.* Meditation is quiet contemplation aimed at making a connection with God (Western tradition) or emptying the mind (Eastern religious tradition). Foster makes these suggestions for productive meditation. Take 5 to 10 minutes to "center down" (quiet your mind). Then reflect on some aspect of creation or spiritual reading. You might visualize yourself in a beautiful setting or interacting with God, for example.

2. *The discipline of prayer.* Prayer is often seen as the best means of getting something from a higher spiritual power—physical recovery, improved relationships, a better job. However, Foster points out that more often than not, it is the person praying who changes as a result of seeking God. Prayer brings a different perspective. We begin to see the big picture, feel more compassion for those who have wronged us (see our earlier discussion of forgiveness), and become more patient.

3. *The discipline of fasting.* Fasting is going without food for spiritual purposes. For example, we might fast to signal our spiritual commitment, to draw closer to our spiritual center, to increase our concentration on spiritual matters, or to provide more time for meditation and prayer.

4. *The discipline of study.* Study is designed to change the way we think about reality. Meditation is reflective but study is analytical. Changing our perspectives

through study requires repeated effort, concentrated focus, and careful reflection on what we've learned. We can uncover important spiritual principles by reading, observing nature, analyzing relationships, and uncovering the underlying values of society. You might want to study the primary texts of the world's faiths and philosophies (the *Tao Te Ching*, the *Koran*, the *Bible*, the *Analects of Confucius*) or seek out spiritual classics that have withstood the test of time. In Christian tradition, spiritual classics include the writings of Martin Luther, Augustine, Søren Kierkegaard, and Teresa of Avila.[23]

OUTWARD DISCIPLINES

The outward disciplines are visible to others and have an impact on our relationships with others and society at large. The outward disciplines include the following:

5. *The discipline of simplicity.* Simplicity means putting spiritual goals first by relegating material goods to a secondary position in our lives. "Simple" individuals don't worry about status or protecting their assets. Instead, they speak plainly and honestly, give things away, and avoid excessive debt.

6. *The discipline of solitude.* Setting aside time to be alone may seem selfish. However, after we've been silent, we listen more effectively to others and are more attentive to their needs. Unfortunately, most of us (including the author) avoid silence like the plague. Even when we're alone, we listen to music or watch television. Foster suggests that we take advantage of the "little solitudes" that occur during the average day. These include the first few moments after waking up, our morning cup of coffee or tea, being stuck in traffic, or walking to an appointment. Create a space at home or work (a room, chair, corner of the garage) for silence and set aside 3 to 4 hours several times a year to reexamine and reset your goals.

7. *The discipline of submission.* Submission means putting aside our need to always have our way. With this attitude, we can decide to give up our rights for the benefit of other people. Acts of submission include the following:
    - Yielding to God
    - Following the tenets of sacred texts
    - Commitment to other family members
    - Acts of kindness toward neighbors
    - Helping the disadvantaged
    - Recognizing our commitment to an interdependent world and future generations.

8. *The discipline of service.* Foster makes a clear distinction between "self-righteous" and "true" service. Self-righteous service looks for immediate visible results and wants public recognition. Those engaged in this kind of service pick who they want to serve and when. They only serve when they feel like it. True service is motivated by need, not mood. It is a lifestyle that quietly goes

about caring for others on a regular basis. True service produces humility in the server. Ways to serve include protecting the reputation of coworkers, common courtesy, practicing hospitality, empathetic listening, and sharing spiritual insights. I'll have more to say about the relationship between service and leadership in Chapter 6.

CORPORATE DISCIPLINES

The final set of disciplines recognizes that, for most of us, our spiritual formation takes place in the context of a larger community (church, synagogue, temple, worship group). Corporate disciplines are what believers do together to foster the spiritual growth of the entire group.

9. *The discipline of confession.* Confession plays an important role in forgiveness (see our earlier discussion). An honest confession requires careful self-examination, genuine sorrow for the act, and a strong desire to not offend again. When receiving a confession, don't act shocked or pry for further details. Instead, listen quietly, accept the confession, and if appropriate, pray with the offender.

10. *The discipline of worship.* Worship occurs when seekers gather together for singing, praise, prayer, and teaching. Effective worship takes preparation. Those coming to the gathering must be prepared to listen and should expect to be spiritually strengthened. The inward disciplines are excellent preparation for the corporate expression of faith. Engage in meditation and prayer, for instance, before joining with others for worship.

11. *The discipline of guidance.* Wise leaders recognize the importance of receiving feedback from the larger group when making significant individual decisions. They're willing to delay or adjust their plans based on the feedback they receive. Quakers call "meetings for clearness" to seek collective input on important questions like what job an individual should take, the suitableness of a couple for marriage, and how to address social concerns. Corporate guidance can also come through a mentor. Recognizing this fact, members of Catholic religious orders appoint spiritual directors to assist young priests and nuns as well as lay people.

12. *The discipline of celebration.* Celebration is a central component of all the spiritual disciplines, according to Foster. A joyful spirit breathes life into the rest of the practices and is the product of a spiritually disciplined life. Joy encourages us to be disciplined, and spiritual development is something worth celebrating. Celebration (a) relaxes us, (b) acts as an antidote to sadness and depression, (c) gives a new perspective (we can laugh at ourselves), (d) levels out status differences, (e) frees us from judgmental attitudes, and (f) increases the likelihood of more celebration ("joy begets joy"). We can celebrate— through music, dance, fantasy, and play—family gatherings, major holidays, and rituals of our own creation.

Implications and Applications

- Evil takes a variety of forms or faces, including a sense of dreadful pleasure, deception, rational administration, sanctioned devaluation, a series of small but fateful decisions, and an evolving, opportunistic element of the human story. Whatever face it displays, evil is a destructive force that inflicts pain and suffering and ends in death.
- Ultimately, the choice of whether or not to do or participate in evil is yours.
- Forgiveness is one way to defuse or absorb evil. As a leader, you need to seriously consider the role of forgiveness in your relations with followers, peers, supervisors, and outsiders.
- Forgiving does *not* mean forgetting or condoning evil. Instead, forgivers hold offenders accountable for their actions at the same time they offer mercy. Forgiving takes a conscious act of the will, unfolds over time, and replaces hostility and resentment with empathy and compassion.
- Forgiveness breaks cycles of evil and restores relationships. However, you may gain the most from extending mercy. Forgiving can heighten your sense of well-being, give you renewed energy, and improve your health.
- Warring groups can overcome their mutual hatred through facing and judging the past, rejecting revenge in favor of restraint, feeling empathy for their enemies' humanity, and being committed to restoring the broken relationship.
- Spiritual resources can equip you for the demanding work of confronting evil. Spirituality focuses on connection with the deepest elements of the self, with other people, and with larger forces like God, nature, and humanity.
- Spiritual development is an ongoing, lifelong process. Expect to face new challenges and concerns throughout your life span. Anticipate that the nature of your spiritual beliefs and commitments will change.
- Engaging in spiritual disciplines can help your spiritual progress. Common spiritual practices fall into three categories: (a) *inward* (meditation, prayer, fasting, study); (b) *outward* (simplicity, solitude, submission, service); and (c) *corporate* (confession, worship, guidance, celebration).

For Further Exploration, Challenge, and Self-Assessment

1. Which of the perspectives on evil described in the chapter is most useful to you? How does it help you better understand and prevent evil?

2. Develop your own definition of forgiveness. Does your definition set boundaries that limit when forgiveness can be offered? What right do leaders have to offer or accept forgiveness on behalf of the group?

3. Consider a time when you forgave someone who treated you unjustly. Did you move through the stages identified by Enright and his colleagues? What benefits did you experience? Conversely, describe a time when you asked for and

received forgiveness. What process did you go through? How did you and the relationship benefit?

4. Develop your own forgiveness case study based on the life of a leader who prevented or broke a cycle of evil through an act of mercy or reconciliation.

5. What should be the role of spirituality in leadership? Try to reach a consensus on this question in a group.

6. Reflect on your responses to the self-assessment exercise in the chapter. What insights did you gain from completing this activity? What clues does it provide to your possible vocation?

7. Design a strategy for encouraging your spiritual growth as a leader using as many of the 12 spiritual disciplines as possible.

CASE STUDY 4.2

Chapter End Case: Justifying Terror

Do dictators ever feel regret for what they've done? What do they tell their children and grandchildren to justify their actions? What do they tell themselves? Italian journalist Riccardo Orizio set out to answer these questions by interviewing seven former tyrants (or, in some cases, their spouses) who had been driven from power in disgrace:

1. *Idi Amin Dada.* During his tenure as leader of Uganda from 1971 to 1979, Big Daddy was known for his bizarre and cruel behavior. He called himself the Last King of Scotland in honor of the country he admired, addressed the queen of England as "Liz," and enjoyed humiliating Western visitors. Amin expelled 80,000 Indians from Uganda and murdered 300,000 citizens, including members of his own family. He boasted of eating human flesh but declared it too salty. Amin died while living in comfortable exile in Saudi Arabia in 2003.

2. *Jean-Bedel Bokassa.* Bokassa terrorized the Central African Republic from 1966 to 1979. He controlled many of the nation's businesses and took a huge share of ivory profits generated by slaughtering 5,000 elephants a year. He ordered the machine gun massacre of 150 elementary and secondary students and the torture and arrest of university demonstrators. Bokassa allegedly kept the remains of student leaders in a freezer next to his kitchen. He died in 1996.

3. *Wojciech Jaruzelski.* Jaruzelski ordered his troops to fire on unarmed Polish protestors while serving as a Communist general. Later, as Polish chief of state (1981–1989), he declared martial law. Hundreds of dissidents were jailed during the subsequent period of repression. The general is also accused of orchestrating the assassination of a popular priest.

4. *Enver and Nexhmije Hoxha.* Staunch Marxists, Enver (the "Great Leader") and his wife (the "Black Widow") founded and then ruled Albania from the end of World War II until the early 1990s. Afraid that the Great Leader might be profaned, they made it illegal to mention Enver's name except on official occasions or by those officially authorized to use it. Only the Great Leader's work could be studied in the country's schools. The Hoxhas tortured their opponents and required citizens to denounce their neighbors or themselves every year.

5. *Jean-Claude Duvalier ("Baby Doc").* Nearly two thirds of the Haitian government's income was illegally diverted to Baby Doc's friends and family during his regime (1971–1986) while Haiti remained one of the poorest countries on earth. His paramilitary supporters are accused of killing 40,000 and driving a million people into exile.

6. *Mengistu Haile Mariam.* The absolute ruler of Ethiopia from 1977 to 1991, Haile Mariam deported hundreds of thousands of citizens "for their own good" and built Africa's largest army while many starved. He launched a campaign called the "Red Terror" that killed 500,000. In order to retrieve the bodies of their dead relatives, family members had to pay a ransom equivalent to the cost of the bullets used in their executions.

7. *Slobodan Milosevic and Mira Markovic.* Serbia's ruling couple used Serbian nationalism and frustration to unleash a war of genocide in the Balkans. Moslems and Croats were driven from their homes, raped, murdered en masse, and interned in concentration camps. Many prominent Serbian citizens were also eliminated during their regime (1986–2000).

Orizio limited his interviews to dictators who had been driven from power. He thought that, unlike Augusto Pinochet of Chile and Suharto of Indonesia who still enjoy popular support, disgraced tyrants would be more likely to examine their consciences. He soon discovered otherwise. None of the dictators expressed serious regrets. Instead, they offered a variety of justifications for their actions.

Amin claimed that his enemies made up stories of atrocities to discredit him. Rather than expressing any remorse, he felt "only nostalgia." Bokassa was convinced he had been absolved by God as well as by the people of the Central African Republic. Januzelski believes that he had to suppress dissent and impose martial law to prevent the Soviet Union from forcing even harsher measures on the Polish people. Nexhmije Hoxha excuses any "excesses" of her regime as the ruling couple's desire to protect Albania and to defend the government against its enemies. Baby Doc is proud of what he and his father (Papa Doc) did for Haiti, particularly for the poor. Haile Mariam is proud of his record as well. He blames his downfall on Communist allies who failed to come to his aid.

The wife of Serbia's imprisoned leader is particularly unrepentant. Mira Markovic accuses the United States of hypocrisy. The U.S. government has declared war against terrorism, she complains, yet opposes her country's efforts to protect itself from Moslem terrorists. Markovic sees her husband as a hero, not as a villain.

My husband will be seen as the hero of all the little people who are the victims of the arrogance of great powers. He'll go down in history as a great freedom fighter. Mass graves? An invention. I'm proud of my people. The only thing I'm not proud about is that the leader of this people has been illegally arrested and extradited thanks to a puppet government funded by the West.[24]

Based on the responses of Orzio's sample, evil leaders are masters of denial: Many of their so-called crimes never took place. Almost anyone else is at fault— the press, the opposition, foreign governments, allies, overzealous followers. National security and ideology justified their cruelty. Conditions are worse now that they have been removed from office.

Perhaps the extent of the tyrants' self-deception should not surprise us. After all, how could they live with themselves if they accepted full responsibility for their actions? Nevertheless, their failure to repent illustrates the deceptive face of evil. Evildoers deceive themselves at the same time they are deceiving others.

DISCUSSION PROBES

1. What other dictators would you like to interview? What would you want to find out? Do you think they would deny their crimes as well?

2. Is deception always part of evil?

3. How do we avoid deceiving ourselves about our wrongful acts?

4. Should any of these dictators be forgiven? What if they had repented for their actions?

5. What leadership lessons do you draw from this case?

REFERENCE

Orizio, R. (2002). *Talk of the devil: Encounters with seven dictators.* (A. Bardoni, Trans.). New York: Walker.

CASE STUDY 4.3

Chapter End Case: Covering Up Evil

Sometimes evil shows up in the most unexpected places. That's the case with the child sexual abuse scandal involving hundreds of priests in the American Roman Catholic Church. Few could have anticipated that alarming numbers of these dedicated professionals would use their positions as spiritual advisers to victimize children in their care. Few, too, could have anticipated the lengths to which church leaders would go to cover up their crimes.

The problem of priest sex abuse became the focus of national attention in January 2002 with a series of reports in the *Boston Globe*. *Globe* reporters found that child molestation was widespread in the Boston archdiocese, with 90 priests accused of abusing hundreds of victims over 40 years. They soon discovered that the problem was not limited to the Boston area. At least 1,500 U.S. priests from nearly every state have been charged with sexual misconduct with minors since the mid-1980s. According to one estimate, the U.S. Catholic Church spent $1.3 billion settling sexual assault claims during this period. Most cases involved parish priests who abused preteen boys. High-level church officials in the United States, Ireland, Poland, and Wales were also removed from office for sexual misconduct during this same period.

Faithful church members trusted these "servants of God" and welcomed them into their families. Often pedophiles targeted victims from needy, single-parent families whose mothers wanted their boys to develop relationships with godly adult males. Parents blame themselves for letting predators into their homes; victims blame themselves for being victimized. A great many of the abused have left the church or their faith. Others find it hard to trust others, hold jobs, build relationships, or enjoy sex. One victim summarized his feeling of betrayal this way: "A person who would wrap themselves in God and weave themselves into the very fabric of a family who came to know, love, and trust him for the purpose of molesting their children is the incarnation of evil."[25]

Public outrage at pedophiles masquerading as priests has been magnified by the response of church leaders. Bishops and cardinals protected offenders rather than fire them and turn them over to the police. Boston cardinal Bernard Law's reaction to sex abuse allegations was all too typical. Law wrote a letter of recommendation to California church officials for alleged child rapist Paul Shanley after Shanley had been accused of sexual abuse. The cardinal later wrote a "glowing" retirement letter for Shanley after paying off Shanley's victims. He didn't object to Shanley's appointment to a position at a New York guest home that cared for children as well as adults. Law also protected Father John Geoghan, who was later killed in prison after being sentenced for child molestation. He periodically sent Geoghan to treatment and then reinstated him. The cardinal kept shuttling the predatory priest from one position to another. Law didn't inform new congregations about Geoghan's troubled history.

Catholic authorities who refused to confront the problem of priest abuse often acted out of ignorance and compassion. Relying on the advice of psychiatrists, they thought that pedophiles could be "cured." (In other cases, church leaders ignored the warnings of mental health professionals.) Well-meaning cardinals and bishops viewed sex abuse as a sin, not a crime. They wanted to restore offenders to ministry.

Church structure contributed to attempts to cover up the crimes. Catholicism is one of the world's most hierarchical faiths. Church officials wield great power with very little accountability to lay people or outside authorities. Those with lower status (church members, nuns, parish priests, victimized children) are reluctant to challenge the actions of superiors. In such an atmosphere, secrecy flourishes. Worst of all, Cardinal Law and others put loyalty to the image of the church and its staff above the needs of innocent victims, their families, and their congregations. They did everything they could to protect the Catholic faith from scandal and to shelter their fellow priests. Congregation members, particularly the most vulnerable, paid the price. The cover-up itself became part of the evil. According to one prominent lay person hoping to reform the church, "The abusive priest, what he does is evil, but he could be mentally ill. The real evil are those who enable these priests."[26]

The U.S. Roman Catholic hierarchy has taken a number of steps to reform the way it handles sex abuse cases. Church officials have acknowledged the problem and apologized to victims and congregations. All reports of sexual allegations are immediately reported to prosecutors, and those accused are suspended pending investigation. Settlements with victims, which had been kept secret in the past, are now a matter of public record. Cardinal Law was replaced with a bishop noted for taking swift action against sexual offenders.

Dealing with the structural causes of the cover-up will be difficult. Despite pressure to give more power to lay people and women, the worldwide Catholic Church remains a male-dominated hierarchy. The ultimate church authority—Pope John Paul II—remains wedded to traditional church rules and structure.

DISCUSSION PROBES

1. Which leadership shadows were cast in this case? Why?

2. What additional steps can the church officials take to prevent future priest sexual abuse?

3. How can leaders restore trust in the Roman Catholic Church?

4. Should lay people have a greater voice in church operations? If so, what can they do to bring about change?

5. How do you maintain your faith in a secular cause or in a religious belief system when you lose your faith in its leaders?

6. What leadership lessons do you draw from this case?

REFERENCES

Adler, J. (2002, December 23). A cardinal offense. *Newsweek,* 50.

The Boston Globe Investigative Staff. (2002). *Betrayal: The crisis in the Catholic Church.* Boston, MA: Little, Brown.

Burnett, J. (2002, April 22). James Burnett looks at how the Catholic Church might salvage its tainted reputation. *PR Week,* 17.

Cooperman, A. (2003, July 19). Catholic bishops look for leadership: Abuse scandal reshaping hierarchy. *The Washington Post,* p. A7.

Dreher, R. (2002, January 15). Boston travesty. *National Review* [Online]. Retrieved November 15, 2003, from LexisNexis (www.lexisnexis.com/search/).

Gilbert, N. (2003, August 22). Darkness in the Catholic confessional. *The New York Times Higher Education Supplement,* p. 18.

Higgins, M. W. (2003, May 13). A Canadian expert on the Vatican examines the sex abuse scandal. *Maclean's,* p. 48.

Miller, L., & France, D. (2003, March 4). Sins of the father. *Newsweek,* 42.

Paulson, M. (2003, July 1). Florida Bishop O'Malley seen choice to lead Boston diocese has strong record on abusive priests in 2 assignments. *The Boston Globe,* p. A1.

Paulson, M., & Farragher, T. (2003, August 24). Ex-priest Geoghan attacked, dies. *The Boston Globe,* p. A1.

Notes

1. Definitions of evil can be found in the following sources. There are, of course, a host of other definitions offered by major religions and philosophical systems.

Hallie, P. (1997). *Tales of good and evil, help and harm.* New York: HarperCollins.

Katz, F. E. (1993). *Ordinary people and extraordinary evil: A report on the beguilings of evil.* Albany: State University of New York Press.

Peck, M. S. (1983). *People of the lie: The hope for healing human evil.* New York: Touchstone.

Sanford, N., & Comstock, C. (Eds.). (1971). *Sanctions for evil.* San Francisco: Jossey-Bass.

2. Alford, C. F. (1997). *What evil means to us.* Ithaca, NY: Cornell University Press, p. 3.

3. Peck (1983), *People of the lie.*

4. Adams, G. B., & Balfour, D. L. (1998). *Unmasking administrative evil.* Thousand Oaks, CA: Sage. See also Arendt, H. (1964). *Eichmann in Jerusalem: A report on the banality of evil.* New York: Viking Press.

5. Sanford & Comstock (1971), *Sanctions for evil.* For a closer look at the role that sanctions play in genocide, see Staub, E. (1989). *The roots of evil: The origins of genocide and other group violence.* Cambridge, UK: Cambridge University Press.

6. Lewis, C. S. (1946). *The great divorce.* New York: Macmillan.

7. Fromm, E. (1964). *The heart of man: Its genius for good and evil.* New York: Harper & Row, p. 136.

8. Morrow, L. (2003). *Evil: An investigation.* New York: Basic Books, p. 16.

Morrow, L. (1991, June 10). Evil. *Time,* 48–53; Morrow, L. (2003, February 24). The real meaning of evil. *Time,* 74.

9. Material on the definition and psychology of forgiveness is taken from the following:

Enright, R. D., Freedman, S., & Rique, J. (1998). The psychology of interpersonal forgiveness. In R. D. Enright & J. North (Eds.), *Exploring forgiveness* (pp. 46–62). Madison: University of Wisconsin Press.
Enright, R. D., & Gassin, E. A. (1992). Forgiveness: A developmental view. *Journal of Moral Education, 21,* 99–114.
McCullough, M. E., Pargament, K. I., & Thoresen, C. E. (2000). The psychology of forgiveness: History, conceptual issues, and overview. In M. E. McCullough, K. I. Pargament, & C. E. Thoreson (Eds.), *Forgiveness: Theory, research, and practice* (pp. 1–14). New York: Guilford Press.
Thomas, G. (2000, January 10). The forgiveness factor. *Christianity Today,* 38–43.

10. Enright, Freedman, & Rique (1998), The psychology of interpersonal forgiveness, p. 46.
11. For information on the by-products of forgiveness, see the following:

Casarjian, R. (1992). *Forgiveness: A bold choice for a peaceful heart.* New York: Bantam Books.
Enright, Freedman, & Rique (1998), The psychology of interpersonal forgiveness.
McCullough, M. E., Sandage, S. J., & Worthington, E. L. (1997). *To forgive is human: How to put your past in the past.* Downers Grove, IL: InterVarsity Press.
Thoresen, C. E., Harris, H. S., & Luskin, F. (2000). Forgiveness and health: An unanswered question. In M. E. McCullough, K. I. Pargament, & C. E. Thoresen (Eds.), *Forgiveness: Theory, research and practice* (pp. 254–280). New York: Guilford Press.

12. Shriver, D. W. (1995). *An ethic for enemies: Forgiveness in politics.* New York: Oxford University Press. See also Wilmot, W. W., & Hocker, J. L. (2001). *Interpersonal conflict* (6th ed.). New York: McGraw-Hill Higher Education, ch. 10.
13. Shriver (1995), *An ethic for enemies,* p. 8.
14. Mitroff, I., & Denton, E. A. (1999, Summer). A study of spirituality in the workplace. *Sloan Management Review, 40,* 83.
15. Mitroff & Denton (1999), A study of spirituality in the workplace, 83–92.
16. Judge, W. Q. (1999). *The leader's shadow: Exploring and developing executive character.* Thousand Oaks, CA: Sage, p. 108.
17. Information on the benefits and dangers of workplace spirituality taken from the following:

Craigie, F. C. (1999). The spirit and work: Observations about spirituality and organizational life. *Journal of Psychology and Christianity, 18,* 43–53.
Fairholm, G. W. (1996). Spiritual leadership: Fulfilling whole-self needs at work. *Leadership & Organization Development Journal, 17*(5), 11–17.

126 LOOKING INWARD

Galen, M. (1995, June 5). Companies hit the road less traveled. *BusinessWeek*, 76.
Laabs, J. (1995, September). Balancing spirituality and work. *Personnel Journal*, 60–76.
Mirvis, P. H. (1997). "Soul Work" in organizations. *Organization Science, 8,* 193–206.
Tourish, D., & Pinnington, A. (2002). Transformational leadership, corporate cultism and the spirituality paradigm: An unholy trinity in the workplace? *Human Relations, 55,* 147–172.

18. Material on Fowler's stages of faith and discussion of vocation drawn from the following:

Fowler, J. W. (1981). *Stages of faith: The psychology of human development and the quest for meaning.* San Francisco: Harper & Row.
Fowler, J. (1984). *Becoming adult, becoming Christian.* New York: Harper & Row.
Fowler, J. (1991). The vocation of faith development theory. In J. W. Fowler, K. E. Nipkow, & F. Schweitzer (Eds.), *Stages of faith and religious development: Implications for church, education, and society* (pp. 19–36). New York: Crossroad.
Fowler, J. W. (1991). *Weaving the new creation: Stages of faith and the public church.* San Francisco: HarperSanFrancisco.
Fowler, J. (1996). *Faithful change: The personal and public challenges of postmodern life.* Nashville, TN: Abingdon.
Jardine, M. M., & Viljoen, H. G. (1992). Fowler's theory of faith development: An evaluative discussion. *Religious Education, 87,* 74–85.

19. Fritz Oser of Switzerland offers an alternative developmental approach to faith. See Oser, F. (1991). Toward a logic of religious development. In J. W. Fowler, K. E. Nipkow, & F. Schweitzer (Eds.), *Stages of faith and religious development* (pp. 37–64). New York: Crossroad.
20. Buechner, F. (1973). *Wishful thinking: A theological ABC.* New York: HarperCollins, p. 95.
21. Mahan, B. J. (2002). *Forgetting ourselves on purpose: Vocation and the ethics of ambition.* San Francisco: Jossey-Bass, p. xxi.
22. Foster, R. J. (1978). *Celebration of discipline: The path to spiritual growth.* New York: Harper & Row.
23. Foster provides one set of spiritual classics in Foster, R. J., & Smith, J. B. (Eds.). (1993). *Devotional classics: Selected readings for individuals and groups.* San Francisco: HarperSanFrancisco.
24. Orizio, R. (2002). *Talk of the devil: Encounters with seven dictators.* (A. Bardoni, Trans.). New York: Walker, p. 196.
25. The *Boston Globe* Investigative Staff. (2002). *Betrayal: The crisis in the Catholic Church.* Boston, MA: Little, Brown, p. 46.
26. The *Boston Globe* Investigative Staff (2002), *Betrayal,* p. 46.

Part III

Ethical Standards and Strategies

5

General Ethical Perspectives

Leaders are truly effective only when they are motivated by a concern for others.

McGill University business professors
Rabindra Kanungo and Manuel Mendonca

What's Ahead

This chapter surveys widely used ethical perspectives that can be applied to the leadership role. These approaches include utilitarianism, Kant's categorical imperative, Rawls's justice as fairness, communitarianism, and altruism. I provide a brief description of each perspective along with a balance sheet that identifies the theory's advantages and disadvantages.

Learning about well-established ethical systems can help dispel ethical ignorance and expand our ethical capacity. The ethical dilemmas we face as leaders may be unique. However, we can meet these challenges with the same tools that we apply to other ethical problems. I've labeled the ethical approaches or theories described in this chapter as "general" because they were developed for all kinds of moral choices. Yet as we'll see, they have much to say to those of us in leadership positions.

Utilitarianism: Do the Greatest Good for the Greatest Number of People

Utilitarianism is based on the premise that ethical choices should be based on their consequences. Individuals have probably always considered the likely outcomes of their decisions when determining what to do. However, this process wasn't formalized and given a name until the eighteenth and nineteenth centuries. English philosophers Jeremy Bentham (1748–1832) and John Stuart Mill (1806–1873) argued that the best decisions (a) generate the most benefits as compared with their disadvantages, and (b) benefit the largest number of people.[1] In sum, utilitarianism is attempting to do the greatest good for the greatest number of people. Utility can be based on what is best in a specific case (act utilitarianism) or on what is generally best in most contexts (rule utilitarianism). We can decide, for example, that telling a specific lie is justified in one situation (to protect someone's reputation) but, as a general rule, believe that lying is wrong because it causes more harm than good.

Leaders frequently take a utilitarian approach to ethical decision making. America's nuclear weapons program, for instance, was the product of a series of utilitarian decisions. Harry Truman decided to drop the atomic bomb on Japan after determining that the benefits of shortening the war in the Pacific (reduction in the loss of American lives) outweighed the costs of destroying Hiroshima and Nagasaki and ushering in the nuclear age. Federal energy officials later decided that the benefits of nuclear weapons testing—improved national security—outweighed the risks to citizens in Nevada and Utah. Based on this calculation, the Nuclear Energy Commission conducted a series of aboveground nuclear tests in the 1940s and 1950s. Local citizens were not warned in advance, and their exposure to radiation led to abnormally high cancer rates.

BALANCE SHEET

Advantages (+s)

- Is easy to understand
- Is frequently used
- Forces us to examine the outcomes of our decisions

Disadvantages (−s)

- Is difficult to identify and evaluate consequences
- May have unanticipated outcomes
- May result in decision makers reaching different conclusions

---

The notion of weighing outcomes is easy to understand and to apply. We create a series of mental balance sheets for all types of decisions (see Case Study 5.1). Focusing on outcomes encourages us to think through our decisions, and we're less likely to make rash, unreasoned choices. The ultimate goal of evaluating consequences is admirable—to maximize benefits to as many people as possible. Utilitarianism is probably the most defensible approach in a medical combat unit like the one portrayed on the television show *MASH*, for example. Surgeons give top priority to those who are most likely to survive. It does little good to spend time with a terminal patient while another soldier who would benefit from treatment dies.

Identifying possible consequences can be difficult, particularly for leaders who represent a variety of constituencies or stakeholders. Take the case of a college president who must decide what academic programs to cut in a budget crisis. Many different groups have a stake in this decision, and each will likely reach a different conclusion about potential costs and benefits. Every department believes that it makes a valuable contribution to the university and serves the mission of the school. Powerful alumni may be alienated by the elimination of their majors. Members of the local community might suffer if the education department is terminated and no longer supplies teachers to local schools or if plays and concerts end because of cutbacks in the theater and music departments. Unanticipated consequences further complicate the choice. If student enrollments increase, the president may have to restore programs that she eliminated earlier. Yet failing to make cuts can put the future of the school in jeopardy.

Even when consequences are clear, evaluating their relative merits can be daunting. As I noted in Chapter 2, we tend to favor ourselves when making decisions. Thus, we are likely to put more weight on consequences that most directly affect us. It's all too easy to confuse the "greatest good" with our selfish interests.

Based on the difficulty of identifying and evaluating potential costs and benefits, utilitarian decision makers sometimes reach different conclusions when faced with the same dilemma. Historians still debate the wisdom of dropping the atomic bomb on Japan. Some contend that the war would have ended soon without the use of nuclear weapons and that no military objective justifies such widespread destruction.

CASE STUDY 5.1

The Reference Letter

Being asked to write a letter of reference can pose a thorny ethical dilemma. Writing or giving a reference for a competent, well-liked employee or student is not a problem. However, deciding what to do in the case of a marginal or poor performer is an entirely different matter. On the one hand, as a supervisor or professor, you don't want to exaggerate or lie about the person's qualifications. On the other hand, refusing the request may alienate the person and endanger your relationship. Writing a critical letter could provoke a lawsuit. That's why many former employers will only confirm the dates that an individual worked for their organization. Further complicating matters is the possibility that writing the letter may help you get rid of a marginal follower, saving you the hassle of having to fire or demote this individual.

Imagine that you are a college professor. What would you do if a marginal (C-) student asked you for a job reference? for a reference to another university or to another program at your school? Would your response be different if this were a bad (D or F) student?

Imagine that you are a supervisor. What would you do if a marginal employee (one that barely meets minimal work standards) asked you for a letter of reference to seek another position or a transfer to another division of your corporation? What would you say if another employer called and asked you to comment on someone you had fired earlier?

Once you've made your decisions, identify the consequences you weighed when making these choices. Describe how the benefits outweighed the costs in each case.

Kant's Categorical Imperative: Do What's Right No Matter What the Cost

In sharp contrast to the utilitarians, German philosopher Immanuel Kant (1724–1804) argued that individuals should do what is morally right no matter what the consequences.[2] (The term *categorical* means "without exception.") His approach to moral reasoning is the best known example of deontological ethics. Deontological ethicists argue that we ought to make choices based on our duty (*deon* is the Greek word for duty) to follow universal truths that are imprinted on our consciences. Guilt is an indication that we have violated these moral laws.

According to Kant, what is right for one is right for all. We need to ask ourselves one question: "Would I want everyone else to make the decision I did?" If the answer is yes, the choice is justified. If the answer is no, the decision is wrong. Based on this reasoning, certain behaviors like truth telling and helping the poor are always right. Other acts, such as lying, cheating, and murder, are always wrong. Testing and grading would be impossible if everyone cheated, for example, and cooperation would be impossible if no one could be trusted to tell the truth.

Kant lived well before the advent of the automobile, but violations of his decision-making rule could explain why law enforcement officials now have to crack down on motorists who run red lights. So many Americans regularly disobey traffic signals (endangering pedestrians and other drivers) that some communities have installed cameras at intersections to catch violators. Drivers have failed to recognize one simple fact. They may save time by running lights, but they shouldn't do so because the system breaks down when large numbers of people ignore traffic signals.

Kant also emphasized the importance of "treating humanity as an end." That is, although others can help us reach our goals, they should never be considered solely as tools. We should, instead, respect and encourage the capacity of others to think and choose for themselves. Under this standard, it is wrong for companies to expose neighbors living near manufacturing facilities to dangerous pollutants without their knowledge or consent. Coercion and violence are immoral because such tactics violate freedom of choice. Failing to help a neighbor is unethical because ignoring this person's need limits his or her options.

BALANCE SHEET

Advantages (+s)

- Promotes persistence and consistency
- Is highly motivational
- Demonstrates respect for others

Disadvantages (−s)

- Exceptions exist to nearly every "universal" law
- Actors may have warped consciences
- Is demonstrated through unrealistic examples
- Is hard to apply, particularly under stress

Emphasis on duty encourages persistence and consistent behavior. Those driven by the conviction that certain behaviors are either right or wrong no

---

Box 5.1

Leadership Ethics at the Movies: *The Pianist*

Key Cast Members: Adrien Brody, Emilia Fox, Thomas Kretschmann, Frank Finlay, Maureen Lipman

Synopsis: Based on the wartime experiences of Polish pianist Wladyslaw Szpilman (Brody). A Jew, Szpilman relocates to the Warsaw ghetto when the Nazis invade in 1939. He flees the ghetto after his family is deported to the Treblinka death camp. Szpilman spends the rest of the war eluding capture with the help of friends, strangers, and a German officer. Along the way, he is witness to the senseless brutality of the occupiers as well as the heroism of the Jewish and Polish resistance movements. The film won three Academy Awards: Best Director (Roman Polanski), Best Actor (Brody), and Best Adapted Screenplay.

Rating: R for brutal violence and strong language

Themes: duty, altruism, kindness, perseverance, courage, loyalty, beauty, ethical decision making, injustice, cruelty, evil

---

matter what the situation are less likely to compromise their personal ethical standards (see Box 5.1). They are apt to "stay the course" despite group pressures and opposition and to follow through on their choices. Transcendent principles serve as powerful motivational tools. Seeking justice, truth, and mercy is more inspiring than pursuing selfish concerns. Respecting the right of others to choose is an important guideline to keep in mind when making moral choices. This standard promotes the sharing of information and concern for others while condemning deception, coercion, and violence.

Most attacks on Kant's system of reasoning center on his assertion that there are universal principles that should be followed in every situation. In almost every case, we can think of exceptions. For instance, many of us believe that lying is wrong yet would lie or withhold the truth to save the life of a friend. Countries regularly justify homicide during war. Then, too, how do we account for those who seem to have warped or dead consciences, like serial killers Jeffrey Dahmer and Ted Bundy? They didn't appear to be bothered by guilt. Psychological factors and elements of the environment, such as being born to an alcoholic mother or to abusive parents, can blunt the force of conscience.

Despite the significant differences between the categorical and utilitarian approaches, both theories involve the application of universal rules or principles to specific situations. Dissatisfaction with rule-based approaches is growing.[3] Some contemporary philosophers complain that these ethical guidelines are applied to extreme situations, not the types of decisions we typically make. Few of us will be faced with the extraordinary scenarios (stealing to save a life or lying to the secret police to protect a fugitive) that are frequently used to illustrate principled decision making. Our dilemmas are less dramatic. We have to determine whether or not to confront a coworker about a sexist joke or tell someone the truth at the risk of hurting their feelings. We also face time pressures and uncertainty. In a crisis, we don't always have time to carefully weigh consequences or to determine which abstract principle to follow.

Justice as Fairness: Guaranteeing Equal Rights and Opportunities Behind the Veil of Ignorance

Many disputes in democratic societies center on questions of justice or fairness. Is it just to give more tax breaks to the rich than to the poor? What is equitable compensation for executives? Should a certain percentage of federal contracts be reserved for minority contractors? Is it fair that Native Americans are granted special fishing rights? Why should young workers have to contribute to the Social Security system that may not be around when they retire?

During the last third of the twentieth century, Harvard philosopher John Rawls addressed questions like these in two books and a series of articles.[4] He set out to identify principles that would foster cooperation in a society made up of free and equal citizens who, at the same time, must deal with inequalities (status and economic differences, varying levels of talent and abilities, etc.). Rawls rejected utilitarian principles because generating the greatest number of benefits for society as a whole can seriously disadvantage certain groups and individuals. Consider the impact of cutting corporate taxes, for example. This policy may spur a region's overall economic growth, but most of the benefits of this policy go to the owners of companies. Other citizens have to pay higher taxes to make up for the lost revenue. Those making minimum wage, who can barely pay for rent and food, are particularly hard hit. They end up subsidizing wealthy corporate executives and stockholders.

Instead of basing decisions on cost/benefit analyses, Rawls argues that we should follow these principles of justice and build them into our social institutions:

Principle 1: Each person has an equal right to the same basic liberties that are compatible with similar liberties for all.

Principle 2: Social and economic inequalities are to satisfy two conditions: (A) They are to be attached to offices and positions open to all under conditions of fair equality of opportunity. (B) They are to be to the greatest benefit of the least advantaged members of society.

The first principle, the "principle of equal liberty," has priority. It states that certain rights, like the right to vote and freedom of speech, are protected and must be equal to what others have. Attempts to deny voting rights to minorities would be unethical according to this standard. Principle 2A asserts that everyone should have an equal opportunity to qualify for offices and jobs. Discrimination based on race, gender, or ethnic origin is forbidden. Further, everyone in society ought to have access to the training and education needed to prepare for these roles. Principle 2B, "the difference principle," recognizes that inequalities exist but that priority should be given to meeting the needs of the poor, immigrants, minorities, and other marginalized groups.

Rawls introduces the "veil of ignorance" to back up his claim that his principles provide a solid foundation for a democratic society like the United States. Imagine, he says, a group of people who are asked to come up with a set of principles that will govern society. These group members are ignorant of their characteristics or societal position. Standing behind this veil of ignorance, these individuals would choose (a) equal liberty, because they would want the maximum amount of freedom to pursue their interests; (b) equal opportunity, because if they turned out to be the most talented members of society, they would likely land the best jobs and elected offices; and (c) the difference principle, because they would want to be sure they were cared for if they ended up disadvantaged.

BALANCE SHEET

Advantages (+s)

- Nurtures both individual freedom and the good of the community
- Highlights important democratic values and concern for the less fortunate
- Encourages leaders to treat followers fairly
- Provides a useful decision-making guide

Disadvantages (−s)

- Principles can only be applied to democratic societies
- Groups disagree about the meaning of justice and fairness
- Lack of consensus about the most important rights

Rawls offers a system for dealing with inequalities that encompasses both individual freedom and the common good. More talented, skilled, or fortunate people are free to pursue their goals, but the fruits of their labor must also benefit their less fortunate neighbors. His principles also uphold important democratic values like equal opportunity, freedom of thought and speech, and the right to own and sell property. Following Rawls's guidelines would ensure that everyone receives adequate health care, decent housing, and a quality education. At the same time, the glaring gap between the haves and have nots would shrink.

The justice-as-fairness approach is particularly relevant to leaders who, as we noted in Chapter 1, cast shadows by acting inconsistently. Inconsistent leaders violate commonly held standards of fairness, arbitrarily giving preferential treatment to some followers while denying the same benefits to others who are equally deserving (or more so). Rawls encourages leaders to be fair. They have a responsibility (a) to guarantee basic rights to all followers; (b) to ensure that followers have equal access to promotion, training, and other benefits; and (c) to make special efforts to help those followers who have special needs.

Stepping behind a veil of ignorance is a useful technique to use when making moral choices. Behind the veil, wealth, education, gender, and race disappear. The least advantaged usually benefit when social class differences are excluded from the decision-making process. Our judicial system is one example of an institution that should treat disputants fairly. Unfortunately, economic and racial considerations influence the selection of juries, the determination of guilt and innocence, the length of sentences (and where they are served), and nearly every other aspect of the judicial process.

Rawls's theory of justice as fairness has come under sharp attack. Rawls himself acknowledged that his model only applies to liberal democratic societies. It would not work, for example, in cultures governed by royal families or religious leaders (Saudi Arabia, Iran, Nepal) who are given special powers and privileges denied to everyone else. In fact, the more diverse democratic nations become, the more difficult it is for groups to agree on common values and principles.[5]

Rawls's critics note that definitions of justice and fairness vary widely, a fact that undermines the usefulness of his principles. What seems fair to one group or individual often appears grossly unjust to others. Evidence of this fact is found in disputes over college admissions criteria. Minorities claim that they should be favored in admissions decisions to redress past discrimination and to achieve equal footing with whites. Caucasians, on the other hand, feel that such standards are unfair because they deny equality of opportunity and ignore legitimate differences in abilities.

Some philosophers point out that there is no guarantee that parties who step behind the veil of ignorance would come up with the same set of principles as Rawls. Rather than emphasize fairness, these individuals might decide to make decisions based on utilitarian criteria or to emphasize certain rights. Libertarians, for example, hold that freedom from coercion is the most important human right. Every individual should be able to produce and sell as he or she chooses regardless of impact on the poor. Capitalist theorists believe that benefits should be distributed based on the contributions each person makes to the group. They argue that helping out the less advantaged rewards laziness while discouraging productive people from doing their best. Because decision makers may reach different conclusions behind the veil, skeptics contend that Rawls's guidelines lack moral force. Other approaches to managing society's inequities are just as valid as the notion of fairness.

Communitarianism: Shoulder Your Responsibilities/Seek the Common Good

The modern communitarian movement began in 1990 when a group of 15 ethicists, social scientists, and philosophers led by sociologist Amitai Etzioni met in Washington, D.C., to express their concerns about the state of American society. Members of this gathering took the name "communitarian" to highlight their desire to shift the focus of citizens from individual rights to communal responsibilities. The next year the group started a journal and organized a teach-in that produced the communitarian platform. In 1993, Etzioni published the communitarian agenda in a book entitled *The Spirit of Community: The Reinvention of American Society.*[6] Etzioni suggests (a) a moratorium on the generation of new individual rights; (b) recognition that citizenship means accepting civic responsibilities (serving on a jury) along with rights and privileges (the right to a trial by jury); (c) acknowledgment that certain duties may not bring any immediate payoffs; and (d) reinterpretation of some legal rights in order to improve public safety and health. For example, sobriety checkpoints mean less personal freedom but are justified because they can significantly reduce traffic deaths.

Many communitarians resemble evangelists more than philosophers. They are out to recruit followers to their movement that promotes moral revival. American society is fragmenting and in a state of moral decline, they proclaim. Evidence of this decay is all around us in the form of high divorce and crime rates, campaign attack ads, and the growing influence of special interest groups in politics. The United States needs renewal that can only come through the creation of healthy local, regional, and national communities. According to political activist and educator John Gardner, healthy or responsive communities are made up of the following:[7]

- *Wholeness incorporating diversity.* The existence of community depends on sharing some vision of a common good or purpose that makes it possible for people to live and work together. Yet at the same time, segments within the system are free to pursue their diverse and often competing interests.
- *A reasonable set of shared values.* Responsive communities agree on a set of core values that are reflected in written rules and laws, unwritten customs, a shared view of the future, and so on. Important ideals include justice, equality, freedom, the dignity of the individual, and the release of human talent and energy.
- *Caring, trust, and teamwork.* Healthy communities foster cooperation and connection at the same time they respect individual differences. Citizens feel a sense of belonging as well as a sense of responsibility. They recognize the rights of minorities, engage in effective conflict resolution, and work together on shared tasks.
- *Participation.* To function effectively, large, complex communities depend on the efforts of leaders disbursed throughout every segment of society.
- *Affirmation.* Healthy collectives sustain a sense of community through continuous reaffirmation of the history, symbols, and identity of the group.
- *Institutional arrangements for community maintenance.* Responsive communities ensure their survival through such structures as city and regional governments, boards of directors, and committees.

Creation of the kinds of communities envisioned by Gardner and others requires citizens to shoulder a number of collective responsibilities. Communitarian citizens should stay informed about public issues and become active in community affairs. They must serve on juries, work with others on common projects, care for the less fortunate, clean up corruption, provide guidance to children, and so forth. These tasks are often accomplished through voluntary associations such as environmental groups, churches, neighborhood patrols, youth sports leagues, and service organizations. (Complete the self-assessment in Box 5.2 to determine if you are shouldering your share of community responsibilities.)

Concern for the common good may be the most useful ethical principle to come out of the communitarian movement. Considering the needs of the broader community discourages selfish, unethical behavior. Lying, polluting, or manufacturing dangerous products may serve the needs of a leader or an organization, but such actions are unethical because they rarely benefit society as a whole. Further, if each group looks out only for its own welfare, the community as a whole suffers. Communitarians address the problems posed by competing interests by urging leaders and followers to put the needs of the whole above the needs of any one individual, group, or organization. By promoting the common good, the communitarian movement encourages dialogue and discussion within and among groups. Consensus about ethical choices may come out of these discussions.

Box 5.2

Self-Assessment

COMMUNITY INVOLVEMENT SCALE

Instructions

The following set of questions will help you determine your level of involvement in your school, local, and national communities. Circle either T (true) or F (false) for each item.

1. T or F I have participated in a service project designed to help my college or university within the last year.

2. T or F I have participated in a service project designed to help my hometown or the community where my college or university is located within the last year.

3. T or F I voted in the last school election.

4. T or F I ran for office, or worked on the campaign of someone who ran, during the last school election.

5. T or F I voted in the last state or local election (if eligible to vote).

6. T or F I voted in the last national election (if eligible to vote).

7. T or F I regularly watch or listen to the news to keep up on local and national events.

8. T or F I can identify the congressperson who represents my home district.

9. T or F I have called or e-mailed a local, state, or national government official in the last year.

10. T or F I am a member of at least one club or religious organization at my college or university.

11. T or F I am a member of at least one club or religious organization in my hometown or in the community where my college or university is located.

12. T or F I have participated in an informal discussion of political or social issues within the last month.

13. T or F I have attended a school-sponsored activity (play, lecture, athletic contest) during the past month.

14. T or F I have participated in a formal or informal residence hall activity during the past month.

15. T or F I participate in group recreational activities outside of class (intramural sports, band, choir) on an ongoing basis.

(Continued)

Box 5.2 *(Continued)*

Scoring

Total up the number of times you circled T and record the number. _____

The higher your score, the greater your involvement in your school, local, and national communities based on your willingness to serve, to be involved in politics, to keep up on current events, and to participate in shared activities. You'll need to adjust the following scale downward if you are not eligible to vote or if you live off campus. A score of 13–15 indicates that you are highly active in community affairs. A score of 10–12 indicates moderate involvement. A score of 9 or below suggests that you might want take a serious look at your commitment to your college or home region. Consider why your score was so low and how you might become more active.

BALANCE SHEET

Advantages (+s)

- Discourages selfish individualism
- Fosters disbursed leadership and ethical dialogue
- Encourages collaborative leadership strategies
- Promotes character development

Disadvantages (−s)

- Evangelistic fervor of its leaders
- Promotes one set of values in a pluralistic society
- May erode individual rights
- Fails to resolve competing community standards

Communitarianism is a promising approach to moral reasoning, particularly for leaders. First, communitarianism addresses selfishness head on, encouraging us to put responsibilities above rights and to seek the common good. We're less tempted to abuse power or to accumulate leadership perks, for example, if we remember that we have obligations both to our immediate followers and to the entire communities in which we live.

Second, communitarianism promotes the benefits of disbursed leadership and ethical dialogue. Healthy nations are energized networks of leaders operating in every segment of society—business, politics, health care, unions, social service, religion, and education. Leaders in these countries create a framework (characterized by equality, openness, and honesty) that encourages discussion of moral questions.

Third, communitarianism encourages collaborative leadership, a new way of solving public problems based on partnership.[8] Collaborative leaders bring together representatives of diverse groups to tackle civic problems like failing schools, substandard housing, economic blight, and uncontrolled development. They focus on the decision-making process rather than promote a particular solution. Collaborative leaders have little formal power but function as "first among equals," convening discussions, providing information, finding resources, helping the group reach agreement, and seeing that the solution is implemented. Collaborative efforts have produced concrete, tangible results in cities both large (Phoenix, Denver, Baltimore) and small (Missoula, Montana, and Sitka, Alaska). Perhaps just as important, these efforts change the way that communities do business. Trust is created, new communication networks form, the focus shifts from serving special interests to serving a common vision, and citizens are more likely to collaborate again in the future.

Fourth, the rise of communitarianism coincides with renewed interest in virtue ethics, which was our focus in Chapter 3. Both are concerned with the development of moral character. The communitarian movement fosters the development of the virtues by supporting strong families, schools, religious congregations, and governments. A "virtue cycle" is created. Virtuous citizens build moral communities that, in turn, encourage further character formation.

The communitarian movement has its share of detractors. Some critics are uncomfortable with the fact that its founders are out to make converts. Others worry about promoting one set of values in a pluralistic society. Who decides, for example, which values are taught in the public schools? Christians want the Ten Commandments displayed in courtrooms (see Chapter 8), but Buddhists, Moslems, and other religious groups object. Still other critics fear that focusing on the needs of the community will erode individual rights.

Competing community standards may pose the greatest threat to communitarianism. Communities frequently have conflicting moral guidelines. For example, debate over flying the Confederate battle flag in South Carolina's state capitol erupted during the 2000 presidential primary. Many white South Carolinians treat the flag as part of their cultural heritage. Minorities (as well as many white citizens in other parts of the country) see the flag as a symbol of racial discrimination. The Confederate banner was moved from the capitol building to another public location in the same complex after the election, but civil rights leaders continue to object to the flag's presence on state property.

Communitarians turn first to community agreement when resolving conflicts such as these.[9] Local values should be respected because they reflect the unique history of the group. Community standards can be oppressive, however. After all, segregation was the norm in the South until the 1960s. Communitarian thinkers turn next to societal values in such cases. Local preferences need to be accountable to the larger society. Attempts to deny blacks the right to vote, for instance, were eventually overturned because they violated rights guaranteed by the U.S. Constitution. Based on this reasoning, the Confederate flag ought to be removed from South Carolina state property because it undermines such national principles as equality, tolerance, and diversity.

Applying societal norms does not always resolve intercommunity moral conflicts. This is the case with Oregon's "Death With Dignity Act" that sanctions physician-assisted suicide. Twice state voters approved this measure despite strong opposition from medical and religious groups. The attorney general tried to outlaw the use of painkillers for medically assisted suicide under the federal Controlled Substances Act. However, he was prevented from doing so by a federal court ruling.[10] Both sides in the dispute claim that their positions are based on widely shared societal principles. Proponents of death with dignity believe that suicide is justified by such values as compassion, quality of life, free will, and self-determination. Opponents give more priority to the sanctity of life and argue that extending life is more compassionate than prematurely ending it.

Altruism: Love Your Neighbor

Advocates of altruism argue that love of neighbor is the ultimate ethical standard. People are never a means to an end; they *are* the ends. Our actions should be designed to help others whatever the personal cost. The altruistic approach to moral reasoning, like communitarianism, shares much in common with virtue ethics. Many of the virtues that characterize people of high moral character, such as compassion, hospitality, empathy, and generosity, reflect concern for other people. Clearly, virtuous leaders are other-, not self-, centered.

Altruism appears to be a universal value, one promoted in cultures from every region of the world. The Dalai Lama urges followers to practice an ethic of compassion, for instance, and Western thought has been greatly influenced by the altruistic emphasis of Judaism and Christianity. The command to love God and to love others as we love ourselves is our most important obligation in Judeo-Christian ethics. Because humans are made in the image of God and God is love, we have an obligation to love others no matter who they are and no matter what their relationship to us. Jesus drove home this point in the parable of the Good Samaritan.

A man was going down from Jerusalem to Jericho when he fell into the hands of robbers. They stripped him of his clothes, beat him, and went away, leaving him half dead. A priest happened to be going down the same road, and when he saw the man, he passed by on the other side. So too, a Levite, when he came to the place and saw him, passed by on the other side. But a Samaritan, as he traveled, came where the man was; and when he saw him, he took pity on him. He went to him and bandaged his wounds, pouring on oil and wine. Then he put the man on his own donkey, took him to an inn, and took care of him. The next day he took out two silver coins and gave them to the innkeeper. "Look after him," he said, "and when I return, I will reimburse you for any extra expense you may have."

Which of these three do you think was a neighbor to the man who fell into the hands of robbers?

The expert replied, "The one who had mercy on him."

Jesus told him, "Go and do likewise." (Luke 10:30–35, New International Version)

Hospice volunteers provide a modern-day example of the unconditional love portrayed in the story of the Good Samaritan. They meet the needs of the dying regardless of a person's social or religious background, providing help at significant personal cost without expecting anything in return.

Concern for others promotes healthy social relationships. Society as a whole functions more effectively when individuals help one another in their daily interactions.[11] Altruism is the driving force behind all kinds of movements and organizations designed to help the less fortunate and to eliminate social problems. Name almost any nonprofit group, ranging from a hospital or medical relief team to a youth club or crisis hotline, and you'll find that it was launched by someone with an altruistic motive. (See the Curing One Patient at a Time Chapter End Case, for example.) In addition, when we compare good to evil, altruistic acts generally come to mind. Moral heroes and moral champions shine so brightly because they ignore personal risks to battle evil forces.

From the discussion above, it's easy to see why altruism is a significant ethical consideration for all types of citizens. Management professors Rabindra Kanungo and Manuel Mendonca believe, however, that concern for others is even more important for leaders than it is for followers.[12] By definition, leaders exercise influence on behalf of others. They can't understand or articulate the needs of followers unless they focus on the concerns of constituents. To succeed, leaders may have to take risks and sacrifice personal gain. According to Kanungo and Mendonca, leaders intent on benefiting followers will pursue organizational goals, rely on referent and expert power bases, and give power away. Leaders intent on benefiting themselves will focus on personal achievements; rely on legitimate, coercive, and reward power bases; and try to control followers.

Followers prefer selfless leaders to selfish ones.[13] Self-focused leaders destroy loyalty and trust and are more likely to lead their communities into disaster. On the other hand, leaders who sacrifice on behalf of the group demonstrate their commitment to its mission. They set a powerful example that encourages followers to do the same. Higher performance often results.

BALANCE SHEET

Advantages (+s)

- Ancient yet contemporary
- Important to society and leaders
- Powerful and inspiring

Disadvantages (–s)

- Failure of many who profess to love their neighbor to act like as if they do
- Many different, sometimes conflicting forms

Altruism is an attractive ethical perspective for several reasons. First, concern for others is an ancient yet contemporary principle. Two thousand years have passed since Jesus told the story of the Good Samaritan. However, we're still faced with the same type of dilemma as the characters in the story. Should we stop to help a stranded motorist or drive on? Should we give our spare change to the homeless person on the street or ignore him? Do we help a fallen runner in a 10K race or keep running? (The Parable of the Sadhu at the end of the chapter is a modern version of the Samaritan dilemma, one that may have involved life or death consequences.) Second, as I noted earlier, altruism is essential to the health of society in general and leaders in particular. In recognition of this fact, social scientists have joined theologians and philosophers in studying the roots of altruistic behavior.[14] Third, altruism is both powerful and inspiring. Acting selflessly counteracts the effects of evil and inspires others to do the same.

Although attractive, love of neighbor is not an easy principle to put into practice. Far too many people who claim to follow the Christian ethic fail miserably, for instance. They come across as less, not more, caring than those who don't claim to follow this approach. Some of the bitterest wars are religious ones fought by believers who seemingly ignore the altruistic values of their faiths. There's also disagreement about what constitutes loving behavior. For example, committed religious leaders disagree about the legitimacy of war. Some view military service as an act of love, one designed to defend their families and friends. Others oppose the military, believing that nonviolence is the only way to express compassion for others.

Ethical Pluralism

I've presented these five ethical perspectives as separate and sometimes conflicting approaches to moral reasoning. In so doing, I may have given you the impression that you should select one theory and ignore the others. That would be a mistake. Often you'll need to combine perspectives (practice *ethical pluralism*) in order to resolve an ethical problem. I suggest that you apply all five approaches to the same problem and see what insights you gain from each one. You might find that a particular perspective is more suited to some kinds of ethical dilemmas than others. For example, when discussing the Sadhu case at the end of the chapter, you may conclude that communitarianism is less helpful than utilitarianism or the categorical imperative. We'll return to the importance of multiple approaches when we examine ethical decision-making formats in Chapter 7.

Implications and Applications

- Well-established ethical systems can help you set your ethical priorities as a leader.
- Utilitarianism weighs the possible costs and benefits of moral choices. Seek to do the greatest good for the greatest number of people.
- The categorical imperative urges you to do what's right no matter what the consequences. By this standard, some actions (lying, cheating, murder) are always wrong. Respect the right of followers to choose for themselves.
- The justice-as-fairness approach guarantees the same basic rights and opportunities to everyone in a democratic society. When these basic requirements are met, your responsibility as a leader is to give special consideration to the least advantaged.
- Communitarians focus attention on responsibility to the larger community and the need to make decisions that support the common good.
- Altruism encourages you to put others first, no matter what the personal cost.
- Don't expect perfection from any ethical perspective. Ethical approaches, like leaders themselves, have their strengths and weaknesses.
- Two well-meaning leaders can use the same ethical system and reach different conclusions.
- Whenever possible, you should practice ethical pluralism by applying more than one perspective to the same problem.

For Further Reflection, Challenge, and Assessment

1. Can you think of any absolute moral laws or duties that must be obeyed without exception?

2. Reflect on one of your recent ethical decisions. What ethical system(s) did you follow? Were you satisfied with your choice?

3. What items can you add to each of the balance sheets in this chapter?

4. Given that inequalities will always exist, what is the best way to allocate wealth, education, health care, and other benefits in a democratic society?

5. In a group, create a list of the characteristics of healthy and unhealthy communities. Then evaluate a town or city of your choice based on your list. Overall, how would you rate the health of this community?

6. Create your own ethics case based on your personal experience or on current or historical events. Describe the key ethical issues raised in the case and evaluate the characters in the story according to each of the five ethical standards.

7. Apply each of the five perspectives to the Sadhu case at the end of the chapter, either on your own or in a group. Write up your conclusions.

CASE STUDY 5.2

Chapter End Case: The Parable of the Sadhu

The following case first appeared in the September-October 1983 issue of the *Harvard Business Review.* Since that time, it has been discussed in thousands of business schools, churches, and corporations. The author, business professor Bowen H. McCoy, believes that the story of the Sadhu reminds us of the constant tension between reaching our goals and the claims of strangers.

The Sadhu

The Nepal experience was more rugged than I had anticipated. Most commercial treks last two or three weeks and cover a quarter of the distance we traveled.

My friend Stephen, the anthropologist, and I were halfway through the sixty-day Himalayan part of the trip when we reached the high point, an 18,000-foot pass over a crest that we'd have to traverse to reach the village of Muklinath, an ancient holy place for pilgrims.

Six years earlier, I had suffered pulmonary edema, an acute form of altitude sickness, at 16,500 feet in the vicinity of Everest base camp—so we were understandably concerned about what would happen at 18,000 feet. Moreover, the Himalayas were having their wettest spring in twenty years; hip-deep powder and ice had already driven us off one ridge. If we failed to cross the pass, I feared that the last half of our once-in-a-lifetime trip would be ruined.

The night before we would try the pass, we camped in a hut at 14,500 feet. In the photos taken at that camp, my face appears wan. The last village we'd passed through was a sturdy two-day walk below us, and I was tired.

During the late afternoon, four backpackers from New Zealand joined us, and we spent most of the night awake, anticipating the climb. Below, we could see the fires of two other parties, which turned out to be two Swiss couples and a Japanese hiking club.

To get over the steep part of the climb before the sun melted the steps cut in the ice, we departed at 3:30 A.M. The New Zealanders left first, followed by Stephen and myself, our porters and Sherpas, and then the Swiss. The Japanese lingered in their camp. The sky was clear, and we were confident that no spring storm would erupt that day to close the pass.

At 15,500 feet, it looked to me as if Stephen were shuffling and staggering a bit, which are symptoms of altitude sickness. (The initial stage of altitude sickness brings a headache and nausea. As the condition worsens, a climber may encounter difficult breathing, disorientation, aphasia, and paralysis.) I felt strong—my adrenaline was flowing—but I was very concerned about my ultimate ability to get across. A couple of our porters were also suffering from the height, and Pasang, our Sherpa sirdar (leader), was worried.

Just after daybreak, while we rested at 15,500 feet, one of the New Zealanders, who had gone ahead, came staggering down toward us with a body slung across his shoulders. He dumped the almost naked, barefoot body of an Indian holy man—a sadhu—at my feet. He had found the pilgrim lying on the ice, shivering and suffering from hypothermia. I cradled the sadhu's head and laid him out on the rocks. The New Zealander was angry. He wanted to get across the pass before the bright sun melted the snow. He said, "Look, I've done what I can. You have porters and Sherpa guides. You care for him. We're going on!" He turned and went back up the mountain to join his friends.

I took a carotid pulse and found that the sadhu was still alive. We figured he had probably visited the holy shrines at Muklinath and was on his way home. It was fruitless to question why he had chosen this desperately high route instead of the safe, heavily traveled caravan route through the Kali Gandaki gorge. Or why he was shoeless and almost naked, or how long he had been lying in the pass. The answers weren't going to solve our problem.

Stephen and the four Swiss began stripping off their outer clothing and opening their packs. The sadhu was soon clothed from head to foot. He was not able to walk, but he was very much alive. I looked down the mountain and spotted the Japanese climbers, marching up with a horse.

Without a great deal of thought, I told Stephen and Pasang that I was concerned about withstanding the heights to come and wanted to get over the pass. I took off after several of our porters who had gone ahead.

On the steep part of the ascent where, if the ice steps had given way, I would have slid down about 3,000 feet, I felt vertigo. I stopped for a breather, allowing the Swiss to catch up with me. I inquired about the sadhu and Stephen. They said that the sadhu was fine and that Stephen was just behind them. I set off again for the summit.

Stephen arrived at the summit an hour after I did. Still exhilarated by victory, I ran down the slope to congratulate him. He was suffering from altitude sickness—walking fifteen steps, then stopping, walking fifteen steps, then stopping. Pasang accompanied him all the way up. When I reached them, Stephen glared at me and said: "How do you feel about contributing to the death of a fellow man?"

I did not completely comprehend what he meant, "Is the sadhu dead?" I inquired.

"No," replied Stephen, "but he surely will be!"

After I had gone, followed not long after by the Swiss, Stephen had remained with the sadhu. When the Japanese had arrived, Stephen had asked to use their horse to transport the sadhu down to the hut. They had refused. He had then asked Pasang to have a group of our porters carry the sadhu. Pasang had resisted the idea, saying that the porters would have to exert all their energy to get themselves over the pass. He believed they could not carry a man down 1,000 feet to the hut, reclimb the slope, and get across safely before the snow melted. Pasang had pressed Stephen not to delay any longer.

The Sherpas had carried the sadhu down to a rock in the sun at about 15,000 feet and pointed out the hut another 500 feet below. The Japanese had given him food and drink. When they had last seen him, he was listlessly throwing rocks at the Japanese party's dog, which had frightened him.

We do not know if the sadhu lived or died.

For many of the following days and evenings, Stephen and I discussed and debated our behavior toward the sadhu. Stephen is a committed Quaker with deep moral vision. He said, "I feel that what happened with the sadhu is a good example of the breakdown between the individual ethic and the corporate ethic. No one person was willing to assume ultimate responsibility for the sadhu. Each was willing to do his bit just so long as it was not too inconvenient. When it got to be a bother, everyone just passed the buck to someone else and took off. Jesus was relevant to a more individualistic stage of society, but how do we interpret his teaching today in a world filled with large, impersonal organizations and groups?"

I defended the larger group, saying, "Look, we all cared. We all gave aid and comfort. Everyone did his bit. The New Zealander carried him down below the snow line. I took his pulse and suggested we treat him for hypothermia. You and the Swiss gave him clothing and got him warmed up. The Japanese gave him food and water. The Sherpas carried him down to the sun and pointed out the easy trail toward the hut. He was well enough to throw rocks at a dog. What more could we do?"

"You have just described the typical affluent Westerner's response to a problem. Throwing money—in this case food and sweaters—at it, but not solving the fundamentals!" Stephen retorted.

"What would satisfy you?" I said. "Here we are, a group of New Zealanders, Swiss, Americans, and Japanese who have never met before and who are at the apex of one of the most powerful experiences of our lives. Some years the pass is so bad no one gets over it. What right does an almost naked pilgrim who chooses the wrong trail have to disrupt our lives? Even the Sherpas had no interest in risking the trip to help him beyond a certain point."

Stephen calmly rebutted. "I wonder what the Sherpas would have done if the sadhu had been a well-dressed Nepali, or what the Japanese would have done if the sadhu had been a well-dressed Asian, or what you would have done, Buzz, if the sadhu had been a well-dressed Western woman?"

"Where, in your opinion," I asked, "is the limit of our responsibility in a situation like this? We had our own well-being to worry about. Our Sherpa guides were unwilling to jeopardize us or the porters for the sadhu. No one else on the mountain was willing to commit himself beyond certain self-imposed limits."

Stephen said, "As individual Christians or people with a Western ethical tradition, we can fulfill our obligations in such a situation only if one, the sadhu dies in our care, two, the sadhu demonstrates to us that he can undertake the two-day walk down to the village; or three, we carry the sadhu for two days down to the village and persuade someone there to care for him."

"Leaving the sadhu in the sun with food and clothing—where he demonstrated hand-eye coordination by throwing a rock at a dog—comes close to fulfilling items one and two," I answered. "And it wouldn't have made sense to take him to the village where the people appeared to be far less caring than the Sherpas, so the third condition is impractical. Are you really saying that, no matter what the implications, we should, at the drop of a hat, have changed our entire plan?"

DISCUSSION PROBES

1. Which ethical standard did the author follow? What perspective did Stephen take?
2. Did McCoy make the right choice? How would you evaluate the responses of the other people in the story?
3. How far should we go to help strangers?
4. What parallels can you draw between the parable of the Sadhu and the kinds of ethical choices made by groups and organizations?
5. Is there any way to prepare ourselves for an ethical crisis like this one?
6. What leadership lessons do you draw from this case?

REFERENCE

McCoy, B. H. (1998). The parable of the Sadhu. In J. R. Katzenbach (Ed.), *The work of teams* (pp. 3–13). Boston, MA: Harvard Business Review Press. Used by permission.

CASE STUDY 5.3

Chapter End Case: Curing One Patient at a Time

When asked to name someone who exemplifies service to others, most people think immediately of Mother Teresa. Yet Mother Teresa is only one example of altruism in action. There are many other leaders who help the less fortunate at great cost to themselves. Pulitzer Prize–winning journalist Tracy Kidder profiles the life of one such modern hero, Dr. Paul Farmer, in a book entitled *Mountains Beyond Mountains*.

Paul Farmer is both a medical doctor and an anthropologist, who teaches at Harvard medical school. He is a past recipient of a MacArthur Foundation "genius" grant and an international authority on infectious diseases. With credentials like these, Farmer could enjoy the lifestyle of a wealthy doctor. Farmer runs a clinic in the impoverished highlands of Haiti instead. He splits his time between Boston and his work among the desperately poor peasants who flock to his Zanmi Lasante medical complex to be treated for everything from malnutrition and gangrene to meningitis and cancer. The organization he cofounded to support his work in Haiti, Partners in Health (PIH), also oversees efforts to eradicate drug-resistant tuberculosis in the prisons and slums of Peru and Russia.

Farmer is consumed with bringing health care to the poor, one patient at a time. Dokte Paul, as the Haitians call him, never turns away a sick person. He and his staff go to extraordinary lengths to make sure their clients follow through on treatment plans. (Failure to ensure that patients take their medications often undermines medical projects in developing nations.) According to Farmer, "The only noncompliant people are physicians. If the patient doesn't get better, it's your own fault. Fix it" (p. 36). Farmer walks for hours over mountain paths to visit his patients in their huts to make sure that they are taking their medicines. Along the way, he stops frequently to talk with former patients and recruits new clients for the clinic. On his frequent trips back to the United States, he shops on behalf of his patients, returning with watches, Bibles, radios, and nail clippers.

Not satisfied just to treat disease, Dokte Paul established a public health system to root out the causes of illness. Zanmi Lasante administers a variety of educational and health programs, including schools, sanitation systems, vaccination and feeding programs, and literacy campaigns. These efforts have paid off. Malnutrition and infant mortality rates in the clinic's service area have dropped dramatically. The mother-to-baby HIV transmission rate is half that of the United States. No one in the region has died from tuberculosis in over 10 years.

Farmer's medical successes have come at significant personal cost. He works constantly, sleeping only a few hours a night in a small house on clinic grounds. His teaching salary and book royalties largely go toward supporting the clinic. When Farmer does have personal funds, he may give the money to a needy patient. Expansion of Partners in Health has increased his already demanding travel schedule. He can spend weeks on the road, traveling between project sites, speaking at international conferences, and stopping in at PIH headquarters in Boston. He rarely sees his wife and daughter.

Some would like to call Dokte Paul a saint for his self-sacrifice, but he resists this designation. Farmer believes that sacrifice for the poor should be the norm rather than the exception. He is convinced that God has special concern for the less fortunate. They are in misery because the wealthy have refused to share: "God gives us humans everything we need to flourish, but he's not the one who's supposed to divvy up the loot. That charge was laid upon us" (p. 79).

Although most admire his efforts, Farmer does have his critics. The majority of international health decisions are made on a cost/benefit basis with money going where it can help the most people. Farmer ignores utilitarian considerations by spending what it takes to meet the needs of a particular patient. As a result, a few could benefit at the expense of the many. Even sympathetic observers argue that Farmer is wasting his time by making rural house calls when he should be addressing global health issues. Not many others will follow his example, they say. Even if they do, only a handful of the sick will be cured. However, these "journeys to the sick" keep Farmer going by helping him connect as a doctor to his patients. Failing to hike to isolated families would mean that their lives matter less than the lives of others. Farmer refuses to make this distinction. Such treks also reflect his philosophy, which is taken from the Haitian proverb that serves as the inspiration for the title of Kidder's biography of Farmer. Haitians say, "Beyond mountains there are mountains." When you cross one mountain range (solve one problem), another mountain or problem will appear. So you travel on to solve that problem as well.

DISCUSSION PROBES

1. What are the advantages and disadvantages of Farmer's methods?

2. Is Farmer wasting his time by investing so much in individual patients?

3. Do leaders have an obligation to give special consideration to the poor as Farmer believes? Why or why not?

4. Do you think that Dokte Paul will experience burnout from sacrificing so much for others? Should he expect that others would follow his example?

5. Should altruism or utilitarianism be the basis for making medical decisions in poor regions?

6. If you could sit down and talk to Dr. Farmer, what would you ask him or say to him?

7. What leadership lessons do you draw from this case?

REFERENCE

Kidder, T. (2003). *Mountains beyond mountains*. New York: Random House.

Notes

1. See, for example, the following:

Barry, V. (1978). *Personal and social ethics: Moral problems with integrated theory.* Belmont, CA: Wadsworth.

Bentham, J. (1948). *An introduction to the principles of morals and legislation.* New York: Hafner.

De George, R. T. (1995). *Business ethics* (4th ed.). Englewood Cliffs, NJ: Prentice Hall, ch. 3.

Gorovitz, S. (Ed.). (1971). *Utilitarianism: Text and critical essays.* Indianapolis, IN: Bobbs-Merrill.

2. Kant, I. (1964). *Groundwork of the metaphysics of morals* (H. J. Ryan, Trans.). New York: Harper & Row; Christians, C. G., Rotzell, K. B., & Fackler, M. (1990). *Media ethics* (3rd ed.). New York: Longman; Leslie, L. Z. (2000). *Mass communication ethics: Decision-making in postmodern culture.* Boston, MA: Houghton Mifflin; Velasquez, M. G. (1992). *Business ethics: Concepts and cases* (3rd ed.). Englewood Cliffs, NJ: Prentice Hall, ch. 2.

3. Meilander, G. (1986). Virtue in contemporary religious thought. In R. J. Nehaus (Ed.), *Virtue: Public and private* (pp. 7–30). Grand Rapids, MI: Eerdmans; Alderman, H. (1997). By virtue of a virtue. In D. Statman (Ed.), *Virtue ethics* (pp. 145–164). Washington, DC: Georgetown University Press.

4. Material on Rawls's theory of justice and criticism of his approach is taken from Rawls, J. (1971). *A theory of justice.* Cambridge, MA: Belknap Press. See also the following:

Rawls, J. (1993). Distributive justice. In T. Donaldson & P. H. Werhane (Eds.), *Ethical issues in business: A philosophical approach* (pp. 274–285). Englewood Cliffs, NJ: Prentice Hall.

Rawls, J. (2001). *Justice as fairness: A restatement* (E. Kelly, Ed.). Cambridge, MA: Belknap Press.

Velasquez, M. G. (1992). *Business ethics: Concepts and cases* (3rd ed.). Englewood Cliffs, NJ: Prentice Hall, ch. 2.

Warnke, G. (1993). *Justice and interpretation.* Cambridge: MIT Press, ch. 3.

5. See Rawls, J. (1993). *Political liberalism.* New York: Columbia University Press.
6. Etzioni, A. (1993). *The spirit of community: The reinvention of American society.* New York: Touchstone. See also the following:

Bellah, N., Madsen, R., Sullivan, W. M., Swidler, A., & Tipton, S. M. (1991). *The good society.* New York: Vintage Books.

Eberly, D. E. (1994). *Building a community of citizens: Civil society in the 21st century.* Lanham, MD: University Press of America.

Etzioni, A. (Ed.). (1995). *New communitarian thinking: Persons, virtues, institutions, and communities.* Charlottesville: University Press of Virginia.

Etzioni, A. (Ed.). (1995). *Rights and the common good: A communitarian perspective.* New York: St. Martin's, pp. 271–276.

Johnson, C. E. (2000). Emerging perspectives in leadership ethics. *Proceedings of the International Leadership Association, USA,* 48–54.

7. Gardner, J. (1995). Building a responsive community. In A. Etzioni (Ed.), *Rights and the common good: The communitarian perspective* (pp. 167–178). New York: St. Martin's.

8. Chrislip, D. D., & Larson, C. E. (1994). *Collaborative leadership: How citizens and civic leaders can make a difference.* San Francisco: Jossey-Bass; Chrislip, D. D. (2002). *The collaborative leadership fieldbook.* San Francisco: Jossey-Bass.

9. Etzioni, A. (1996). *The new golden rule: Community and morality in a democratic society.* New York: Basic Books.

10. Liptak, A. (2002, April 18). Judge blocks U.S. bid to ban suicide law. *The New York Times,* p. A16.

11. Altruistic behavior can be critical to organizational success. See Organ, D. W. (1988). *Organizational citizenship behavior: The good soldier syndrome.* Lexington, MA: Lexington Books.

12. Kanungo, R. N., & Mendonca, M. (1996). *Ethical dimensions of leadership.* Thousand Oaks, CA: Sage.

13. Avolio, B. J., & Locke, E. E. (2002). Contrasting different philosophies of leader motivation: Altruism versus egoism. *Leadership Quarterly, 13,* 169–191.

14. See, for example, the following:

Batson, C. D. (1991). *The altruism question: Toward a social-psychological answer.* Hillsdale, NJ: Erlbaum.

Kanungo, R. N., & Conger, J. A. (1993). Promoting altruism as a corporate goal. *Academy of Management Executive, 79*(3), 37–49.

6

Normative Leadership Theories

The Presidency is . . . preeminently a place of moral leadership.

Franklin D. Roosevelt

What's Ahead

In this chapter, we continue to look at ethical perspectives but narrow our focus to approaches that directly address the behavior of leaders. These include transformational leadership, the postindustrial model, Taoism, and servant leadership. As in the last chapter, I'll describe each theory and then offer a balance sheet outlining some of its advantages and disadvantages.

In Chapter 5, we looked at well-established ethical systems or theories. I referred to them as general perspectives because they can be applied to any situation or role in which we find ourselves. In this chapter, we'll examine what philosopher and ethicist Joanne Ciulla of the University of Richmond calls "normative leadership theories."[1] Normative leadership theories tell leaders how they ought to act. They are built on moral principles or norms but unlike general ethical perspectives, deal directly with the leader-follower relationship.

Transformational Leadership: Raising the Ethical Bar

Social scientists offered a series of explanations for leadership behavior over the course of the twentieth century. Until the 1940s, researchers believed that leaders were born, not made. Only individuals who inherited the necessary mental and physical characteristics or traits (intelligent, extroverted, tall, good-looking) could be leaders. When investigators had trouble isolating one set of traits common to all leaders, this model was largely (but not completely) abandoned. The next group of scholars assumed that, in order to be effective, leaders had to adapt to elements of the situation, such as the nature of the task, the emotional, motivational, and skill level of followers, and the quality of the leader-follower relationship. New workers will need more direction than experienced ones, for example. These situational or contingency theories are still popular but suffer from two major shortcomings. First, they are hard to apply. It's not easy to decide what leadership style to use because so many factors must be taken into consideration. Second, contingency theories give too much weight to contextual factors. Elements of the situation are important, but there are strategies that can be effective in a variety of settings.

The transformational approach addressed the limitations of both the traits and situational perspectives by isolating sets of behaviors (which are learned, not inherited) that can produce positive results in many different contexts. Interest in transformational leadership began in 1978 with the publication of the book entitled *Leadership* by James McGregor Burns, a former presidential adviser, political scientist, and historian.[2]

Burns contrasted traditional forms of leadership, which he labeled "transactional," with a more powerful form of leadership he called "transforming." Transactional leaders appeal to lower-level needs of followers, that is, the need for food, shelter, and acceptance. They exchange money, benefits, recognition, and other rewards in return for the obedience and labor of followers; the underlying system remains unchanged. Transformational leaders, in contrast, speak to higher-level needs, like esteem, competency, self-fulfillment, and self-actualization. In so doing, they change the very nature of the groups, organizations, or societies they guide. Burns points to Franklin Roosevelt and Mahatma Gandhi as examples of leaders who transformed the lives of followers and their cultures as a whole. (Another famous transformational leader is profiled in Leadership Ethics at the Movies: *The Gathering Storm,* described in Box 6.1.) In his most recent work, *Transforming Leadership,* Burns argues that the greatest task facing transformational leaders is defeating global poverty, which keeps the world's poorest people from meeting their basic needs for food, medicine, education, and shelter.[3]

Moral commitments are at the heart of Burns's definition of transforming leadership. "Such leadership," states Burns, "occurs when one or more persons *engage* with others in such a way that leaders and followers raise one another to higher levels of motivation and morality."[4] Transformational leaders focus on terminal values like liberty, equality, and justice. These values mobilize and energize followers, create an agenda for action, and appeal to larger audiences.[5] In contrast, transactional leaders emphasize instrumental values, such as responsibility, fairness, and honesty, that make routine interactions go smoothly.

Box 6.1

Leadership Ethics at the Movies: *The Gathering Storm*

Key Cast Members: Albert Finney, Vanessa Redgrave, Linus Roache, Jim Broadbent, Lena Headey

Synopsis: Winston Churchill (Finney) suffers through a period of despair prior to becoming one of the twentieth century's best-known transformational leaders. During most of the 1930s, he is broke, plagued by the "black dog" of depression, dependent on his wife (Redgrave) for emotional support, and largely ignored by other members of Parliament. Churchill mounts a campaign to warn the English people about the dangers of Nazism despite these obstacles. He is reinstated as lord of the Admiralty when Britain declares war in 1939. Roache plays the role of a young government official who risks his career to aid Churchill in his efforts to change public opinion.

Rating: Not rated but likely PG-13 for language and brief nudity

Themes: courage, dealing with hardship, persistence, personal mission, loyalty, whistle-blowing, the power of public speaking

---

In a series of studies, leadership experts Bernard Bass, Bruce Avolio, and their colleagues identified the factors that characterize transactional and transformational forms of leadership.[6] They found that transactional leadership has both active and passive elements. Active transactional leaders engage in *contingent reward* and *management-by-exception*. They provide rewards and recognition contingent on followers carrying out their roles and reaching their objectives. After specifying standards, as well as the elements of acceptable performance, active transactional leaders then discipline followers when they fall short. *Passive-avoidant* or *laissez-faire* leaders wait for problems to arise before taking action, or they avoid taking any action at all. These leaders fail to provide goals and standards or clarify expectations.

According to Bass and Avolio, transformational leadership is characterized by the following:

1. *Idealized influence.* Transformational leaders become role models for followers who admire, respect, and trust them. They put followers' needs above their own, and their behavior is consistent with the values and principles of the group.

2. *Inspirational motivation.* Transformational leaders motivate by providing meaning and challenge to the tasks of followers. They arouse team spirit, are

enthusiastic and optimistic, and help followers develop desirable visions for the future.

3. *Intellectual stimulation.* Transformational leaders stimulate innovation and creativity. They do so by encouraging followers to question assumptions, reframe situations, and approach old problems from new perspectives. Transforming leaders don't criticize mistakes but instead solicit solutions from followers.

4. *Individualized consideration.* Transformational leaders act as coaches or mentors who foster personal development. They provide learning opportunities and a supportive climate for growth. Their coaching and mentoring is tailored to the individual needs and desires of each follower.

Burns believed that leaders display either transactional or transformational characteristics, but Bass found otherwise. Transforming leadership utilizes both transactional *and* transformational elements. Explains Bass: "Many of the great transformational leaders, including Abraham Lincoln, Franklin Delano Roosevelt, and John F. Kennedy, did not shy away from being transactional. They were able to move the nation as well as play petty politics."[7] The transformational leader uses the active elements of the transactional approach (contingent reward and management-by-exception) along with idealized influence, inspirational motivation, intellectual stimulation, and individualized consideration.[8]

The popularity of the transformational approach probably has more to do with practical considerations than with ethical ones. Evidence from over 100 empirical studies establishes that transforming leaders are more successful than their transactional counterparts.[9] Their followers are more committed, form stronger bonds with colleagues, work harder, and persist in the face of obstacles. As a result, organizations led by transforming figures often achieve extraordinary results—higher quality, greater profits, improved service, military victories, and better win-loss records. James Kouzes, Barry Posner, Tom Peters, Warren Bennis, and Burt Nanus are just some of the popular scholars, consultants, and authors who promote the benefits of transformational leadership.[8]

Burns originally believed that the transforming leader is a moral leader because the ultimate product of transformational leadership is higher ethical standards and performance. However, his definition didn't account for the fact that some leaders can use transformational strategies to reach immoral ends. A leader can act as a role model, provide intellectual stimulation, and be passionate about a cause. Yet the end product of her or his efforts can be evil. Hitler was a charismatic figure who had a clear vision for Germany but left a trail of unprecedented death and destruction.

Acknowledging the difference between ethical and unethical transformational leaders, Bass adopted the terms "authentic" and "pseudo-transformational" to distinguish between the two categories.[11] Authentic transformational leaders are motivated by altruism and marked by integrity. (See Box 6.2 for one

Box 6.2

Self-Assessment

PERCEIVED LEADER INTEGRITY SCALE

You can use this scale to measure the integrity of your immediate supervisor or, as an alternative, ask a follower to rate you. The higher the score (maximum 124), the lower the integrity of the leader rated.

The following items concern your immediate supervisor. You should consider your immediate supervisor to be the person who has the most control over your daily work activities. Circle responses to indicate how well each item describes your immediate supervisor.

Response choices: 1 = Not at all; 2 = Somewhat; 3 = Very much; 4 = Exactly

1. Would use my mistakes to attack me personally

2. Always gets even

3. Gives special favors to certain "pet" employees, but not to me

4. Would lie to me

5. Would risk me to protect himself or herself in work matters

6. Deliberately fuels conflict among employees

7. Is evil

8. Would use my performance appraisal to criticize me as a person

9. Has it in for me

10. Would allow me to be blamed for his or her mistake

11. Would falsify records if it would help his or her work reputation

12. Lacks high morals

13. Makes fun of my mistakes instead of coaching me as to how to do my job better

14. Would deliberately exaggerate my mistakes to make me look bad when describing my performance to his or her superiors

15. Is vindictive

16. Would blame me for his or her own mistake

17. Avoids coaching me because she or he wants me to fail

(Continued)

Box 6.2 *(Continued)*

18. Would treat me better if I belonged to a different ethnic group

19. Would deliberately distort what I say

20. Deliberately makes employees angry at each other

21. Is a hypocrite

22. Would limit my training opportunities to prevent me from advancing

23. Would blackmail an employee if she or he could get away with it

24. Enjoys turning down my requests

25. Would make trouble for me if I got on his or her bad side

26. Would take credit for my ideas

27. Would steal from the organization

28. Would risk me to get back at someone else

29. Would engage in sabotage against the organization

30. Would fire people just because she or he doesn't like them if she or he could get away with it

31. Would do things which violate organizational policy and then expect subordinates to cover for him or her

Total Score _____

SOURCE: Bartholomew, C. S., & Gustafson, S. B. (1998). Perceived leader integrity scale: An instrument for assessing employee perceptions of leader integrity. *Leadership Quarterly, 9,* 143–144. Used by permission.

measure of leader integrity.) They don't impose ethical norms but allow followers free choice, hoping that constituents will voluntarily commit themselves to moral principles. Followers are viewed as ends in themselves, not as a means to some other end. Pseudotransformational leaders are self-centered. They manipulate followers in order to reach their personal goals. Envy, greed, anger, and deception mark the groups they lead. Mahatma Gandhi and Martin Luther King, Jr., deserve to be classified as transformational because they promoted universal brotherhood. Iran's Ayatollah Khomeini was pseudotransformational because he taught followers to hate outsiders. A list of the products of transformational and pseudotransformational leadership is found in Box 6.3.

BALANCE SHEET

Advantages (+s)

- Strives for higher morality
- Reflects higher-level ethical reasoning
- Is highly effective
- Is inspirational
- Recognizes that leaders are made, not born
- Not bound by the context or culture

Disadvantages (−s)

- Practitioners often overlook moral principles
- Is leader-centric
- Creates dependency

Transformational leadership rests on a clear ethical foundation. The goal of a transforming leader is to raise the level of morality in a group or organization. Pursuit of this goal will increase the ethical capacity of followers, create a more moral climate, foster independent action, and serve the larger good. Indeed, there is evidence to suggest that those exhibiting transformational leadership behaviors demonstrate higher levels of moral reasoning.[12] Transformational leaders also get results. Identify a successful corporation, team, or military unit, many experts say, and you'll find the guiding hand of a transformational leader. This combination of morality and pragmatism makes transformational leadership very attractive. After all, who wouldn't want to be an extraordinary leader who is both good and effective?

The transformational approach holds promise for those wanting to become better, more ethical leaders. If transforming leadership consists of a set of practices, then anyone can function as a transformational leader by adopting these behaviors. The same set of practices works in every context, ranging from small informal groups and military units to large complex organizations. No longer do leaders have to balance a host of situational factors when making decisions. Instead, they display the same set of characteristics that they adapt to their particular context. Further, transforming leadership appears to be effective in a variety of cultures. Researchers at the Global Leadership and Organizational Behavior Effectiveness (GLOBE) Research Project asked managers in 62 cultures to identify the characteristics of successful leaders. Nine charismatic/transformational attributes were universally associated with outstanding leadership: foresight, encouraging,

Box 6.3

Products of Transformational and Pseudotransformational Leadership

Transformational Leaders

Raise awareness of moral standards

Highlight important priorities

Increase followers' need for achievement

Foster higher moral maturity in followers

Create an ethical climate (shared values, high ethical standards)

Encourage followers to look beyond self-interests to the common good

Promote cooperation and harmony

Use authentic, consistent means

Use persuasive appeals based on reason

Provide individual coaching and mentoring

Appeal to the ideals of followers

Allow followers freedom of choice

Pseudotransformational Leaders

Promote special interests at the expense of the common good

Encourage dependency of followers and may privately despise them

Foster competitiveness

Pursue personal goals

Foment greed, envy, hate, and deception

Engage in conflict rather than cooperation

Use inconsistent, irresponsible means

Use persuasive appeals based on emotion and false logic

Keep their distance from followers and expect blind obedience

Seek to become idols for followers

Manipulate followers

SOURCES: Bass, B. M. (1995). The ethics of transformational leadership. In J. B. Ciulla (Ed.), *Ethics: The heart of leadership* (pp. 169–192). Westport, CT: Praeger.

Bass, B. M., & Steidlmeier, P. (1999). Ethics, character, and authentic transformational leadership behavior. *Leadership Quarterly, 10,* 181–217.

communicative, trustworthy, dynamic, positive, confidence builder, and motivational.[13]

Unfortunately, the ethical assumptions underlying transformational leadership have often been overlooked in the pursuit of greater results. Many writers and researchers appear more interested in what works than in what is right. To them, transformational leadership is another name for successful or effective leadership; leaders are transforming because they achieve extraordinary, tangible results, like rescuing failing corporations or winning battles. These theorists are less concerned with whether leaders foster higher moral standards or if transforming tactics serve ethical ends. Thus, Attila the Hun can be held up as an example of transformational leadership although he pillaged the lands that he conquered.[14]

Writers who fail to distinguish between pseudotransformational and transformational leadership engage in the blind hero worship I criticized in the introduction to this book. There are true leadership heroes, but let's not confuse them with the villains. Remember, too, that all leaders suffer from the uneven character development we described in Chapter 3. No leader is perfect but is a mix of virtues and vices.

Some scholars label transformational theorists as "leader-centric" for paying too much attention to leaders while downplaying the contributions of followers. These skeptics have reason for concern. Burns, Bass, and other proponents of transformative leadership argue that leaders play the most important role in determining group morality and performance. Leaders craft the vision, challenge the status quo, and inspire. At times, they may decide to transform the organization in spite of, not because of, followers, as in the case of the CEO who overrules his staff in order to bring about change. Critics of transformational leadership argue that stakeholders are just as important to the success of a group as leaders, if not more so. After all, followers do most of the work. Worse yet, transforming leaders can silence dissent and encourage followers to sacrifice their legitimate self-interests in order to meet the needs of the larger group.[15]

So much focus on the leader can create dependency and undermine such values as shared decision making and consensus. Followers won't act independently if they continually look to the leader for guidance. Leaders may also get an inflated sense of their own importance, tempting them to cast shadows. Bass believes that the distinction between pseudo- and authentic transformational leadership addresses these concerns. Transforming leaders are much less prone to ethical abuses, he asserts, because they put the needs of others first, treat followers with respect, and seek worthy objectives. You'll need to decide for yourself if transformational theorists have adequately responded to the dangers posed by their perspective.

Postindustrial Leadership:
Ethics in Relational Process

James Rost is one of the most influential opponents of transformational leadership and other modern leadership theories. Rost, a retired professor of leadership studies, contends that most definitions of leadership are based on an industrial model. In this model, leaders function as "super managers." They set the goals and then get followers to reach these objectives. The higher the group's productivity, as measured by such yardsticks as profits, service, and growth, the more effective the leader.

The industrial model of leadership, according to Rost, is ill suited to the new postindustrial age that will put a greater value on collaboration, consensus, diversity, and participation. In addition, theories based on this foundation (including the transformational approach) overlook the "essential nature" of what leadership is—the relationship between leaders and followers that enables them to get things done.

Rost highlights this partnership in his definition. Leadership, he says, "is an influence relationship among leaders and followers who intend real changes that reflect their mutual purposes."[16] Four elements are key to this definition:

1. *The relationship is based on influence.* Leaders influence followers, followers influence leaders, and followers influence other followers. Followers can disagree with their leaders and decide to end the relationship.

2. *Leaders and followers are the people in this relationship.* This principle seems self-evident, but Rost wants to highlight the fact that followers are active partners with leaders. At one point, he rejects the "follower" label because it implies passivity, opting instead for such alternative terms as "constituent" and "participant." Leaders have more power to influence, but they work together with constituents. In fact, Rost contends that "followers do not do followership, they do leadership. Both leaders and followers form one relationship that is leadership."[17]

3. *Leaders and followers intend real changes.* Real changes are both purposeful and substantive. They don't happen by accident but are designed to make a significant difference in the lives of individuals, groups, organizations, and societies. Unlike approaches based on the industrial model, the postindustrial perspective emphasizes process rather than product. The key is the intent of both parties. Few immediate changes may result, but leadership occurs when leaders and their constituents share the same intentions and engage in the ongoing relational process.

4. *Leaders and followers develop mutual purposes.* Leaders and participants don't have to have identical purposes but need to share at least some in common. Purposes are different from goals. Goals are quantifiable, are aimed at producing specific end products, and are achievable. Purposes are broad statements that address the quality of life. They are never reached (in fact, they may

change) but allow leaders and followers to create communities. Leaders don't create purposes and then impose them on followers. Instead, leaders and constituents come to a common agreement about what they hold to be important.

Rost believes that ethicists have not paid enough attention to the interaction between leaders and followers. Leaders need to generate ethical products or content (decisions, policies, programs), but they ought to do so in an ethical manner. The *process* should follow certain criteria: (a) influence in the leader-follower relationship should be based on persuasion, not coercion (physical force, psychological intimidation, obedience to authority); (b) influence should flow in both directions; (c) followers must be able to choose whether or not to participate; and (d) goals ought to be jointly created through discussion and argument. Rost concludes by offering the following ethical standard: "The leadership process is ethical if the people in the relationship (the leaders and followers) *freely* agree that the intended changes *fairly* reflect their mutual purposes.[18]

The developer of the postindustrial model doesn't totally ignore the outcomes of the leadership process. Rost rejects utilitarianism, Kant's categorical imperative, and other popular ethical perspectives as too individualistic. Instead, he believes that leaders and followers must work together to develop ethical standards by which to judge their actions. Rost wants to shift the focus from individual choices to those made by the community. Drawing from communitarianism, he argues that leaders and followers should pursue the common good.

BALANCE SHEET

Advantages (+s)

- Focuses on persuasion, mutual influence, and joint purposes
- Shifts attention from leaders to followers
- Is highly creative
- Recognizes the importance of ethical leadership process

Disadvantages (−s)

- Blurs the distinction between leaders and followers
- Limits leadership to major change efforts
- Is idealistic
- Discards well-established ethical theories

Rost's postindustrial model generated an enthusiastic response from many leadership scholars when it first came out. Supporters liked its emphasis on process, persuasion, collaboration, mutual influence, and shared purposes. This approach seemed to reverse the trend, reflected in transformational leadership, toward glorifying leaders at the expense of followers. Even casual readers had to be impressed by Rost's thorough review of previous definitions of leadership. The postindustrial model is a creative attempt to develop a new understanding of leadership better suited to a new era. Important ethical values—empowerment, nonviolence, community, honesty, and equality—run throughout its definitional elements. Rost rightly recognizes the fact that *how* we carry out our tasks as leaders is extremely important.

The advantages of the postindustrial model must be weighed against a number of significant disadvantages. First, Rost blurs the distinction between leaders and followers (participants, constituents). If followers "do" leadership, how do their roles differ from those of leaders? Second, leaders can intend small, immediate changes in addition to significant, long-term, "real" changes described in the postindustrial model. Third, Rost appears to limit leadership to only those relationships marked by persuasion, mutual purposes, participation, and equality. He doesn't seem to acknowledge the reality that many leaders use coercion to get their way, withhold power and information, put their goals first, and distance themselves from constituents. Even leaders who do want to build partnerships with followers must sometimes punish poor behavior and closely supervise followers who lack skills and experience. Fourth, Rost is too quick to reject well-established ethical perspectives. General ethical perspectives, as we saw in the last chapter, can provide plenty of moral guidance to leaders. Rost makes community standards the sole guideline for making ethical choices about leadership products. In our discussion of communitarianism, however, we saw that communities often pursue conflicting standards or goods.

Taoism: Lead Nature's Way

Taoism (pronounced Daoism) is one of the world's oldest philosophies, dating back to ancient China (600–300 B.C.). The nation had enjoyed peace and prosperity under a series of imperial dynasties but was now a patchwork of warring city-states. Groups of philosophers traveled from one fiefdom to another offering leaders advice for restoring harmony. The Taoists were one of these "100 Schools of Thought."[19]

The *Tao Te Ching* (usually translated as *The Classic of the Way and Its Power and Virtue*) is Taoism's major text. According to popular tradition, a royal librarian named Lao-tzu authored this book as he departed China for self-imposed exile. Most scholars, however, believe that this short volume (5,000 words) is a collection of the teachings of several wise men or sages.

Taoism divided into religious and philosophical branches by A.D. 200. Religious Taoists sought to extend their lives through diet and exercise and developed a priesthood that presided over elaborate temple rituals. Today Taoist religious practices are popular in both the East and the West, but those interested in Taoist leadership principles generally draw from the movement's philosophical roots. These principles are described for Western audiences in such books as *The Tao of Leadership, The Tao of Personal Leadership* and *Real Power: Business Lessons from the Tao Te Ching.*

Understanding the "Way" or Tao is the key to understanding Taoist ethical principles. The Tao is the shapeless, nameless force or "Non-Being" that brings all things into existence, or being, and then sustains them. The Tao takes form in nature and reveals itself through natural principles. These principles then become the standards for ethical behavior. Ethical leaders and followers develop *te,* or character, by acting in harmony with the Tao, not by following rules and commandments. Laws reflect a distrust of human nature and create a new class of citizens—lawbreakers—instead of encouraging right behavior. Efforts to reduce crime, for example, seem to increase it instead:

Throw away holiness and wisdom,

And people will be a hundred times happier.

Throw away morality and justice,

And people will do the right thing.

Throw away industry and profit, and there won't be any thieves.[20]

"Leave well enough alone" seems to capture the essence of Taoist ethics. Consistent with their hands-off approach, Taoist sages argue that he or she governs best who governs least. Leading is like cooking a small fish—don't overdo it. The ideal Taoist leader maintains a low profile, leading mostly by example and by letting followers take ownership.

When the Master governs, the people

Are hardly aware that he [she] exists.

Next best is a leader who is loved.

Next, one who is feared.

The worst is one who is despised.

If you don't trust the people,

You make them untrustworthy.

The Master doesn't talk, he [she] acts.

When his [her] work is done,

The people say, "Amazing:

We did it, all by ourselves!"[21]

Taoists rely on images or metaphors drawn from nature and daily life to illustrate the characteristics of model leaders. The first image is that of an uncarved block. An uncarved block of stone or wood is nameless and shapeless like the Tao itself. Leaders should also be blocklike, avoiding wealth, status, and glory at the same time they leave followers alone.

The second image is the child. Children serve as another reminder that wise leaders don't get caught up in the pursuit of power and privilege but remain humble. Mahatma Gandhi demonstrated childlike character. He dressed simply in clothes he made himself, owned almost nothing, and did not seek political office. Yet he emerged as one of history's most influential leaders.

The third image is water. Water provides an important insight into how leaders ought to influence others by illustrating that there is great strength in weakness. Water cuts through the hardest rock given enough time. In the same way, the weak often overcome the powerful.[22] Authoritarian governments in Soviet Russia, Argentina, and the Philippines were overthrown, not by military means but through the efforts of ordinary citizens. Leaders who use "soft" tactics (listening, empowering, and collaborating) rather than "hard" ones, like threats and force, are more likely to overcome resistance to change. Flexibility or pliability is an important attribute of water as well. Water seeks new paths when it meets resistance.

The fourth image is the valley. To the Taoists, the universe is made up of two forces: the yin (negative, dark, cool, female, shadows) and the yang (positive, brightness, warmth, male, sun). Creation operates as it should when these forces are in balance. Although both the yin and yang are important, Taoists highlight the importance of the yin, or feminine side of leadership, which is represented by the valley metaphor. Leaders should seek to be valleys (which reflect the yin) rather than prominent peaks (which reflect the yang).

The fifth image is the clay pot, which celebrates emptiness by elevating nothing to higher status than something. The most useful part of a pot is the emptiness within. Similarly, the most useful part of a room is the empty space between the walls. Leaders ought to empty themselves, putting aside empty words, superficial thinking, technology, and selfishness. By being empty, leaders can use silence, contemplation, and observation to better understand the workings of the Tao and its ethical principles.

BALANCE SHEET

Advantages (+s)

- Provides an alternative to Western approaches
- Is suited to the modern work environment
- Parallels trends in leadership studies
- Emphasizes inner peace, silence, contemplation, and service
- Focuses on character
- Addresses the leader's use of power and privilege, and his or her relationship to nature

Disadvantages (–s)

- Denies reason
- Rejects codes and laws
- Is ambiguous about many moral issues
- Promotes ethical pragmatism and ethical relativism
- Does not adequately explain evil

Nearly all the concepts presented in the typical Western leadership or ethics text are drawn from the United States, Great Britain, and Europe. Taoism is one of the few non-Western approaches to attract much attention. It's easy to see why Taoist thought is catching on with leaders and scholars alike. Taoist principles provide an ethical framework for such important trends or themes in leadership studies as empowerment, innovation, teamwork, spirituality, and collaboration. Taoist philosophy seems particularly well suited to leaders working in fast-paced, rapidly changing, and decentralized work environments. Taoist thinkers encourage us to be flexible and to use "soft" tactics like listening and negotiation that facilitate teamwork in leaner, flatter organizations. They urge us to embrace silence and contemplation, to develop a sense of inner peace, to reject ambition, and to serve (see our discussion of servant leadership in the next section). Focusing on being rather than doing (being "block-like" and "childlike") encourages leaders to develop character, our focus in Chapter 3.

Taoism speaks most directly to the leader's use of power and privilege. The authors of the *Tao Te Ching* reject the use of force except as a last resort. They criticize the feudal lords of their day for living in splendor while their people sink into poverty and starvation. It is difficult to imagine that Taoist sages would approve of the vast difference in pay between American executives and employees, for example, or give their blessing to such perks as company jets, private chauffeurs, and executive dining rooms.

The Taoist perspective also addresses environmental issues. According to Taoists, we need to work with nature instead of controlling or managing it. The natural world seems to renew itself when left alone. When cows are kept out of streams, for instance, vegetation returns to the riverbank, providing shade that cools the water and encourages the return of native fish. On the other hand, attempts to manage the environment frequently end in disaster. Consider our attempts to suppress forest fires. Putting out wildfires allows tinder to build up over a period of years. When a blaze does take hold, it is much more likely to burn out of control.

There are some serious disadvantages to Taoist ethics. In their attempt to follow nature, Taoists encourage leaders to empty themselves of, among other things, reason. Intuition has its place, but we need to learn how to make more reasoned decisions, not to abandon logic. Taoists are rightly skeptical about the effectiveness of moral codes and laws. Nevertheless, laws can change society for the better. For example, civil rights legislation played a significant role in reducing racial discrimination and changing cultural norms. In organizations, reasonable rules, professional guidelines, and codes of conduct can and do play a role in improving ethical climate (see Chapter 9).

Although Taoism has much to say about the shadow of power and our relationship to the world around us, it is silent on many common ethical dilemmas, such as the case of the manager asked to keep information about an upcoming merger to herself (see Chapter 1). What does it mean to follow nature's example when faced with this decision? Perhaps the manager should keep quiet to keep from intruding into the lives of followers. Nonetheless, withholding information would put her in the position of a mountain instead of a valley, giving her an advantage.

Basing moral decision making on conformity to principles manifested in the natural world promotes ethical pragmatism and relativism. The Taoist is pragmatic, believing that the ethical action is the one that blends with natural rhythms to produce the desired outcome. In other words, what works is what is right. This pragmatic approach seems to ignore the fact that what may "work" (generate profits, create pleasure, ensure job security, earn a raise) may be unethical (result in an unsafe product, destroy public trust, exploit workers). The follower of the Tao also practices ethical relativism. Natural conditions are always changing—seasons shift, plants and animals grow and die. The flexible leader adapts to shifting circumstances. However, this makes it impossible to come to any definite conclusion about right or wrong. What is the right moral choice in one context may be wrong in another.

One final concern should be noted: Taoism's firm conviction that humans, in their natural state, will act morally seems to deny the power of evil. My thesis has been that leaders and followers can and do act destructively, driven by the monsters lurking in their shadow side.

Servant Leadership: Put the Needs of Followers First

Servant leadership has roots in both Eastern and Western thought. Whereas the Taoist sages encouraged leaders to be humble valleys, Jesus told his disciples that "whoever wants to become great among you must be your servant, and whoever wants to be first must be slave of all" (Mark 10:43–44, New International Version). Robert Greenleaf sparked contemporary interest in leaders as servants. Greenleaf, who spent 40 years in research, development, and education at AT&T and 25 years as an organizational consultant, coined the term "servant leader" in the 1970s to describe a leadership model that puts the concerns of followers first.[23] Later he founded a center to promote servant leadership. A number of businesses (Southwest Airlines, The Container Store, AFLAC), nonprofit organizations, and community leadership programs have adopted his model.[24] Margaret Wheatley, Peter Block, Max DePree, and James Autry have joined Greenleaf in urging leaders to act like servants.

The basic premise of servant leadership is simple yet profound. Leaders should put the needs of followers before their own needs. In fact, what happens in the lives of followers should be the standard by which leaders are judged. According to Greenleaf, when evaluating a leader we ought to ask, "Do those served grow as persons? Do they, while being served, become healthier, wiser, freer, more autonomous, more likely themselves to become servants?"[25]

By continually reflecting on what would be best for their constituents, servant leaders are less likely to cast shadows by taking advantage of the trust of followers, acting inconsistently, or accumulating money and power. Four related concepts are central to servant leadership:

1. *Stewardship.* Being a servant leader means acting on behalf of others.[26] Leaders function as the agents of followers who entrust them with special duties and opportunities for a limited time. (See the Betraying the Small Investor Chapter End Case for a description of one group of leaders who failed to carry out their stewardship responsibilities.) Servant leaders are charged with protecting and nurturing their groups and organizations while making sure that these collectives serve the common good. Stewardship implies accountability for results. However, stewards reach their objectives through collaboration and persuasion rather than through coercion and control.

2. *Obligation.* Servant leaders take their obligations or responsibilities seriously. Max DePree, former CEO of Herman Miller, a major office furniture manufacturer, offers one list of what leaders "owe" their followers and institutions:[27]

- *Assets.* Leaders need to ensure financial stability as well as the relationships and reputation that will ensure future prosperity. Leaders must also provide followers with adequate tools, equipment, and facilities.
- *A legacy.* When they depart, leaders ought to leave behind people who find more meaning, challenge, and joy in their work.
- *Clear institutional values.* Servant leaders articulate principles that shape both individual and organizational behavior.
- *Future leadership.* Current leaders are obligated to identify and then to develop their successors.
- *Healthy institutional culture.* Servant leaders are responsible for fostering such organizational characteristics as quality, openness to change, and tolerance of diverse opinions.
- *Covenants.* Covenants are voluntary agreements that serve as reference points for organizational members, providing them with direction. Leaders and followers who enter into a covenant are bound together in pursuit of a common goal.
- *Maturity.* Followers expect a certain level of maturity from their leaders. Mature leaders have a clear sense of self-worth, belonging, responsibility, accountability, and equality.
- *Rationality.* Leaders supply the reason and understanding that helps followers make sense of organizational programs and relationships. A rational environment builds trust, allows followers to reach their full potential, and encourages ongoing organizational learning.
- *Space.* Space refers to a sense of freedom that allows followers and leaders to be and express themselves. Leaders who create adequate space allow for the giving and receiving of such gifts as new ideas, healing, dignity, and inclusion.
- *Momentum.* Servant leaders help create the feeling that the group is moving forward and achieving its goals. Momentum arises out of a clear vision and strategy supported by productive research, operations, financial, and marketing departments.
- *Effectiveness.* Effectiveness comes from enabling followers to reach their personal and institutional potential. Servant leaders allow followers to assume leadership roles when conditions warrant.
- *Civility and values.* A civilized institution is marked by good manners, respect for others, and service. Wise leaders can distinguish between what is healthy for the organization (dignity of work, hope, simplicity) and what is superficial and unhealthy (consumption, instant gratification, affluence).

3. *Partnership.* Servant leaders view followers as partners not subordinates. As a consequence, they strive for equity or justice in the distribution of power. Strategies for empowering followers include sharing information, delegating authority to carry out important tasks, and encouraging constituents to develop and exercise their talents. Concern for equity extends to the distribution of rewards as well. For example, at Herman Miller, every employee with a year or more of service can purchase company stock. The compensation of the CEO is limited to 20 times the salary of the lowest paid factory worker.

4. *Elevating purpose.* In addition to serving followers, servant leaders also serve worthy missions, ideas, and causes. Seeking to fulfill a high moral purpose, and understanding the role one plays in the process, makes work more meaningful to leaders and followers alike. Consider the example of three bricklayers at work in the English countryside. When asked by a traveler to describe what they were doing, the first replied, "I am laying bricks." The second said, "I am feeding my family by laying bricks." The third bricklayer, who had a clearer sense of the purpose for his labor, declared, "Through my work of laying bricks, I am constructing a cathedral, and thereby giving honor and praise to God."

BALANCE SHEET

Advantages (+s)

- Is altruistic
- Incorporates simplicity
- Promotes self-awareness
- Incorporates moral sensitivity

Disadvantages (−s)

- Seems unrealistic
- May not work in every context
- Poses the danger of serving the wrong cause or offering unwise service
- Carries a negative connotation in the term "servant"

Altruism is the first strength of servant leadership. Concern for others, in this case followers, comes before concern for self. We can only serve if we commit ourselves to the principle that others should come first.

Simplicity is the second strength of servant leadership. We are far less likely to cast shadows if we approach our leadership roles with one goal in mind—the desire to serve. A great number of ethical abuses, as we emphasized in Chapter 2, stem from leaders putting their personal interests first. Instead, servant leaders act out of a sense of stewardship and obligation, promoting the growth of followers and the interests of the larger community. They share, rather than hoard, power, privilege, and information.

Self-awareness is the third strength of servant leadership. Servant leaders listen to themselves as well as to others, take time for reflection, and recognize the importance of spiritual resources.

Moral sensitivity is the fourth strength of servant leadership. Servant leaders are acutely aware of the importance of pursuing ethical purposes that bring meaning and fulfillment to work. Serving a transcendent goal means that every act of leadership has a moral dimension.

Despite its strengths, servant leadership has not met with universal approval. Cynicism is often the first response when this model is presented. "Sounds good in principle," listeners respond, "but it would never work at my company, in my family, at my condominium association meeting, or _____ " (fill in the blank). Skeptics report that they have been "walked on" whenever they've tried to be nice to poor performers at work, rebellious teenagers, or nasty neighbors. Others equate a servant attitude with passivity.

Skepticism about servant leadership may stem, in part, from a misunderstanding that equates service with weakness. Servant leaders need to be tough. Sometimes the best way to serve someone is to reprimand or fire that individual. Nevertheless, there may be situations in which servant leadership is extremely difficult, if not impossible, to implement (see Case Study 6.1).

CASE STUDY 6.1

Servant Leadership Behind Bars

A federal penitentiary filled with some of the nation's most notorious criminals seems an unlikely setting for servant leadership. Prison guards must deal with hostile, manipulative inmates. Their jobs are monotonous but quickly become dangerous when prisoners take hostages or riot. Do the principles of servant leadership apply in this situation? That was the challenge Les, an experienced federal custodial officer, posed after hearing my presentation on servant leadership. He wanted to abandon his old, authoritarian approach to his job but was afraid that inmates would take advantage of him if he adopted a "softer" leadership style.

For the next half hour, the group wrestled with the question of whether or not Les could serve prisoners in his role as a guard. We concluded that Les could demonstrate at least some of the characteristics of a servant leader. He could (a) listen more, (b) remember that inmates are valuable human beings, (c) try persuasion first, before giving orders or using force, and (d) encourage prisoners to take advantage of educational and training opportunities while in prison.

Evaluate the suggestions of the group. Can Les be a servant leader? Are there situations in which it is impossible to serve followers?

Misplaced goals are problems for servant leaders and followers alike. The butler in the novel *Remains of the Day* by Kazuo Ishiguro illustrates the danger of misspent service. He devotes his entire life to being the perfect servant who meets the needs of his English employer. Sadly, his sacrifice is wasted because the lord of the manor turns out to be a Nazi sympathizer. The desire to serve needs to be combined with careful reasoning and values clarification. We must carefully examine who and what we serve, asking ourselves questions such as the following: Is this group, individual, or organization worthy of our service? What values are we promoting? What is the product of our service—light or darkness?

We are also charged with giving wise service. Lots of well-intentioned efforts to help others are wasted when leaders fail to do their homework. Following the devastation of Hurricane Mitch in Honduras, for example, one well-known humanitarian organization built a large housing development miles from the nearest town or city. Years later nearly all the homes stand empty because the neighborhood is too far from jobs, schools, and shopping.

Finally, members of some minority groups, particularly African Americans, associate the word *servant* with a history of slavery, oppression, and discrimination. The negative connotations surrounding the word may keep you from embracing the *idea* of servant leadership. You may want to abandon this term and focus instead on related concepts like altruism and the virtues of concern and compassion.

Implications and Applications

- Many popular leadership theories are built on moral principles. Try to understand a perspective's underlying values and standards before you adopt it as your blueprint for leadership.
- Contrary to popular belief, being ethical makes us more, not less successful. Being a "good" leader means being both ethical *and* effective.
- Seek to be a transforming leader who raises the level of morality in a group or organization. Transformational leaders speak to higher-level needs and bring about profound changes. They are motivated by altruism and marked by personal integrity.
- *How* you interact with followers is critical. Ethical leader-follower relationships are based on free choice, mutual persuasion, and joint goal setting.
- Taoists argue that nature and elements of everyday life serve as a source of leadership lessons. You can learn from uncarved blocks, children, water, valleys, and clay pots.
- Putting the needs of followers first reduces the likelihood that you'll cast ethical shadows. Servant leaders are stewards who have significant obligations to both their followers and their institutions, practice partnership, and serve worthy purposes.
- Be careful who and what you serve. Make sure your efforts support worthy people and goals and are carefully thought out.

For Further Exploration, Challenge, and Self-Assessment

1. What additional advantages and disadvantages can you add for each approach described in the chapter? Which perspective do you find most useful? Why?

2. Brainstorm a list of pseudotransformational and transformational leaders. What factors distinguish between the two types of leaders? How do your characteristics compare with those presented in the chapter?

3. Develop a definition of ethical leadership that addresses both leadership processes and products.

4. Discuss the following proposition in a group: "The most successful leaders are also the most ethical leaders." Do you agree? Why or why not?

5. Make a diligent effort to serve your followers for a week. At the end of this period, reflect on your experience. Did focusing on the needs of followers

change your behavior? What did you do differently? What would happen if you made this your leadership philosophy?

6. Which natural image from Taoism do you find most interesting and helpful? Why? Can you think of additional natural metaphors that would be useful to leaders?

7. Read a popular book on transformational leadership or on a transformational leader. Write a review. Summarize the contents for those who have not read it. Next, evaluate the book. What are its strengths and weaknesses from an ethical point of view? Would you recommend it to others? Why or why not?

CASE STUDY 6.2

Chapter End Case: Transforming Clear Lake College

Clear Lake College was in serious trouble in 1992. Enrollment at the Midwestern school had dropped from 650 to 600 undergraduates. Because it had no emergency endowment fund, Clear Lake counted on tuition revenue to pay its bills. The loss of so many students threatened to close the 90-year-old school. The college's president, who seemed unable to respond to the crisis, resigned.

The school's board of directors appointed Samuel (Sam) Thomas as the next president. Thomas had a PhD in higher education but came to Clear Lake directly out of a marketing position in business. Unlike his predecessor, Thomas didn't hesitate to make bold, sometimes risky decisions. He hired a new admissions staff, convinced faculty to agree to a salary and benefits freeze, and spent several hundred thousand dollars to launch the college's first graduate degree program.

Initially, Clear Lake seemed to go backward rather than forward under Sam's direction. Enrollment dropped still further during the first year of his administration, but 1994 saw a surge in new students. The graduate program was a big success, and Sam used his marketing background to improve the college's visibility. An entrepreneur at heart, he encouraged faculty and staff to develop additional programs for new markets. During the next 10 years, enrollment grew to nearly 2,000 students. The college added more graduate degrees and several new undergraduate majors. Clear Lake College earned a national listing as "one of America's educational bargains."

Thomas had many admirable leadership qualities. To begin, he was a "people person" who enjoyed mixing with donors, students, faculty, and administrators at other schools. No one would think of calling him "Dr. Thomas." He was "Sam" to everyone. Second, he was more than willing to tackle tough problems and fire those who weren't performing up to standards. Third, he kept his word to faculty and staff. When the financial picture of the school improved, he raised faculty salaries dramatically. Fourth, he had an uncanny ability to sense new educational markets. He never made a major miscalculation when it came to proposing additional programs.

Yet all was not well under Sam's leadership. His friendly exterior masked an explosive temper. He dressed down faculty and other employees in public meetings and made personnel decisions on his own, based on his instincts rather than on hard data. A number of employees were let go without warning, and many of his hires lasted less than a year. In several instances, the college had to offer generous severance packages to dismissed employees in order to avoid costly lawsuits. Sam's autocratic style wasn't limited strictly to personnel decisions. He would change the school's governance structure without consulting faculty, who expected to participate in these choices. In addition, Sam engaged in micromanagement. He read minutes from every department meeting held on campus, for example, and didn't hesitate to send scathing memos if he disagreed with the group's conclusions.

Sam received lots of accolades for his success at Clear Lake College. He was credited for the school's turnaround and was named as the area's outstanding citizen one year. He was popular with other university presidents, serving on national collegiate boards and commissions. The board of the college was eager to renew his contract despite the concerns of the faculty. Unfortunately, Sam's successes made him less, not more, flexible. Frustrated by faculty criticism, he made even fewer efforts to consult them when making decisions. He began to call students who had offended him into his office to berate them.

By the late 1990s, it looked as if the college had "outgrown" Sam's leadership style. After all, the school was much bigger and more complex than it had been when he took over. Sam had no intention of stepping down, however. He referred to Clear Lake as "my" college and continued to be involved in every detail of college life. In fact, Sam had to be forced to resign when he contracted Parkinson's disease in 1999. The college has continued to grow under the leadership of a new president who, while maintaining a good deal of decision-making power, relies heavily on his vice presidents and has very little input in the day-to-day operations of most departments.

DISCUSSION PROBES

1. What elements of transactional and transforming leadership did Sam exhibit?

2. Was Sam a transformational or a pseudotransformational leader?

3. Have you ever had to confront a leader about her or his behavior? What did you say or do? What was the outcome of the encounter? Would you do anything differently next time?

4. Does success make leaders more dangerous, more likely to cast shadows?

5. How do you determine when to remove a leader, particularly one that has a proven track record of success?

6. What leadership lessons do you draw from this case?

CASE STUDY 6.3

Chapter End Case: Betraying the Small Investor

Mutual funds are the most popular way for average citizens to invest in the stock market. Small investors can choose from among 8,200 funds when saving for retirement, new homes, and other long-range goals. All told, the mutual fund industry manages $7 trillion in assets for 95 million Americans.

Mutual funds long enjoyed a reputation for integrity and transparency, avoiding the insider trading and accounting scandals associated with brokerage firms and investment banks (see the Salomon case at the end of Chapter 2). Their wholesome image was shattered, however, when allegations of late-day trading and market timing surfaced in 2003. In illegal late trading, large clients were allowed to place orders after the fund price (based on the collective value of all the stocks held by the fund) was set for the day. Their orders were based on late-breaking financial news that would drive the price of a mutual fund up in the next trading session the following day. In market timing, wealthy investors moved their money rapidly in and out of funds. Market timing is not against the law, but most fund families prohibit the practice because frequent trades increase costs and reduce share values.

At first, regulators thought that late trading and market timing practices were limited to a few fund companies. In reality, abuses appear widespread with a quarter of all brokerage houses reporting that they helped major clients trade after hours. Half of the biggest firms said they allowed market timing. Investigators have unearthed new allegations involving high management fees and steering customers toward certain funds in return for commissions. Former Securities and Exchange Commission Chairman Arthur Levitt called the spreading scandal the worst in 50 years. Companies accused of violating federal regulations include Putnam Investments, Charles Schwab, Alliance Capital, Janus Capital, Canary Capital Partners, Morgan Stanley, and PBHG Funds. Punishments have been meted out to both individuals (felony charges, fines, forced resignations, lifetime bans from the securities industry) and fund families (refunds, civil penalties, federal supervision).

Mutual funds belong to investors, not to the firms that manage them. Yet the interests of small investors were almost totally ignored in the mutual fund scandal. Fund managers accused of late-day trading and market timing served themselves, not their average customers. They wanted to keep big clients happy in order to generate more commissions. In some instances, dishonest brokers also took a share of the profits generated by late trading or engaged in market timing in their own accounts. Fund boards failed to exercise proper oversight because they are often overworked. At Janus Capital Group, for example, nine people oversaw 113 funds.

The Securities and Exchange Commission (SEC) is the government agency charged with regulating the mutual fund industry. Unfortunately, the agency looked the other way as illegal practices (which were no secret to industry insiders) continued. Understaffed and distracted by other financial scandals, SEC regulators bowed to pressure from the industry's trade organization to keep regulations to a minimum. They even ignored whistle-blowers who tried to alert them to illegal trading activities. As a result, state regulators in New York and Massachusetts, not the SEC, filed the initial charges against fund management companies and their officers.

Offending fund firms face the prospect of losing millions of dollars in management fees as investors both small and large flee to more reputable companies. In the end, their losses are likely to far outweigh any gains they made by engaging in late trading, market timing, and other shady practices. The fund industry as a whole will have to regain the trust of disillusioned investors.

DISCUSSION QUESTIONS

1. Who is most to blame for the mutual fund scandal? Why?

2. Will the mutual fund industry be permanently damaged by this scandal? Why or why not?

3. What steps should the mutual fund industry take to restore public trust? What role should the SEC and state regulators play in this process?

4. Can you think of other examples of organizational leaders who lost sight of the fact that they were stewards acting on behalf of organizational members and society as a whole? What price did they pay? What price did their organizations pay?

5. What leadership lessons do you draw from this case?

REFERENCES

Fuerbringer, J. (2003, November 9). The mysterious world of mutual fund costs. *The New York Times,* section 3, p. 6.

Labaton, S. (2003, November 18). Looking the other way. *The Oregonian,* p. A8.

Masters, B. A. (2003, October 3). SEC finds illegal fund trading; Survey discloses after-hours deals. *Washington.post.com.* Retrieved November 15, 2003, from LexisNexis (www.lexisnexis.com/).

Masters, B. A. (2003, October 5). A big scandal rattles the little guy. *The Washington Post,* p. F1.

Shell, A. (2003, September 5). Anatomy of a tricky trading scheme. *USA Today,* Money, p. 18.

Sloan, D. A. (2003, October 7). Mutual fund machinations may be the most troubling of recent scandals. *The Washington Post,* p. E3.

Notes

1. Ciulla, J. B. (1995). Ethics: Mapping the territory. In J. B. Ciulla (Ed.), *Ethics: The heart of leadership* (pp. 3–25). Westport, CT: Praeger.

2. Burns J. M. (1978). *Leadership.* New York: Harper & Row.

3. Burns, J. M. (2003). *Transforming leadership: A new pursuit of happiness.* New York: Atlantic Monthly Press.

4. Burns (1978), *Leadership*, p. 20.

5. Burns (2003), *Transforming leadership*, ch. 12.

6. See, for example, the following:

Bass, B. M. (1996). *A new paradigm of leadership: An inquiry into transformational leadership.* Alexandria, VA: U.S. Army Research Institute for the Behavioral and Social Sciences.

Bass, B. M., Avolio, B. J., Jung, D. I., & Berson, Y. (2003). Predicting unit performance by assessing transformational and transactional leadership. *Journal of Applied Psychology, 88*, 207–218.

7. Bass, B. M. (1990). *Bass & Stogdill's handbook of leadership* (3rd ed.). New York: Free Press, p. 53.

8. See, for example, the following:

Bass, B. M., & Avolio, B. J. (1993). Transformational leadership: A response to critiques. In M. M. Chemers & R. Ayman (Eds.), *Leadership theory and research: Perspectives and directions* (pp. 49–60). San Diego: Academic.

Waldman, D. A., Bass, B. M., Yammarino, F. J. (1990). Adding to contingent-reward behavior: The augmenting effect of charismatic leadership. *Group and Organizational Studies, 15*, 381–394.

9. For evidence of the effectiveness of transformational leadership, see Bass, Avolio, Jung, & Berson (2003), Predicting unit performance, and the following:

DeGroot, T., Kiker, D. S., & Cross, T. C. (2000). A meta-analysis to review organizational outcomes related to charismatic leadership. *Canadian Journal of Administrative Sciences, 17*, 356–371.

Fiol, C. M., Harris, D., & House, R. J. (1999). Charismatic leadership: Strategies for effecting social change. *Leadership Quarterly, 10*, 449–482.

Lowe, K. B., & Kroeck, K. G., (1996). Effectiveness correlates of transformational and transactional leadership: A meta-analytic review. *Leadership Quarterly, 7*, 385–425.

10. A few examples of popular leadership sources based on a transformational approach include the following:

Bennis, W., & Nanus, B. (1985). *Leaders: The strategies for taking charge.* New York: Harper & Row.

Kotter, J. P. (1990). *A force for change: How leadership differs from management.* New York: Free Press.

Kouzes, J. M., & Posner, B. (1987). *The leadership challenge: How to get extraordinary things done in organizations.* San Francisco: Jossey-Bass.

Nanus, B. (1992). *Visionary leadership.* San Francisco: Jossey-Bass.

Peters, T. (1992). *Liberation management.* New York: Ballantine.

11. Bass, B. M. (1995). The ethics of transformational leadership. In J. Ciulla (Ed), *Ethics: The heart of leadership* (pp. 169–192). Westport, CT: Praeger.

12. Turner, N., Barling, J., Epitropaki, O., Butcher, V., & Milner, C. (2002, April). Transformational leadership and moral reasoning. *Journal of Applied Psychology, 87,* 304–311.

13. Den Hartog, D. N., House, R. J., Hanges, P. U., Ruiz-Quintanilla, S. A., & Dorfman, P. W. (1999). Culture-specific and cross-culturally generalizable implicit leadership theories: Are attributes of charismatic/transformational leadership universally endorsed? *Leadership Quarterly, 10,* 219–257.

14. Roberts, W. (1987). *Leadership secrets of Attila the Hun.* New York: Warner Books.

15. Criticisms of transformational leadership can be found in the following:

Kelley, R. (1992). *The power of followership.* New York: Doubleday/Currency.

Tourish, D., & Pinnington, A. (2002). Transformational leadership, corporate cultism and the spirituality paradigm: An unholy trinity in the workplace? *Human Relations, 55*(2), 147–172.

16. Rost, J. (1991). *Leadership for the twenty-first century.* New York: Praeger, p. 102. See also the following:

Rost, J. (1993). Leadership in the new millennium. *Journal of Leadership Studies, 1,* 92–110.

17. Rost (1991), *Leadership for the twenty-first century,* p. 161.

18. Rost (1991), *Leadership for the twenty-first century,* p. 109.

19. Material on key components of Taoist thought is adapted from the following:

Johnson, C. E. (2000). Taoist leadership ethics. *Journal of Leadership Studies, 7,* 82–91.

Johnson, C. E. (1997, Spring). A leadership journey to the East. *Journal of Leadership Studies, 4,* 82–88.

For an alternative perspective on the origins of Taoism, see the following:

Kirkland, R. (2002). Self-fulfillment through selflessness: The moral teachings of the Daode Jing. In M. Barnhart (Ed.), *Varieties of ethical reflection: New Directions for ethics in a global context* (pp. 21–48). Lanham, MD: Lexington Books.

20. Mitchell, S. (1988). *Tao te ching.* New York: Harper Perennial, p. 19.

21. Mitchell (1988), *Tao te ching,* p. 17.

22. Chan, W. (1963). *The way of Lao Tzu.* Indianapolis: Bobbs-Merrill, p. 236.

23. Greenleaf, R. K. (1977). *Servant leadership.* New York: Paulist Press.

24. Spears, L. (1998). Introduction: Tracing the growing impact of servant-leadership. In L. C. Spears (Ed.), *Insights on leadership* (pp. 1–12). New York: Wiley; Ruschman, N. L. (2002). Servant-leadership and the best companies to work for in America. In L. C. Spears & M. Lawrence (Eds.), *Focus on leadership: Servant-leadership for the twenty-first century* (pp. 123–139). New York: Wiley.

25. Greenleaf (1977), *Servant leadership*, pp. 13–14.

26. Block, P. (1996). *Stewardship: Choosing service over self-interest.* San Francisco: Berrett-Koehler; DePree, M. (2003). Servant-leadership: Three things necessary. In L. C. Spears & M. Lawrence (Eds.), *Focus on leadership: Servant-leadership for the 21st century.* New York: Wiley.

27. DePree, M. (1989). *Leadership is an art.* New York: Doubleday.

7

Ethical Decision-Making Formats

As we practice resolving dilemmas we find ethics to be less a goal than a pathway, less a destination than a trip, less an inoculation than a process.

Ethicist Rushworth Kidder

What's Ahead

This chapter introduces systematic approaches to ethical problem solving. We'll take a look at five decision-making formats: (1) Kidder's ethical checkpoints, (2) Nash's 12 questions, (3) the SAD formula, (4) Cooper's active process model, and (5) the case study method. After presenting each approach, I'll discuss its relative advantages and disadvantages.

Pick a Format, Any Format

Decision-making guidelines or formats can help us make better ethical choices. Taking a systematic approach encourages teams and individuals to carefully define the problem, gather information, apply ethical standards and values, identify and evaluate alternative courses of action, and follow through on their choices. They're also better equipped to defend their decisions. I'll describe five ethical decision-making formats in the pages to come. All five approaches are useful. You may want to use just one or a combination of all of them. The particular format you use is not as important as being systematic. You can practice these guidelines by applying them to the scenarios described at the end of the chapter.

Kidder's Ethical Checkpoints

Ethicist Rushworth Kidder suggests that nine steps or checkpoints can help bring order to otherwise confusing ethical issues.[1]

1. Recognize that there is a problem. This step is critically important because it forces us to acknowledge that there is an issue that deserves our attention and helps us separate moral questions from disagreements about manners and social conventions. Being late for a party, for example, may be bad manners and violate cultural expectations. However, this act does not translate into a moral problem involving right or wrong. Deciding whether or not to accept a kickback from a supplier, on the other hand, is an ethical dilemma.

2. Determine the actor. Once we've determined that there is an ethical issue, we then need to decide who is responsible for addressing the problem. I may be concerned that the owner of a local business treats his employees poorly. Nonetheless, unless I work for the company or buy its products, there is little I can do to address this situation.

3. Gather the relevant facts. Adequate, accurate, and current information is important for making effective decisions of all kinds, including ethical ones. Details do make a difference. In deciding whether or not it is just to suspend a student for fighting, for instance, a school principal will want to hear from teachers, classmates, and the offender to determine the seriousness of the offense, the student's reason for fighting, and the outcome of the altercation. The administrator will probably be more lenient if this is the offender's first offense and he was defending himself.

4. Test for right-versus-wrong issues. A choice is generally a poor one if it (a) gives you a negative, gut-level reaction (the stench test), (b) would make you uncomfortable if it appeared on the front page of tomorrow's newspaper (the front page test), or (c) would violate the moral code of someone that you care a lot about (the Mom test). If your decision violates any of these criteria, you had better reconsider.

5. Test for right-versus-right values. Many ethical dilemmas pit two core values against each other. Determine if two good or right values are in conflict with one another in this situation. Right-versus-right value clashes include

- Truth telling versus loyalty to others and institutions. Telling the truth may threaten our allegiance to another person or to an organization, such as when a leader must determine whether or not to "blow the whistle" on corporate wrongdoing.

- Personal needs versus the needs of the community. Our desire to serve our immediate group or ourselves can run counter to the needs of the larger group or community.
- Short-term benefits versus long-term negative consequences. Sometimes satisfying the immediate needs of the group (giving a hefty pay raise to employees, for example) can lead to long-term negative consequences (endangering the future of the business).
- Justice versus mercy. Being fair and evenhanded, as Leadership Ethics at the Movies: *Catch Me If You Can* (Box 7.1) demonstrates, may conflict with our desire to show love and compassion.

Kidder believes that truth versus loyalty is the most common type of conflict involving two deeply held values. He offers the case described in Case Study 7.1, The Board Chairman's Question, as an example of the tension caused by this type of choice.

6. *Apply the ethical standards/perspectives.* Apply the ethical principle(s) that is most relevant and useful to this specific issue. Is it communitarianism? utilitarianism? Kant's categorical imperative? a combination of perspectives?

7. *Look for a third way.* Sometimes seemingly irreconcilable values can be resolved through compromise or the development of a creative solution. Negotiators frequently seek a third way to bring competing factions together. Such was the case in the deliberations that produced the Camp David peace accord. Egypt demanded that Israel return land on the West Bank seized in the 1967 War. Israel resisted because it wanted a buffer zone to protect its security. The dispute was settled when Egypt pledged that it would not attack Israel again. Assured of safety, the Israelis agreed to return the territory to Egypt.[2]

8. *Make the decision.* At some point we need to step up and make the decision. This seems a given (after all, the point of the whole process is to reach a conclusion). We may be mentally exhausted from wrestling with the problem, however, or we may get caught up in the act of analysis or lack the necessary courage to come to a decision. In Kidder's words,

> At this point in the process, there's little to do but decide. That requires moral courage—an attribute essential to leadership and one that, along with reason, distinguishes humanity most sharply from the animal world. Little wonder, then, that the exercise of ethical decision-making is often seen as the highest fulfillment of the human condition.[3]

9. *Revisit and reflect on the decision.* Learn from your choices. Once you've moved on to other issues, stop and reflect. What lessons emerge from this case that you can apply to future decisions? What ethical issues did it raise?

BALANCE SHEET

Advantages (+s)

- Is thorough
- Considers problem ownership
- Emphasizes the importance of getting the facts straight
- Recognizes that dilemmas can involve right-versus-right as well as right-versus-wrong choices
- Encourages the search for creative solutions
- Sees ethical decision making as a learning process

Weaknesses (−s)

- Not easy to determine who has the responsibility to solve a problem
- The facts are not always available or there may not be enough time to gather them
- Decisions don't always lead to action

Box 7.1

Leadership Ethics at the Movies: *Catch Me If You Can*

Key Cast Members: Leonardo DiCaprio, Tom Hanks, Christopher Walken

Synopsis: This film recounts the story of real-life con artist Frank Abagnale, Jr. During the 1960s, Abagnale (DiCaprio) talked his way into jobs as a teacher, surgeon, lawyer, and airline pilot. He also passed hundreds of forged checks. Hanks plays the lonely FBI agent assigned to track Frank down. The chase goes on for years. During this period, the agent and forger develop a genuine affection for one another. After finally bringing Abagnale to justice, Hanks has him released from prison in order to help the bureau catch other counterfeiters. The con man turned lawman then goes on to a lucrative career as a crime prevention consultant.

Themes: justice versus mercy, moral decision making, deceit, betrayal, character, redemption, forgiveness

---

There is a lot to be said for Kidder's approach to ethical decision making. For one thing, he seems to cover all the bases, beginning with defining the issue all the way through to learning from the situation after the "dust has settled." He acknowledges that there are some problems that we can't do much about and that we need to pay particular attention to gathering as much information as possible. The ethicist recognizes that some decisions involve deciding between two "goods" and leaves the door open for creative solutions. Making a choice can be an act of courage, as Kidder points out, and we can apply lessons learned in one dilemma to future problems.

On the flip side, some of the strengths of Kidder's model can also be seen as weaknesses. Determining responsibility or ownership of a problem, as we'll see in Chapter 10, is getting harder in an increasingly interdependent world. Who is responsible for poor labor conditions in Third World countries, for instance? the manufacturer? the subcontractor? the store that sells the products made in sweatshops? those who buy the items? Kidder also seems to assume that leaders will have the time to gather necessary information. Unfortunately, in crisis situations, time is in short supply. When an employee goes public with a charge of sexual harassment against a manager, his supervisor must decide immediately whether to fire or suspend the accused, what information to release to the press, and so on. Finally, the model seems to equate deciding with doing. As we saw in our discussion of moral action in Chapter 3, we can decide on a course of action but not follow through. Kidder is right to say that making ethical choices requires courage. However, it takes even more courage to put the choice into effect.

CASE STUDY 7.1

The Board Chairman's Question

In his position as the number two in a loan organization, Andrew was appointed directly by the board of directors, as was the president. The organization, a nonprofit with some $10 million in assets, had a good record of dispensing loans to families in need. It proved to be a very attractive entity to a similar and slightly larger organization, whose principals approached the president and suggested a merger.

For some months, the talks between the organizations continued, with the president as the chief negotiator for Andrew's side. The board of directors was aware of the activity. As the situation seemed to be approaching a decision point, however, the board got cold feet and one day instructed the president to cease and desist in his negotiations, explaining that from now on all contacts with the other organization should flow through the board.

Several days later, the president told Andrew he had invited the senior officers from the other loan organization to town for a daylong site visit during which they could examine the loan files and learn about the procedures of this organization. Andrew was taken aback: "Wasn't this in direct violation of the board's directive?" he asked. The president admitted it was but asserted that he was tired of being run around by the board. He told Andrew that he was going ahead with plans for what seemed to him a very good merger, not only for the two organizations but for the client base they served. And he asked Andrew to be present for the daylong meeting.

Andrew's initial dilemma was clear. As an appointee of the board, he had more than the usual commitment of a number two to an organization's governing board. Yet he knew that, were he to cross the president on such a matter, his tenure in the organization could be short-lived. What's more, he liked and respected the president. What to do?

He explained to the president that although he did not feel he could stand in his way, his conscience would not let him participate. They agreed that he should work at home on the day of the visit. The day came, and Andrew was at home when, early in the afternoon, the phone rang. It was the chairman of the board, who asked why Andrew was at home.

Now the dilemma was immediate. It was right, Andrew knew, to support his president, show the kind of loyalty that he knew the president would show him in similar circumstances, and not play the tattletale. What's more, it would have been easy to create an explanation that was acceptable and unrevealing—pleading, for example, a health-related problem. Yet it was right to tell the truth—especially when the question was a legitimate one, coming from an individual who had every right to know what was happening.

If you were Andrew, how would you answer the board chairman's question? Why?

REFERENCE

Kidder, R. M. (1995). *How good people make tough choices: Resolving the dilemmas of ethical living.* New York: Fireside, pp. 124–125. Reprinted by permission of HarperCollins Publishers, Inc.

Nash's 12 Questions

Ethics consultant Laura Nash offers 12 questions that can help businesses and other groups identify the responsibilities involved in moral choices.[4] She argues that discussions based on these queries can be useful, even if the group doesn't reach a conclusion. Managers who answer the questions surface ethical concerns that might otherwise remain hidden, identify common moral problems, clarify gaps between stated values and performance, and explore a variety of alternatives.

1. Have you defined the problem accurately? The ethical decision-making process begins with assembling the facts. Determine how many employees will be affected by layoffs, how much the cleanup of toxic materials will cost, or how many people have been injured by faulty products. Finding out the facts can help defuse the emotionalism of some issues (perhaps the damage is not as great as first feared).

2. How would you define the problem if you stood on the other side of the fence? Asking how others might feel forces self-examination. From a company's point of view, expanding a local plant by increasing production and efficiency may make good sense. Government officials and neighbors might have an entirely different perspective. A larger plant means more workers clogging already overcrowded roads and contributing to urban sprawl.

3. How did this situation occur in the first place? This question separates the symptoms from the disease. Lying, cheating customers and strained labor relations are generally symptoms of deeper problems. Firing an employee for unethical behavior is a temporary solution. Probe to discover the underlying causes. Many dubious accounting practices, for example, are the result of pressure to produce high quarterly profits.

4. To whom and to what do you give your loyalties as a person or group and as a member of the organization? Conflicts of loyalty, as we saw in Chapter 1, are hard to sort through. However, wrestling with the problem of ultimate loyalty (work group? family? self? corporation?) can clarify the values operating in an ethical dilemma.

5 & 6. What is your intention in making this decision? How does this intention compare with the likely results? These questions probe both the group's intentions and the likely products. Honorable motives don't guarantee positive results. Make sure that the outcomes reflect your motivations.

7. Whom could your decision or action injure? Too often groups consider possible injury only after being sued. Try, in advance, to determine harmful consequences. What will happen if customers ignore label warnings and spread your pesticide indiscriminately, for example? Will the guns you manufacture end up in the hands of urban gang members? Based on these determinations, you may decide to abandon your plans to make these items or revise the way they are marketed.

8. Can you engage the affected parties in a discussion of the problem before you make your decision? Talking to affected parties is one way to make sure that you understand how your actions will affect them. Few of us would want other people to decide what's in our best interest. Yet we often push forward with projects assuming we know what's in the best interests of others.

9. Are you confident that your position will be as valid over a long period of time as it seems now? Make sure that your choice will stand the test of time. What seem like compelling reasons for a decision may not seem so important months or years later. Consider the U.S. decision to invade Iraq, for instance. American intelligence experts and political leaders linked Saddam Hussein to terrorist groups and claimed that he was hiding weapons of mass destruction. After the invasion, no solid ties between Iraqis and international terrorists or weapons of mass destruction were discovered. The decision to wage this war doesn't appear as justified now as it did in the months leading up to the conflict.

10. Could you disclose without qualms your decision or action to your boss, your CEO, the board of directors, your family, or society as a whole? No ethical decision is too trivial to escape the disclosure test. If you or your group wouldn't want to disclose this action, then you'd better reevaluate your choice.

11. What is the symbolic potential of your action if understood? misunderstood? What you intend may not be what the public perceives (see questions 5 & 6). If your company is a notorious polluter, contributions to local arts groups may be seen as an attempt to divert attention from your firm's poor environmental record, not as a generous civic gesture.

12. Under what conditions would you allow exceptions to your stand? Moral consistency is critical, but is there any basis for making an exception? Dorm rules might require that visiting hours end at midnight on weekdays. However, as a resident assistant, is there any time when you would be willing to overlook violations? during finals week? on the evening before classes start? when dorm residents and visitors are working on class projects?

BALANCE SHEET

Advantages (+s)

- Highlights the importance of gathering facts
- Encourages perspective taking
- Forecasts results and consequences over time

Disadvantages (–s)

- Is extremely time consuming
- May not always reach a conclusion
- Ignores implementation and important ethical perspectives

Like the ethical checkpoints, the 12 questions highlight the importance of problem identification and information gathering. They go a step further, however, by encouraging us to engage in perspective taking. We need to see the problem from the other party's point of view, consider the possible injury we might cause, invite others to give us feedback, and consider how our actions will be perceived. Perspective-taking skills will play a critical role in managing ethical-cultural diversity, our topic in Chapter 10. We also need to envision results and take a long-term perspective, imagining how our decisions will stand the test of time. Stepping back can keep us from making choices we might regret later. For example, the decision to test nuclear weapons without warning citizens may have seemed justified to officials waging the Cold War. However, now even the federal government admits that these tests were immoral. Test your perspective-taking skills by analyzing the case described in the self-assessment in Box 7.2.

I suspect that some groups will be frustrated by the amount of time it takes to answer the 12 questions. Not only is the model detailed, but discussing the problem with affected parties could take a series of meetings over a period of weeks and months. Complex issues like determining who should clean up river pollution involve a great many constituencies with very different agendas (government agencies, company representatives, citizens groups, conservation clubs). Some decision makers may also be put off by the model's ambiguity. Nash admits that experts may define problems differently, that there may be exceptions to the decision, and that groups may use the procedure and never reach a conclusion. Finally, none of the questions utilize the ethical standards we identified in Chapter 5 or address the problem of implementing the choice once it is made.

Box 7.2

Self-Assessment:

THE GIFT

Instructions

Test your ability to take other perspectives into account by reading the following case and answering the questions that follow.

Alfredo Ruiz is director of development at a small liberal arts college in the South. He supervises a small staff that raises funds for the school. Every 3 or 4 years, his office organizes capital campaigns to complete new buildings on campus. Between capital campaigns, Ruiz and his colleagues spend most of their time raising money for the college's annual fund. The annual fund covers shortfalls in projected revenue and underwrites small remodeling projects. The development office also works with donors on an ongoing basis to establish student scholarships.

Recently a donor died and left the university with an estate gift of $200,000. The will does not state a specific designation or use for the money. Alfredo knows that during the donor's lifetime she gave $10,000 a year to fund student scholarships, however. At the same time, this year's annual fund drive is falling seriously short of projections. Ruiz will be called on to explain the shortfall and his use of the $200,000 gift at the upcoming board of trustees meeting.

Alfredo is very tempted to use the gift to meet the college's annual fund goal instead of establishing an endowed scholarship in the donor's name. Before making this choice, he comes to you for advice about how others will respond if he applies the money to the annual fund drive.

How do you think the donor's family would view such a choice? other donors? students? the public? the board of trustees? What would be the long-term consequences of such a decision? After considering these various viewpoints, do you think that Ruiz should use the money for the annual fund?

Reference

Dana Miller, George Fox University

The SAD Formula

Media ethicist Louis Alvin Day of Louisiana State University developed the SAD formula in order to build important elements of critical thinking into moral reasoning.[5] Critical thinking is a rational approach to decision making that emphasizes careful analysis and evaluation. It begins with an understanding of the subject to be evaluated; moves to identifying the issues, information, and assumptions surrounding the problem; and then concludes with evaluating alternatives and reaching a conclusion.

Each stage of the SAD formula—Situation definition, Analysis of the situation, Decision—addresses a component of critical thinking (see Box 7.3). To demonstrate this model, I'll use a decision made by a government official following a weather emergency.

SITUATION DEFINITION

In January 2004, an ice and snowstorm paralyzed the Portland, Oregon, region for 4 days. Essential city and county employees made it to work to clear the roads and provide emergency services. Other government workers either stayed home or came to their offices for 2 half days during the storm. When the weather cleared, city and county leaders had to decide whether or not to pay hourly workers for time missed from work. Salaried employees must be paid for partial workweeks according to federal law; hourly workers not covered by union contracts have no such protection.

The city of Portland decided to reimburse workers only for the time when city offices were officially closed. Other city employees had to take vacation days or go without pay. However, Dianne Linn, the chair of the Multnomah County Board of Commissioners (the county encompassing the Portland metro area), opted to pay county employees who didn't make it into work when county facilities were open. She offered to pay double time to those who did. Commissioner Linn justified her generosity as a reward to county workers (many of whom worked from their homes during the storm) demoralized by a recent series of budget cuts. Critics were outraged, claiming that the chairwoman was wasting taxpayers' money by being more generous than the vast majority of private employers. Later Linn was forced to withdraw her double-time offer because she had overstepped her authority.[6]

Competing principles and values came into play in this situation. Linn was motivated by concern for the welfare of her employees. Cutting their wages would be one more blow to loyal workers who had been hit with a series of salary freezes and layoffs. Justice was another important consideration for the chairwoman. Only hourly nonunion county employees would lose wages as a result of the storm. Their salaried colleagues (who generally earn more) would be unaffected. The union's contract with the county requires that hourly employees be paid during weather emergencies.

Linn's opponents (including her fellow county commissioners) put a higher value on stewardship. To them, the government operates on behalf of its citizens who did not approve of her pay decision. Opponents argued that it is not fair to treat county employees better than city employees and most workers in the private sector.

Ethicist Day says that the ethical question to be addressed in his model should be as narrow as possible. In our example, we will seek to answer the following query: Was the county chair ethically justified in paying the wages of workers who didn't make it to work during the storm when their offices were officially open?

ANALYSIS

Evaluation of values and principles. In the storm scenario both sides can claim moral justification for their positions. Concern for employees is admirable, and denying pay to hourly workers means that they will bear a disproportionate burden for the shutdown. All leaders, however, particularly government officials, are stewards acting on behalf of constituents. The interests of the public ought to be taken into consideration. Private-sector workers often complain that public employees are overpaid and receive too many benefits.

External factors. The county's weather closure policy is vague, with no clear statement of whether or not hourly workers should be paid. Commission Chair Linn didn't feel that she needed the approval of her fellow commissioners to make her decision. Another important external factor was an upcoming vote on a proposed tax increase. This bond measure failed 3 weeks after the storm, requiring further cutbacks in county services. Voters might have been angered by the board chair's decision and expressed their frustration in the voting booth.

Moral duties or loyalties. Professor Day borrows from theologian Ralph Potter for this part of his model. Potter believes that we need to take into account important duties or loyalties whenever making ethical choices.[7] In this case, the moral agent (the board chair) had to keep the following duties in mind:

- Loyalty to her conscience
- Loyalty to county employees

- Loyalty to fellow board members

- Loyalty to others in the same profession

- Loyalty to taxpayers

- Loyalty to the society and community

The board chair made her conscience and loyalty to county employees top priority with the hope that her choice would benefit the community as well. Her opponents asserted that taxpayers ought to come first. Linn's decision cast her colleagues in other government agencies, which refused to pay their workers, in a bad light.

Moral theories. Each of the ethical perspectives outlined in Chapter 5 can be applied to this dilemma. From a utilitarian perspective, the immediate benefits to employees must be balanced against the potential long-term costs of alienating voters and possibly undermining the long-term financial health of the county. Based on Kant's categorical imperative, the board chair had an obligation or duty to carry through on her decision regardless of the consequences. However, it's not clear that we would want all government officials to make the same choice in similar situations because the cost could be prohibitive. According to Rawls's theory of justice as fairness, the decision to pay workers was justified because it benefited less advantaged hourly workers. Citizens standing behind the veil of ignorance would likely approve of this choice because they would want to be paid if they ended up being hourly employees. The communitarianism and altruism approaches also appear to support the chairwoman's decision. Paying personnel may encourage the ethic of caring and teamwork reflected in communitarianism, and it demonstrates altruistic concern for others.

DECISION

Decisions often emerge out of careful definition and analysis of the problem. It may be clear which course of action is best after identifying and evaluating external constraints, principles, duties, and moral theories. In our example, however, observers can reach and defend different conclusions. Refusing to pay for missed work hours reflects a concern for stewardship, puts the highest priority on loyalty to the public, and may generate the most benefits in the long run. Paying for lost hours, on the other hand, puts a higher premium on fairness and loyalty to employees.

Box 7.3

The Moral Reasoning Process

Situation Definition

Description of facts
Identification of principles and values
Statement of ethical issue or question

↓

Analysis

Weighing of competing principles and values
Consideration of external factors
Examination of duties to various parties
Discussion of applicable ethical theories

↓

Decision

Rendering of moral agent's decision
Defense of that decision based on moral theory

SOURCE: Day. L. A. (2003). *Ethics in media communications: Cases & controversies.* Belmont, CA: Wadsworth/Thompson, p. 67. Used by permission.

BALANCE SHEET

Advantages (+s)

  – Encourages orderly, systematic reasoning
  – Incorporates situation definition, duties, and moral theories

Disadvantages (−s)

  – May fail to reach consensus
  – Limits creativity
  – Ignores implementation

As advertised, the SAD formula does encourage careful reasoning by building in key elements of the critical thinking process. Following the formula keeps decision makers from reaching hasty decisions. Instead of jumping immediately to solutions, they must carefully identify elements of the situation, examine and evaluate ethical alternatives, and then reach a conclusion.

Three elements of the SAD formula are particularly praiseworthy. First, the formula recognizes that the keys to solving a problem often lie in clearly identifying and describing it. Groups are far less likely to go astray when members outline the question they are to answer. Second, Day's formula highlights duties or loyalties. In the case of the snowstorm dispute, prioritizing loyalties is key to supporting or opposing the board chair's determination to pay workers for lost time. Third, the formula incorporates moral theories directly into the decision-making process.

The strengths of the SAD model must be balanced against some troubling weaknesses. Day implies that a clear choice will emerge after defining and analyzing the problem. Nevertheless, our example demonstrates that this is not always the case. Focusing on a narrowly defined question may exclude creative options and make it hard to apply principles from one decision to other settings. Finally, the formula, because it was developed for use in discussing cases in classroom settings, leaves out the important implementation stage.

Cooper's Active Process Model

Ethics professor Terry Cooper developed his decision-making system for public administrators, but leaders in other fields will also find it useful.[8] Cooper believes that government officials develop their ethical character through solving a series of ethical dilemmas. As leaders encounter a series of ethical challenges, both large and small, they form an "ethical identity." They can strengthen their ethical identities by understanding how best to make ethical choices and then by practicing their skills.

According to Cooper, we typically respond to ethical problems at four levels: expressive, moral rules, ethical analysis, and postethical. The lowest level—*expressive*—is our emotional response to ethical situations. Our first reaction to an ethical dilemma may be to vent our frustrations: "How could he do that?" "Why do I always get stuck with these types of decisions?" At the next level—*moral rules*—we begin to consider alternatives and consequences. Imagine that you're a low-level manager at a construction company who suspects that your supervisor is using substandard building materials on a major building project in order to reduce costs. Should you ignore the violations? confront your supervisor? go directly to your boss's boss? report your suspicions directly to city building inspectors? Moral rules play a key role in solving these types of dilemmas. You may decide that honesty is the best policy (so you decide to confront the problem) and that you should always follow the organizational chain of command (you first take your concerns directly to your supervisor). Most ethical problems are resolved at this level. Further analysis is required if (a) the moral rules don't seem to apply, (b) if they conflict with one another, or (c) the actions just don't feel right.

At the level of *ethical analysis,* we link our values with specific actions and determine our priorities. Let's say that you value integrity above all else, followed by fairness and loyalty. As the construction manager in our example, you determine that you must air your concerns no matter what the cost. To be fair, however, you will first give your supervisor an opportunity to dispel your fears. To display loyalty, you will try to resolve the problem internally before going to the press or outside regulators. You come up with a plan of action that begins with confronting your boss and, if he doesn't provide a satisfactory explanation, working your way up the company chain of command. You will go to inspectors and the press only as a last resort.

The *postethical* level of decision making occurs in those cases when we are faced with particularly thorny problems. We ask ourselves "Why should I act morally?" "What's so important about integrity or truth or loyalty?" We may then turn to religion or philosophy for answers to these questions. This level comes to a close when we identify a motive for striving to be ethical.

Cooper emphasizes that decision makers routinely move between the levels. They may react emotionally, search for moral reasons, get frustrated, and then move on to in-depth analysis. They may reach a decision and stop to ponder why morality matters. It's important to recognize that group members may be functioning at different levels at the same time. One may be ready to apply moral rules while others are still venting, for instance.

As we saw earlier, emotions do play a role in ethical decision making, but leaders must have a reasoned justification for their actions. To that end, Cooper offers the following steps to help leaders move beyond the expressive level to careful analysis.

Examining the ethical issue. Too often public administrators (and likely the rest of us) define moral problems as practical ones instead. In Chapter 1, for instance, we described the ethical quandary faced by the manager who knows about an upcoming merger but has been ordered to keep silent. If she focuses on how to please her boss or her followers, she'll overlook the fact that this is an ethical dilemma involving deception.

Identifying alternative courses of action. Many choice makers fall into the either/or trap, believing that right course of action consists of either one action or another. Leaders sometimes reinforce this mode of thinking by insisting on obedience ("my way or the highway"). Keep from falling into this trap by first brainstorming lists of alternatives and consequences.

Projecting the probable consequences. After identifying a variety of alternatives, project the anticipated positive and negative consequences of each one. This requires visualizing what might happen—complete with characters, script, and vivid imagery. In our construction case, this would mean mentally rehearsing your encounters with each party. What will you say? How will they react? How will you feel if they ignore your concerns? threaten you? What will happen to the firm if you succeed or fail in your attempts to focus attention on this problem?

Finding a fit. No alternative will be perfect. The key, instead, is to find a balance between four elements. First, determine which moral rules support each course of action. Second, consider how the decision can be defended. How would the company feel, for example, if it had to defend its choice to ignore evidence of faulty materials on the local news? Third, consider which ethical principles and their priorities come into play. How can the firm give higher priority to earning profits than public safety? Fourth, consider how the decision fits with your self-image. How would you feel about yourself if you chose to keep silent about your supervisor's illegal activity? How will you feel about yourself if you turn her in to the authorities? The more satisfied you are with your choices, the more inclined you'll be to act in a similar way in the future. If you consistently combine sound reasoning with positive feelings about your decisions, you'll develop a strong sense of ethical autonomy.

BALANCE SHEET

Advantages (+s)

- Acknowledges the expressive or emotional element in ethical decision making
- Recognizes that some decisions will be more serious than others and require a deeper level of analysis
- Links action and character. Character emerges out of patterns of ethical behavior over time
- Highlights the role of moral imagination
- Admits that ethical decision making is an imperfect process; strives for balance

Disadvantages (−s)

- Puts action before reflection
- Ignores implementation

The active process approach adds some elements that are missing from the first three models. The first new component is emotion. Our gut-level reactions shouldn't drive our choices, but it's okay to vent and to check our emotions to see if we're comfortable with our decisions. The second new component is level of ethical difficulty. Some decisions are going to be more taxing than others and will take more concentrated analysis to resolve. The third additional component is a link between action and character. Cooper argues that our character emerges out of patterns of ethical behavior that unfold over extended periods of time. The fourth new component is visualization. The fifth and final additional component is balance. We shouldn't expect to find a perfect solution but strive instead to reach one that fits well with our moral rules, can be adequately defended, reflects our ethical principles and priorities, and is congruent with our self-image.

Cooper's model broadens our understanding of moral reasoning by adding the elements listed above. However, its creator seems to put action before reflection. According to Cooper, we only wrestle with the question of *why* we ought to be moral when faced with particularly difficult dilemmas. This ought to be the first, not the last, level of ethical analysis. Making reasoned ethical choices is hard, time-consuming work. We need to determine early on that moral reasoning is worth the effort. Only then will we be willing to invest the time and energy we need to improve our ethical fitness. Cooper also omits the implementation step. Once we've found a decision that fits, we need to put it into effect.

The Case Study Method

The case study method is widely used when making medical diagnoses. At many hospitals, groups made up of doctors, nurses, and other staff meet regularly to talk about particularly troublesome cases. They may be unable to determine the exact nature of the illness or how to best treat a patient. Many of these deliberations involve ethical issues like whether or not to keep a terminally ill person on life support or how to respond to patients who demand unnecessary tests and procedures. The group solicits a variety of viewpoints and gathers as much information as possible. Members engage in analogical reasoning, comparing the specifics of a particular case with other similar cases by describing the patient, her illness, and relationships with her family. Instead of focusing on how universal principles and standards can be applied in this situation, hospital personnel are more concerned about the details of the case itself. Participants balance competing perspectives and values, reach tentative conclusions, and look for similarities between the current case and earlier ones.

Medical ethicist and communication scholar David H. Smith argues that the case-based approach is a powerful technique because it is based on narrative or story.[9] When decision makers describe cases, they are telling stories. These narratives say as much about the storyteller as they do about the reality of the case. "Facts" are not objective truth but reflections of what the narrator thinks is true and important. Stories knit these perceptions into a coherent whole. When discussing the fate of patients, it is not enough to know medical data. Hospital personnel need to learn about the patient's history, the costs and benefits of various treatment options, and other factors like the wishes of relatives and legal issues. Smith outlines the following steps for case-based decision making:

1. *Foster storytelling.* Alert participants to the fact that they will be sharing their story about the problem. Framing the discussion as a storytelling session invokes a different set of evaluation criteria than is generally used in decision making. We judge evidence based on such factors as the quality of sources and logical consistency (see the discussion of argumentation in Chapter 8). We judge stories by how believable they seem to be, how well the elements of the story fit together and mesh with what we know of the world, and the values reflected in the narrative.[10]

2. *Encourage elaboration of essential events and characters.* Details are essential to the case study method. Additional details make it easier to draw comparisons with other examples.

3. *Encourage the sharing of stories by everyone with an interest in the problem.* Bringing more perspectives to bear on the problem reveals more details. In the end, a better shared story emerges. Consider the case of an elderly man refusing a heart operation that could extend his life. Finding out why he is rejecting the surgery is an important first step to solving this ethical dilemma. As nurses, social workers, and doctors share information, they may discover that the patient is suffering from depression or feels cut off from his family. Addressing these problems may encourage the patient to agree to the operation and thus resolve the moral issue.

4. *Offer alternative meanings.* Change the interpretation of the story by the following:
   a. Provide additional expert information and point out where the facts of the story do not fit with other facts. The first diagnosis may not be correct. Press on when needed. In the case of our patient, claims that he is alienated from his family would be rejected if his children and grandchildren visit him daily.
   b. Focus attention on the characters in the story (the patient) rather than on some overarching ethical issue like utilitarianism or the categorical imperative.
   c. Examine analogies critically to make sure they really hold. Don't assume that the reasons one patient turns down treatment are the same as those of other patients, for example.
   d. Offer alternative futures that might come to pass depending on decisions made by the group. In our case, what will be the likely outcome if treatment is delayed or never given? How much will the patient improve if he has the heart operation? Will attempts to persuade him backfire, locking him into his current position? What might happen if the hospital enlists his family to force him into compliance?

BALANCE SHEET

Advantages (+s)

- Is unique
- Harnesses the power of narrative and analogical reasoning
- Avoids ethical polarization; allows for ethical middle ground

Disadvantages (−s)

- Downplays the importance of objective reality
- Fails to account for the fact that details are not always available to decision makers
- Fails to account for the fact that consensus on the right course of action is not always possible

---

The case study method is significantly different from the rest of the formats presented in this chapter. These other models outline a linear, step-by-step process for resolving ethical dilemmas that for the most part call for the application of universal ethical principles or standards. The case study approach is not linear but circular, calling for participants to share a variety of perspectives. Decision makers keep ethical principles in mind but don't try to invoke them to provide the resolution to a problem. They use them as general guides instead and focus on the case itself. Although unique, the case method still requires decision makers to meet, systematically share information and analyze the problem, evaluate options, and reach a conclusion.

Many of us like to think that we are rational thinkers who decide based on the facts. In reality, I suspect we often make choices based on stories. A good narrative, for instance, is more persuasive than statistical evidence, and we frequently employ the type of analogical reasoning reflected in the case study approach.[11] For example, when faced with an ethical decision about whether or not to tell your current employer about a job offer from another firm, you probably would consider the following: (a) the details of the situation (your relationship to your immediate supervisor, how hard it will be to replace you, your loyalty to the organization); (b) similar situations or cases in your past (what happened when you revealed this information before leaving your last job?); and (c) what your friends did when facing similar circumstances. The case study method takes advantage of our natural tendency to reason through story and analogy.

As I noted in the discussion of character ethics in Chapter 3, universal principles can be difficult to apply to specific situations. There always seem to be exceptions to the rule ("In general, don't lie, but it may be okay to lie if it protects someone else from danger."). A strength of the case study approach is that it acknowledges that specific circumstances often shape how a general principle can be used to resolve a particular dilemma. This approach also avoids polarization caused by invoking ethical absolutes. Take the abortion debate, for example. Proponents and opponents of abortion are locked into their positions due to their interpretation of such values as freedom and sanctity of life. The case study method suggests that some middle ground can be found by examining specific cases. After all, even some pro-life advocates allow abortion when the mother's life is in danger. Some in the pro-choice camp are uncomfortable with late-term abortions.

The case study approach has its downside. To begin, it minimizes objective reality. Although we always see ethical dilemmas through our perceptual filters, there do appear to be verifiable facts that ought to come into play when making decisions. Crime scene evidence should be essential to determining a defendant's guilt or innocence, for instance. Some criticized the verdict in the O. J. Simpson trial because they felt that the jury overlooked factual DNA evidence and accepted the story of police misconduct instead. The same evidence was offered in a later civil trial. Jurors in that case concluded that the football star was indeed guilty of murdering his ex-wife and her friend and forced him to pay damages to the families.

A practical problem with the case study method is its dependence on detail. In real life, leaders may not have the luxury of being able to solicit stories and probe for additional information. They must make decisions quickly, particularly in crisis situations. Students face a similar problem when discussing cases in class. Short cases, like the ones in this text, may leave out details you feel are important. Nevertheless, you have to resolve them anyway.

Finally, consensus, although likely in this format, is not guaranteed. One overall story may emerge, but it may not. This is often the case in medical diagnoses. Two doctors may reach different conclusions about what is wrong with a patient. Differences in values, perspectives, and definitions of "facts" may keep ethical decision makers apart.

Implications and Applications

- The particular format you choose to follow is not as important as taking a systematic approach to ethical problem solving.
- Possible ethical decision-making formats include Kidder's ethical checkpoints, Nash's 12 questions, the SAD formula, Cooper's active process model, and the case study method.
- Get your facts straight. Make every effort to gather in-depth, current, and accurate information.
- Creativity is as vital to ethical decisions as it is to generating new products and programs. Sometimes you can come up with a "third way" that resolves ethical conflicts.

- Moral dilemmas often involve clashes between two core (good) values. Common right-versus-right dilemmas are truth versus loyalty, short-term versus long-term, individual versus community, and justice versus mercy.
- Action is the ultimate test of leadership ethics. You can make reasoned moral choices, but they'll do little practical good unless you put them into practice.
- Think of ethical deliberation as an ongoing process. You may go through a sequence of steps and use them again. Return to your decision later to evaluate and learn from it. As soon as one ethical crisis passes, there's likely to be another on the horizon.
- Emotions play a subservient but significant role in ethical decision making. Use your feelings as one yardstick to determine if you're satisfied with a particular course of action.
- Don't expect perfection. As a leader, make the best choice you can after thorough deliberation but recognize that sometimes you may have to choose between two flawed alternatives.

For Further Exploration, Challenge, and Self-Assessment

1. How do you typically go about making ethical choices? How effective is this strategy?

2. Which of the five formats do you find most useful? Why?

3. What role should emotion play in ethical decision making? Write up your conclusions.

4. Brainstorm a list of possible ethical dilemmas faced by a college student. How many of these problems involve a clash between two important values (right versus right)? Identify which values are in conflict in each situation.

5. Apply each of the formats to one of the chapter end scenarios. Do you reach different conclusions depending on the system you follow? To enhance the experience, first reach your own conclusions and then discuss the situations in a group. See if you can reach a consensus. Make note of the important factors dividing or uniting group members.

6. Use a format from the chapter to analyze an ethical decision facing society (gay marriage or ordination, illegal music file sharing, privacy rights). Write up your analysis and conclusions.

CASE STUDY 7.2

Chapter End Case: Ethical Scenarios for Analysis

SCENARIO A   CLOTHING THE CAMP COUNSELORS

You are a first-year counselor at a camp for needy children, which is subsidized through contributions from individuals and local businesses. Yours is the only camp experience that these disadvantaged kids will ever have. One afternoon, a few hours before the next batch of children is due to arrive, a truck stops by with a donated shipment of new shoes, shirts, and shorts for your campers. Immediately, the other counselors (all of whom have more experience than you do) begin selecting out items for personal use. They encourage you to do the same. When questioned, they argue that there is plenty to go around for both kids and counselors and that the clothes are a "fringe benefit" for underpaid camp staff.

Would you take any shoes or clothing to wear?

REFERENCE

Kristina Hanson, George Fox University

SCENARIO B   CAMPUS BOOKSTORE PROTEST

You are the bookstore manager on your college or university campus. Although not required to make a profit, your store is to break even, generating enough sales to match expenses. Next to textbooks, clothing items with the school name and logo bring in the most revenue. These items have a high profit margin and are particularly popular among alumni who come to campus for games, Parents Day, graduation, and other public events. Recently, students at the University of Michigan and other campuses around the country have protested the sale of licensed school clothing (sweatshirts, T-shirts, hats, shorts) made by suppliers who manufacture their garments in deplorable conditions in Third World countries. Your clothing line is manufactured by one of the firms accused of unfair labor practices.

It's 2 weeks before homecoming (which attracts one of the largest crowds of alumni). A representative from the student government comes to your office to announce that, unless you stop selling your current line of licensed apparel, protestors will picket the bookstore during the upcoming festivities. In addition, students will be urged to buy their books over the Internet and from other sources. There is no way you can replace your current clothing stock in time for homecoming. Besides, you will lose thousands of dollars if you do. Your supervisor is out of town but is noted for his "get tough" attitude toward student protests. You, however, are bothered by the idea of selling products produced in sweatshops and are sympathetic to the students' concerns.

What would you do?

SCENARIO C   THE HIRING DECISION

You are the male owner of a small company that installs printer cable and services printers at automotive dealerships. With the exception of receptionists and billing clerks, very few women work at the stores that buy your parts and services. In this male-dominated atmosphere, females are treated as second-class citizens, and sexist humor is common. Your former service person, Mike, was quite at home in this environment. He kept his clients entertained with a constant stream of dirty jokes and was accepted as "one of the guys."

Mike has given notice that he is going to quit, and you're searching for a replacement. The job market is tight for cable installers, and you can't match the salaries paid by larger firms in the area. After a monthlong search, you finally locate an enthusiastic applicant. Sue, a recent college graduate, has limited experience but appears to be a "go-getter" who mixes well with all types of people. Most importantly, she holds a Class C low voltage license that qualifies her to do all types of installation and maintenance work.

You worry about hiring a young woman for this particular job. Not only do you wonder if she will be as successful as Mike, but you fear that she may be the target of sexist humor. Sue doesn't seem to be easily offended, but you wonder if you could be sued later if she claims sexual discrimination. After all, you would be sending her into a potentially hostile working environment.

Would you hire Sue for this position?

SCENARIO D   THE TERMINAL PATIENT

Determining what to tell patients with life-threatening illnesses is one of the most difficult challenges facing physicians. American doctors have been told to be more honest with patients in recent years, but they have plenty of reasons for concealing or softening the truth. Some of their motivations may be self-serving, as when they don't want to admit that a disease has defeated them or that they misdiagnosed a medical condition. However, doctors are also motivated by altruism. They know that patients are more likely to survive operations and live longer if they are hopeful and optimistic. This holds true even when they are given false hope. European doctors have gone so far as to criticize their U.S. counterparts for being *too truthful* in many such situations, believing that brutal honesty does the patient little good.

Imagine that you are the chief surgeon on an emergency room team. An ambulance has rushed a patient to your hospital following a serious accident. Initial X-rays indicate that the victim is suffering from multiple fractures; damage to his heart, liver, and kidneys; and internal bleeding. Chances are the patient will not live through the night, but you prepare to operate anyway. As you leave the examination room to prep for surgery, the injured man beckons you back to his bedside to ask, "Will I make it?"

What would you say to the accident victim? What would you say to his family waiting in the lobby?

REFERENCE

Ford, C. V. (1996). *Lies! Lies! Lies! The psychology of deceit.* Washington, DC: American Psychiatric Press, ch. 1.

SCENARIO E   THE FAULTY SALES CONTRACT

You are the sales manager for a high-tech firm that makes engineering software for the design of circuit boards, monitors, and other electronics components. One of your salespeople has just landed a contract with a major computer manufacturer. This contract will be the largest in your firm's 10-year history. Due to the importance of the account, you go with the lucky salesman to the final meeting where the sales documents will be signed.

As you are waiting for all the parties to arrive, the company's buying manager begins to talk excitedly about all the features of your product. Only trouble is, your software package doesn't contain a number of the features she is describing. The buying manager has either confused your product with a competitor's or your salesperson (who is out of the room for the moment) has lied in order to make the sale.

Would you go ahead and sign the contract?

REFERENCE

Mark Reed, High Ground Partners, Lake Oswego, Oregon

Notes

1. Kidder, R. M. (1995). *How good people make tough choices: Resolving the dilemmas of ethical living.* New York: Fireside.

2. Fisher, R., & Ury, W. (1991). *Getting to yes* (2nd ed.). New York: Penguin Books.

3. Kidder (1995), *How good people make tough choices*, p. 186.

4. Nash, L. L. (1989). Ethics without the sermon. In K. R. Andrews (Ed.), *Ethics in practice: Managing the moral corporation* (pp. 243–257). Boston, MA: Harvard Business School Press.

5. Day, L. A. (2003). *Ethics in media communications: Cases & controversies* (4th ed.). Belmont, CA: Wadsworth/Thomson Learning, ch. 3.

6. Austin, D. (2004, January 14). At county, snow days are paid. *The Oregonian.* Retrieved January 20, 2004, from oregonian.com; Austin, D. (2004, January 23). Snow days put Linn on icy footing. *The Oregonian,* pp. B1, B6.

7. Potter, R. B. (1972). The logic of moral argument. In P. Deats (Ed.), *Toward a discipline of social ethics* (pp. 93–114). Boston: Boston University Press.

8. Cooper, T. C. (1998). *The responsible administrator* (4th ed.). San Francisco: Jossey-Bass.

9. Smith, D. H. (1993). Stories, values, and patient care decisions. In C. Conrad (Ed.), *The ethical nexus* (pp. 123–148). Norwood, NJ: Ablex. For a history of the case study method, see Jonsen, A. R., & Toulmin, S. (1988). *The abuse of casuistry: A history of moral reasoning.* Berkeley: University of California Press.

10. Fisher, W. (1987). *Human communication as narration: Toward a philosophy of reason, value, and action.* Columbia: University of South Carolina Press.

11. Martin, J., & Powers, M. E. (1983). Truth or corporate propaganda: The value of a good story. In L. R. Pondy, P. J. Frost, G. Morgan, & T. C. Dandridge (Eds.), *Organizational symbolism* (pp. 93–107). Greenwich, CT: JAI.

Part IV

Shaping Ethical Contexts

8

Building an Effective, Ethical Small Group

A monologue is not a decision.

Former British prime minister Clement Attlee

Language is not just one of man's possessions in the world, but on it depends the fact that man has a world at all.

Philosopher Hans-Georg Gadamer

What's Ahead

This chapter examines ethical leadership in the small-group context. Groups are often charged with making ethical decisions because they have the potential to make better choices than individuals. To make the most of the small-group advantage, however, leaders must resist groupthink, as well as false agreement, and engage in productive (enlightening) communication patterns rooted in the pursuit of dialogue.

Parker Palmer, in his metaphor of the leader's light or shadow, emphasizes that leaders shape the settings or contexts around them. According to Palmer, leaders are individuals who have "an unusual degree of power to create the conditions under which other people must live and move and have their being, conditions that can either be as illuminating as heaven or as shadowy as hell."[1] In this final section of the text, I'll describe some of the ways we can create conditions that illuminate the lives of followers in small-group, organizational, and culturally diverse settings. Shedding light means both resisting and exerting

215

influence. We must fend off pressures to engage in unethical behavior while actively seeking to create healthier moral environments.

The Leader and the Small Group

Leaders spend a great deal of their time in small groups, either chairing or participating in meetings. You can expect to devote more of your workday to meetings with every step up the organizational hierarchy. Some top-level executives spend as much as 21 weeks a year working in committees, task forces, and other small-group settings.[2] Meeting expert John Tropman points out that high-quality management is the product of high-quality meetings that render high-quality decisions. Meetings aren't distractions from our work, he argues, they *are* the work. Successful meetings are "absolutely central to the achievement of organizational goals."[3]

Groups meet for many different purposes—to coordinate activities, to pass along important information, to clarify misunderstandings, and to build relationships. In this chapter, however, I'll focus on the role of groups in making ethical decisions. Examples of ethical group dilemmas include the following:

- A congressional subcommittee debating the morality of the estate tax
- Court justices determining if grandparents have visitation rights
- The board of the local United Way responding to a funding request from an abortion clinic or a Boy Scout troop that doesn't allow gay men to be leaders
- Foreign aid officials deciding if their agency should send food to a drought-stricken nation ruled by a dictator
- Student officers disciplining a campus organization that has violated university and student government policies
- Corporate executives devising a plan to dispose of toxic waste

Groups have significant advantages over lone decision makers when it comes to solving ethical problems like those described above as well as the case presented in Case Study 8.1, The Ten Commandments Go to Court. In a group, members can pool their information, divide up assignments, draw from a variety of perspectives, and challenge questionable assumptions. They are more likely to render carefully reasoned, defensible decisions as a result.[4] Of course, groups don't always make good moral choices, as in the case of executives who decide to hide product defects from the public or city officials who bypass regulations and award construction contracts to friends. Our task as leaders is to create the conditions that ensure that teams make the most of the small-group advantage. In particular, we must confront the problems of groupthink and false consensus and engage in productive or "enlightening" communication patterns.

CASE STUDY 8.1

The Ten Commandments Go to Court

Former Alabama chief justice Roy Moore is serious about the Ten Commandments. When he was a circuit judge, he hung a handmade rosewood plaque with the ten edicts in his courtroom. He successfully fended off attempts to remove the plaque and then was elected chief justice of the Alabama Supreme Court, running on the slogan, "Roy Moore: Still the Ten Commandments Judge." After his election, he installed a 5,280-pound granite monument in the lobby of the state judicial building in Montgomery, complete with the commandments and fourteen quotations tying God to government.

Lawyers for the American Civil Liberties Union, the Southern Poverty Law Center, and Americans for Separation of Church and State took issue with the religious display and filed suit. Moore's attorneys argued that U.S. law is founded on the Ten Commandments, which are also displayed in other U.S. government buildings. In his ruling, however, Federal District Judge Myron Thompson agreed with the plaintiffs that the Alabama monument was an unconstitutional use of public facilities for religious purposes. Thompson said that the granite statue was an obtrusive year-round religious display.

Thompson's ruling was upheld by a federal appeals court, but Judge Moore refused to back down, declaring, "I will never, never deny the God upon whom our laws and country depend" (Winters, 2003, p. 53). He also claimed that the federal government has no right to interfere with the state's right to acknowledge its religious heritage. The U.S. Supreme Court refused to stay Thompson's court order, and Alabama faced a $5,000-a-day fine if the statue wasn't removed. Moore's fellow state Supreme Court justices then had the monument (nicknamed "Roy's Rock") taken to a back room. They suspended Moore for disobeying the court order and filed an ethics complaint against him with the Alabama Court of the Judiciary. Moore was then removed from office.

Moore fared better in the court of public opinion. In one poll, 77% of Alabama citizens approved of Roy's Rock, and hundreds rallied in his support. Protestors carrying Bibles and crosses sang hymns and occupied the court building. Others drove around Montgomery in campers decorated with large cardboard versions of the commandments. Moore loyalists compared him to Martin Luther King, Daniel, and Moses and complained of "federal tyranny." One pastor, who was arrested for failure to leave the judicial building, called attempts to cover up the monument or move it "an assault on God."

Moore's critics are just as passionate as his supporters. An anti-Ten Commandments activist complained, "He [Moore] is taking our public facility and making it a place of worship. This is a place where justice is supposed to happen. How do we know a judge is being fair when he is promoting his view?" (Poe & Rankin, 2003, p. 1B). A fellow state Supreme Court justice expressed his concern that the same type of theocracy that has plagued the Middle East would take root in Alabama. An historian compared Moore's crusade to former governor Wallace's attempt to stop integration at the University of Alabama, declaring, "This is southern demagoguery in a very pure and undiluted form" (Poe & Rankin, 2003, p. 1B).

Imagine that you are a member of the U.S. Supreme Court meeting to decide whether or not to overturn the decision to remove the Ten Commandments statue from the Alabama state judicial building. You should come out of your discussions with (a) a final ruling and (b) a list of reasons for your decision.

REFERENCES

Johnson, B. (2003, August 22). Alabama's defiant chief justice, building manager confer in showdown over religious monument. *Associated Press.* Retrieved August 22, 2003, from LexisNexis (www.lexisnexis.com/).

Johnson, B. (2003, August 23). Panel suspends Alabama's chief justice. *The Oregonian,* p. A6.

Poe, J., & Rankin, B. (2003, August 21). Commandments feud spurs arrests. *The Atlanta Journal-Constitution,* p. 1B.

Ringel, J. (2003, June 9). *Miami Daily Business Review,* p. 14.

Roig-Franzia, M. (2003, August 21). Ala. Justices symbolically conceal commandments; Partitions put up briefly to comply with order. *The Washington Post,* p. A2.

Roig-Franzia, M. (2003, August 21). Jurist defies deadline on monument. *The Washington Post,* p. A1.

Winters, R. (2003, September 1). Standoff at Roy's Rock. *Time,* p. 53.

Resisting Groupthink

Social psychologist Irving Janis believed that cohesion is the greatest barrier to groups charged with making effective, ethical decisions. He developed the label "groupthink" to describe groups that put unanimous agreement ahead of reasoned problem solving. Groups suffering from this symptom are both ineffective and unethical.[5] They fail to (a) consider all the alternatives, (b) gather additional information, (c) reexamine a course of action when it's not working, (d) carefully weigh risks, (e) work out contingency plans, or (f) discuss important moral issues. Janis first noted faulty thinking in small groups of ordinary citizens (such as an antismoking support group that decided that quitting was impossible). He captured the attention of fellow scholars and the public, however, through his analysis of major U.S. policy disasters like the failure to anticipate the attack on Pearl Harbor, the invasion of North Korea, the Bay of Pigs fiasco, and the escalation of the Vietnam War. In each of these incidents, some of the brightest (and presumably most ethically minded) political and military leaders in our nation's history made terrible choices. (See the NASA Chapter End Case for a contemporary example of the tragic consequences of groupthink.)

Janis identified the following as symptoms of groupthink. The greater the number of these characteristics displayed by a group, the greater the likelihood that members have made cohesiveness their top priority.

Signs of Overconfidence

1. *Illusion of invulnerability.* Members are overly optimistic and prone to take extraordinary risks.

2. *Belief in the inherent morality of the group.* Participants ignore the ethical consequences of their actions and decisions.

Signs of Closed-mindedness

3. *Collective rationalization.* Group members invent rationalizations to protect themselves from any feedback that would challenge their operating assumptions.

4. *Stereotypes of outside groups.* Underestimating the capabilities of other groups (armies, citizens, teams); thinking that people in these groups are weak or stupid.

Signs of Group Pressure

5. *Pressure on dissenters.* Coercing dissenters to go along with the prevailing opinion in the group.

6. *Self-censorship.* Individuals keep their doubts about group decisions to themselves.

7. *Illusion of unanimity.* Because members keep quiet, the group mistakenly assumes that everyone agrees on a course of action.

8. *Self-appointed mindguards.* Certain members take it on themselves to protect the leader and others from dissenting opinions that might disrupt the group's consensus.

The danger of falling captive to groupthink increases when teams made up of members from similar backgrounds are isolated from contact with other groups. The risks increase still further when group members are under stress (due to recent failure, for instance) and follow a leader who pushes one particular solution.

Resisting groupthink is more important than ever before because more firms are using self-directed work teams (SDWTs). An SDWT is made up of 6 to 10 employees from a variety of departments who manage themselves and their tasks. Self-directed work teams operate much like small businesses within the larger organization, overseeing the development of a service or product from start to finish. SDWTs have been credited with improving everything from attendance and morale to productivity and product quality. Unfortunately, self-directed teams are particularly vulnerable to groupthink. Members, working under strict time limits, are often isolated and undertrained. They may fail at first, and the need to function as a cohesive unit may blind them to ethical dilemmas.[6]

Irving Janis made several suggestions for reducing groupthink. If you're appointed as the group's leader, avoid expressing a preference for a particular solution. Divide regularly into subgroups and then bring the entire group back together to negotiate differences. Bring in outsiders—experts or colleagues—to challenge the group's ideas. Avoid isolation, keeping in contact with other groups. Role-play the reactions of other groups and organizations to reduce the effects of stereotyping and rationalization. Once the decision has been made, give group members one last chance to express any remaining doubts about the decision. Janis points to the ancient Persians as an example of how to revisit decisions. The Persians made every major decision twice—once while sober and again while under the influence of wine!

Interest in the causes and prevention of groupthink remains high.[7] Contemporary researchers have discovered that a group is in greatest danger when the leader actively promotes his or her agenda and when it doesn't have any procedures in place (like those described in the last chapter) for solving problems. With this in mind, don't offer your opinions as a leader but solicit ideas from group members instead. Make sure that the group adopts a decision-making format before discussing an ethical problem.

Management professor Charles Manz and his colleagues believe that self-managing work teams should replace groupthink with "teamthink." In teamthink, groups encourage divergent views, combining the open expression of concerns and doubts with a healthy respect for their limitations. The teamthink process is an extension of *thought self-leadership* (TSL).[8] In thought self-leadership, individuals improve their performance (lead themselves) by adopting constructive thought patterns. They visualize a successful performance (mental imagery), eliminate critical and destructive self-talk, such as "I can't do it," and challenge unrealistic assumptions. For example, the mental statement, "I must succeed at everything or I'm a failure," is irrational because it sets an impossibly high standard. This destructive thought can be restated as, "I can't succeed at everything, but I'm going to try to give my best effort no matter what the task."

Teamthink, like thought self-leadership, is a combination of mental imagery, self-dialogue, and realistic thinking. Members of successful groups use mental imagery to visualize how they will complete a project and jointly establish a common vision ("to provide better housing to the homeless";

"to develop the best new software package for the company"). When talking with each other (self-dialogue), leaders and followers are particularly careful not to put pressure on deviant members, and at the same time, they encourage divergent views.

Teamthink members challenge three forms of faulty reasoning that are common to small groups. The first is "all-or-nothing" thinking. If a risk doesn't seem threatening, too many groups dismiss it and proceed on without a backup plan. Teamthink groups, in contrast, realistically assess the dangers and anticipate possible setbacks. The second common form of faulty group thinking, described earlier, is the assumption that the team is inherently moral. Groups under the grip of this misconception think that anything they do (including lying and sabotaging the work of other groups) is justified. Ethically insensitive, they don't stop to consider the moral implications of their decisions. Teamthink groups avoid this trap, questioning their motivations and raising ethical issues. The third faulty group assumption is the conviction that the task is too difficult, that the obstacles are too great to overcome. Effective, ethical groups instead view obstacles as "opportunities" and focus their efforts on reaching and implementing the decision.

Avoiding False Agreement

Not everyone agrees that conformity is the leading cause of group moral failure. In fact, George Washington University management professor Jerry Harvey believes that blaming group pressure is just an excuse for our individual shortcomings.[9] He calls this the *Gunsmoke* myth. In this myth, the lone Western sheriff (Matt Dillon in the radio and television series) stands down a mob of armed townsfolk out to lynch his prisoner. If group tyranny is really at work, Harvey argues, Dillon stands no chance. After all, he is outnumbered 100 to 1 and could be felled with a single bullet from one rioter. The mob disbands due to the fact that its members really didn't want to lynch the prisoner in the first place. Harvey contends that falling prey to the *Gunsmoke* myth is immoral because as long as we can blame our peers, we don't have to accept personal responsibility. In reality, we always have a choice as to how to respond.

Professor Harvey introduces the Abilene Paradox as an alternative to the *Gunsmoke* myth. He describes a time when his family decided to drive (without air-conditioning) 100 miles across the desert from their home in Coleman, Texas, to Abilene to eat dinner. After returning home, family members discovered that no one had really wanted to make the trip. Each agreed to go to Abilene based on the assumption that everyone else in the group was enthusiastic about eating out. Harvey believes that organizations and small groups, like his family, also take needless "trips":

> I now call the tendency for groups to embark on excursions that no group member wants "the Abilene Paradox." Stated simply, when organizations blunder into the Abilene Paradox, they take actions in contradiction to what they really want to do and therefore defeat the very purposes they are trying to achieve.[10]

Examples of the Abilene Paradox include leaders who continue to pour time and money into projects that no one believes will succeed and teams who carry out illegal activities that everyone in the group is uneasy about. Five psychological factors account for the paradox:

1. *Action anxiety.* Group members know what should be done but are too anxious to speak up.

2. *Negative fantasies.* Action anxiety is driven in part by the negative fantasies members have about what will happen if they voice their opinions. These fantasies ("I'll be fired or branded as disloyal") serve as an excuse for not attacking the problem.

3. *Real risk.* There are risks to expressing dissent—getting fired, losing income, damaging relationships. However, most of the time the danger is not as great as we think.

4. *Fear of separation.* Alienation and loneliness constitute the most powerful force behind the paradox. Group members fear being cut off or separated from others. To escape this fate, they cheat, lie, break the law, and so forth.

5. *Psychological reversal of risk and certainty.* Being trapped in the Abilene Paradox means confusing fantasy with real risk. This confusion produces a self-fulfilling prophecy. Caught up in the fantasy that something bad may happen, decision makers act in a way that fulfills the fantasy. For instance, group members may support a project with no chances of success because they are afraid they will be fired or demoted if they don't. Ironically, they are likely to be fired or demoted anyway when the flawed project fails.

Breaking out of the paradox begins with diagnosing its symptoms in your group or organization. If the group is headed in the wrong direction, call a meeting where you "own up" to your true feelings and invite feedback. (Of course, you must confront your fear of being separated from the rest of the group to take this step.) The team may immediately come up with a better approach or engage in extended conflict that generates a more creative solution. You might suffer for your honesty, but you could be rewarded for saying what everyone else was thinking. In any case, you'll feel better about yourself for speaking up.

Box 8.1

Leadership Ethics at the Movies: *Twelve Angry Men*

Key Cast Members: Jack Lemmon, George C. Scott, Ossie Davis, Tony Danza

Synopsis: This made-for-television remake of the 1957 film starring Henry Fonda features a more ethnically diverse cast than the original film. Eleven members of a jury deciding the fate of a young Latino murder defendant immediately vote for a conviction. Lemmon convinces the rest of the group to reconsider the evidence, however. Several hours later they vote to acquit. George C. Scott gives the most compelling performance in the film (one of his last) as the juror who wants to punish the male defendant because he can't punish his own son. The film is an excellent look at the group process and the ethical issues confronting jurors in capital cases. It is particularly relevant in light of the fact that a number of convicted murderers have been placed on death row, only to be freed later.

Rating: Not rated but probably worthy of a PG-13 ranking due to occasional profanity and emotional intensity

Themes: groupthink, counteractive influence, moral courage, argumentation, critical thinking, ethical responsibility, the value of human life, stereotypes

---

Enlightening Communication

Communication is the key to both the relationships between group members and the quality of their ethical choices. Shadowy groups are marked by ineffective, destructive communication patterns that generate negative emotions while derailing the moral reasoning process. Healthier groups engage in productive or "enlightened" communication strategies that enable members to establish positive bonds and make wise ethical choices. Enlightening communication skills and tactics arise out of the pursuit of dialogue and include comprehensive, critical listening; supportive communication; productive conflict management; and argumentation.

SEEKING DIALOGUE

The attitude we have toward other group members will largely determine whether our interactions with them are destructive or productive. There are two primary human attitudes or relationships according to philosopher

Martin Buber: I-It and I-Thou.[11] Communicators in I-It relationships treat others as objects and engage in monologue. At its best, monologue is impersonal interaction focused on gathering and understanding information about the other party. At its worst, monologue manipulates others for selfish gain and is characterized by deception, exploitation, and coercion. Participants in I-Thou (You) relationships, in contrast, treat others as unique human beings and engage in dialogue. Dialogue occurs between equal partners who focus on understanding rather than on being understood. Communication experts Kenneth Cissna and Robert Anderson identify the following characteristics of dialogue:[12]

- *Presence.* Partners in dialogue are less interested in a specific outcome than in working with others to come up with a solution. Their interactions are unscripted and unrehearsed.
- *Emergent unanticipated consequences.* Dialogue produces unpredictable results that are not controlled by any one person in the group.
- *Recognition of "strange otherness."* If dialogue is to flourish, discussants must refuse to believe that they already understand the thoughts, feelings, or intentions of others in the group, even people they know well. They are tentative instead, continually testing their understanding of the perspectives of other group members and revising their conclusions when needed.
- *Collaborative orientation.* Dialogue demands a dual focus on self and others. Participants don't hesitate to take and defend a position. At the same time, they care about the point of view of their conversational partners and about maintaining relationships. They focus on coming up with a shared, joint solution, not on winning or losing.
- *Vulnerability.* Dialogue is risky because discussants open their thoughts to others and may be influenced by the encounter. They must be willing to change their minds.
- *Mutual implication.* Speakers engaged in dialogue always keep listeners in mind when speaking. In so doing, they may discover more about themselves as well.
- *Temporal flow.* Dialogue takes time and emerges over the course of a group discussion. It is a process that can't be cut into segments and analyzed.
- *Genuineness and authenticity.* Participants in dialogue give each other the benefit of the doubt, assuming that the other person is being honest and sharing from personal experience. Although speakers don't share all their thoughts, they don't deliberately hide thoughts and feelings that are relevant to the topic and to the relationship.

By its nature, "pure" dialogue is difficult to achieve. Focusing on the needs and positions of others is hard work. Nonetheless, striving for dialogue lays the groundwork for the enlightening communication strategies that follow. We are much more likely to listen and to support others when we treat them as equals whose experiences and opinions are just as valid as our own. Dialogue encourages healthy argument and conflict as well. Buber argued that the best example of the I-Thou relationship comes not when friends or intimates interact

Building an Effective, Ethical Small Group   225

but when acquaintances profoundly disagree and yet remain in dialogue.[13] Confrontation tempts us to treat others like obstacles that need to be overcome so that we can win. Dialogue empowers us to remain genuinely present to fellow group members while holding fast to our own positions.

COMPREHENSIVE, CRITICAL LISTENING

We spend much more time listening than speaking in small groups. If you belong to a team with 10 members, you can expect to devote approximately 10% of your time to talking and 90% to listening to what others have to say. All listening involves receiving, paying attention to, interpreting, and then remembering messages. However, our motives for listening will vary.[14] *Discriminative listening* processes the verbal and nonverbal components of a message. It serves as the foundation for the other forms of listening because we can't accurately process or interpret messages unless we first understand what is being said and how the message is being delivered. Tom and Ray Magliozzi of National Public Radio's *Car Talk* demonstrate the importance of discriminative listening on their weekly call-in program. They frequently ask callers to repeat the sounds made by their vehicles. A "clunk" sound can signal one type of engine problem; a "chunk" noise might indicate that something else is wrong.

Comprehensive listening is motivated by the need to understand and to retain messages. We engage in this type of listening when we attend lectures, receive job instructions, attend oral briefings, and watch the evening weather report. *Therapeutic or empathetic listening* is aimed at helping the speaker resolve an issue by encouraging him or her to talk about the problem. Those in helping professions like social work and psychiatry routinely engage in this listening process. All of us act as empathetic listeners, however, when friends and family come to us for help. *Critical listening* leads to evaluation. Critical listeners pay careful attention to message content, logic, language, and other elements of persuasive attempts so that they can identify strengths and weaknesses and render a judgment. *Appreciative listening* is prompted by the desire for relaxation and entertainment. We act as appreciative listeners when we enjoy a CD, live concert, or play.

Group members engage in all five types of listening during meetings, but comprehensive and critical listening are essential to ethical problem solving. Coming up with a high-quality decision is nearly impossible unless group members first understand and remember what others have said. Participants also have to critically analyze the arguments of other group members in order to identify errors (see the discussion of conflict and argumentation that follows).

There are several barriers to comprehensive, critical listening in the group context. In one-to-one conversations, we know that we must respond to the speaker, so we tend to pay closer attention. In a group, we don't have to carry as much of the conversational load, so we're tempted to lose focus or to talk to the person sitting next to us. The content of the discussion can also make listening difficult. Ethical issues can generate strong emotional reactions because they involve deeply held values and beliefs. The natural tendency is to dismiss the speaker ("What does he know?" "He's got it all wrong!") and become absorbed in our own emotions instead of concentrating on the message.[15] Reaching an agreement then becomes more difficult because we don't understand the other person's position while, at the same time, we're more committed than ever to our point of view.

Listening experts Larry Barker, Patrice Johnson, and Kittie Watson make these suggestions for improving your listening performance in a group setting:[16]

1. *Avoid interruptions.* Give the speaker a chance to finish before you respond or ask questions. The speaker may address your concerns before he or she finishes, and you can't properly evaluate a message until you've first understood it.

2. *Seek areas of agreement.* Take a positive approach by searching for common ground. What do you and the speaker have in common? Commitment to solving the problem? Similar values and background?

3. *Search for meanings and avoid arguing about specific words.* Discussions of terms can keep the group from addressing the real issue. Stay focused on what speakers mean; don't be distracted if they use different terminology than you do.

4. *Ask questions/request clarification.* When you don't understand, don't be afraid to ask for clarification. Chances are, others in the group are also confused and will appreciate more information. Asking too many questions, however, can give the impression that you're trying to control the speaker.

5. *Be patient.* We can process information faster than speakers can deliver it. Use the extra time to reflect on the message instead of focusing on your own reactions or daydreaming.

6. *Compensate for attitudinal biases.* All of us have biases based on such factors as personal appearance, age differences, and irritating mannerisms. Among my pet peeves? Men with Elvis hairdos, grown women with little girl voices, and nearly anyone who clutters his or her speech with "ums" and "uhs." I have to suppress my urge to dismiss these kinds of speakers and concentrate on listening carefully. (Sadly, I don't always succeed.)

7. *Listen for principles, concepts, and feelings.* Try to understand how individual facts fit into the bigger picture. Don't overlook nonverbal cues like tone of voice and posture that reveal emotions and, at times, can contradict verbal statements. If a speaker's words and nonverbal behaviors don't seem to match (as in expression of support uttered with a sigh of resignation), probe further to make sure you clearly understand the person's position.

8. *Compensate for emotion-arousing words and ideas.* Certain words and concepts like "fundamentalist," "euthanasia," "gay pride," "terrorist," and "feminist"

spark strong emotional responses. We need to overcome our knee-jerk reactions to these labels and strive instead to remain objective.

9. *Be flexible.* Acknowledge that other views may have merit, even though you may not completely agree with them.

10. *Listen, even if the message is boring or tough to follow.* Not all messages are exciting and simple to digest, but we need to make a concerted effort to understand them anyway. A boring comment made early in a group discussion may later turn out to be critical to the team's success.

DEFENSIVE VERSUS SUPPORTIVE COMMUNICATION

Defensiveness is a major threat to accurate listening. When group members feel threatened, they divert their attention from the task to defending themselves. As their anxiety levels increase, they think less about how to solve the problem and more about how they are coming across to others, about winning, and about protecting themselves. Listening suffers because participants distort the messages they receive, misinterpreting the motives, values, and emotions of senders. Supportive messages, on the other hand, increase accuracy because group members devote more energy to interpreting the content and emotional states of sources. Psychologist Jack Gibb identified six pairs of behaviors (described below) that promote either a defensive or supportive group atmosphere.[17] Our job as team leader or member is to engage in supportive communication, which contributes to a positive emotional climate and accurate understanding. At the same time, we need to challenge comments that spark defensive reactions and lead to poor ethical choices.

Evaluation versus description. Evaluative messages are judgmental. They can be sent through statements ("What a lousy idea!") or through such nonverbal cues as a sarcastic tone of voice or a raised eyebrow. Those being evaluated are likely to respond by placing blame and making judgments of their own ("Your proposal is no better than mine"). Supportive messages ("I think I see where you're coming from," attentive posture, eye contact) create a more positive environment.

Control versus problem orientation. Controlling messages imply that the recipient is inadequate (i.e., uninformed, immature, stubborn, overly emotional) and needs to change. Control, like evaluation, can be communicated both verbally (issuing orders, threats) and nonverbally (stares, threatening body posture). Problem-centered messages reflect a willingness to collaborate, to work together to resolve the issue. Examples of problem-oriented statements might include, "What do you think we ought to do?" "I believe we can work this out if we sit down and identify the issues."

Strategy versus spontaneity. Strategic communicators are seen as manipulators who try to hide their true motivations. They say they want to work with others yet withhold information and appear to be listening when they're not. This "false spontaneity" angers the rest of the group. On the other hand, behavior that is truly spontaneous and honest reduces defensiveness.

Neutrality versus empathy. Neutral messages like "You'll get over it" and "Don't take it so seriously" imply that the listener doesn't care. Empathetic statements, such as "I can see why you would be depressed" and "I'll be thinking about you when you have that appointment with your boss," communicate reassurance and acceptance. Those who receive them enjoy a boost in self-esteem.

Superiority versus equality. Attempts at "one-upmanship" generally provoke immediate defensive responses. The comment "I got an A in my ethics class" is likely to be met with this kind of reply: "Well, you may have a lot of book learning, but I had to deal with a lot of real-world ethical problems when I worked at the advertising agency." Superiority can be based on a number of factors, including wealth, social class, organizational position, and power. All groups contain members who differ in their social standing and abilities. These differences are less disruptive, however, if participants indicate that they want to work with others on an equal basis.

Certainty versus provisionalism. Dogmatic group members (those who are inflexible and claim to have all the answers) are unwilling to change or consider other points of view. As a consequence, they appear more interested in being right than in solving the problem. Listeners often perceive certainty as a mask for feelings of inferiority. In contrast to dogmatic individuals, provisional discussants signal that they are willing to work with the rest of the team in order to investigate issues and come up with a sound ethical decision.

PRODUCTIVE CONFLICT

In healthy groups, members examine and debate the merits of the proposal before the group, a process that experts call *substantive conflict.*[18] Substantive conflicts produce a number of positive outcomes, including these:

- Accurate understanding of the arguments and positions of others in the group
- Higher-level moral reasoning
- Thorough problem analysis
- Improved self-understanding and self-improvement
- Stronger, deeper relationships

- Creativity and change

- Greater motivation to solve the problem

- Improved mastery and retention of information

- Deeper commitment to the outcome of the discussion

- Increased group cohesion and cooperation

- Improved ability to deal with future conflicts

- High-quality solutions that integrate the perspective of all members

It is important to differentiate between substantive conflict and *affective conflict* that is centered on the interpersonal relationships between group members. Those caught in personality-based conflicts find themselves either trying to avoid the problem or, when the conflict can't be ignored, escalating hostilities through name calling, sarcasm, threats, and other means. In this poisoned environment, members aren't as committed to the group process, sacrifice in-depth discussion of the problem in order to get done as soon as possible, and distance themselves from the decision. The end result? A decline in moral reasoning that produces an unpopular, low-quality solution.

There are a number of ways that you as a leader can encourage substantive conflict. Begin by paying attention to the membership of the group. Encourage the emergence of minority opinion by forming teams made up of people with significantly different backgrounds. Groups concerned with medical ethics, for example, generally include members from both inside the medical profession (nurses, surgeons, hospital administrators) and outside (theologians, ethicists, government officials). Individuals and subgroups that disagree with the majority cast doubt on the prevailing opinion and stimulate further thought. In the end, the majority generally comes up with a better solution because members have examined their assumptions and considered more viewpoints and possible solutions.[19]

Next, lay down some procedural ground rules—a conflict covenant—before discussion begins. Come up with a list of conflict guideposts as a group. "Absolutely no name-calling or threats." "No idea is a dumb idea." "Direct all critical comments toward the problem, not the person." "You must repeat the message of the previous speaker—to that person's satisfaction—before you can add your comments." Highlight the fact that conflict about ideas is an integral part of group discussion and caution against hasty decisions. Encourage individuals to stand firm instead of capitulating. If need be, appoint someone to play the role of devil's advocate with the responsibility to cast doubt on the group's proposals.

During the discussion make sure that members follow their conflict covenant and don't engage in conflict avoidance or escalation. Stop to revisit the ground rules when needed. Be prepared to support your position. Challenge and analyze the arguments of others as you encourage them to do the same (see the discussion to follow).

Engaging in Effective Argument

Making arguments is the best way to influence others when the group is faced with a controversial decision. That's why argumentative individuals are more likely to emerge as leaders.[20] An argument is an assertion or claim that is supported by evidence and reasons. In the argumentation process, group members interact with each other using claims, evidence, and reasoning in hopes of reaching the best decision. They avoid personal attacks that characterize affective conflicts.

Argumentation in a small group is not as formal and sophisticated as a legal brief or a debate at a college forensics tournament. In more formal settings, there are strict limits on, among other things, how long arguers can speak, what evidence they can introduce, how they should address the audience, and how the argument should be constructed. Argumentation in a group is much less structured. No one enforces time limits for individual speakers, and members may interrupt each other and get off track. Nonetheless, when you argue in a group, you'll have to carry out the same basic tasks as the members of a university debate team.[21] (Complete the Self-Assessment in Box 8.2 to determine how likely you are to engage in arguments.)

Box 8.2

Self-Assessment

ARGUMENTATIVENESS SCALE

Instructions: This questionnaire contains statements about arguing controversial issues. Indicate how often each statement is true for you personally by placing the appropriate number in the blank to the left of the statement.

Never true = 1

Rarely true = 2

Occasionally true = 3

Often true = 4

Almost always true = 5

(Continued)

Box 8.2 *(Continued)*

____ 1. While in an argument, I worry that the person with whom I am arguing with will form a negative impression of me.

____ 2. Arguing over controversial issues improves my intelligence.

____ 3. I enjoy avoiding arguments.

____ 4. I am energetic and enthusiastic when I argue.

____ 5. Once I finish an argument, I promise myself that I will not get into another.

____ 6. Arguing with a person creates more problems for me than it solves.

____ 7. I have a pleasant, good feeling when I win a point in an argument.

____ 8. When I finish arguing with someone, I feel nervous and upset.

____ 9. I enjoy a good argument over a controversial issue.

____ 10. I get an unpleasant feeling when I realize I am about to get into an argument.

____ 11. I enjoy defending my point of view on an issue.

____ 12. I am happy when I keep an argument from happening.

____ 13. I do not like to miss the opportunity to argue a controversial issue.

____ 14. I prefer being with people who rarely disagree with me.

____ 15. I consider an argument an exciting intellectual challenge.

____ 16. I find myself unable to think of effective points during an argument.

____ 17. I feel refreshed and satisfied after an argument on a controversial issue.

____ 18. I have the ability to do well in an argument.

____ 19. I try to avoid getting into arguments.

____ 20. I feel excitement when I expect that a conversation I am in is leading to an argument.

Argumentativeness Scoring:

1. Add your scores on items 2, 4, 7, 9, 11, 13, 15, 17, 18, 20.

2. Add 60 to the sum obtained in step 1.

(Continued)

Box 8.2 *(Continued)*

3. Add your scores on items 1, 3, 5, 6, 8, 10, 12, 14, 16, 19.

4. To compute your argumentativeness score, subtract the total obtained in step 3 from the total obtained in step 2.

Interpretation:

  73 to 100 = High in Argumentativeness

  56 to 72 = Moderate in Argumentativeness

  20 to 55 = Low in Argumentativeness

SOURCE: Infante, D. A., & Rancer, A. S. (1982). A conceptualization and measure of argumentativeness. *Journal of Personality Assessment, 46,* 72–80. Used by permission.

The first task is to identify just what the controversy is about. All too often teams waste their time debating the wrong issues and end up solving the wrong problem. In Case Study 8.1, The Ten Commandments Go to Court, the controversy surrounded the legality of one religious display in a public place. The conflict is *not* about the truth of the Bible or the role of religion in a jurist's private life. Clarify the controversy by putting it in the form of a proposition or proposal. The Supreme Court must determine its response to the following assertion: "The ban on placing the Ten Commandments statue in the Alabama Judicial Building lobby should remain in place."

Once the controversy is clearly identified, you need to assemble and present your arguments. Arguments, as I noted above, consist of a claim supported by evidence and reasons. Back your claim with examples, personal experience, testimonials from others, and statistics. Also, supply reasons or logic for your position. The most common patterns of logic include (a) analogical (drawing similarities between one case and another, as we saw in Chapter 7), (b) causal (one event leads to another), (c) inductive (generalizing from one or a few cases to many), and (d) deductive (moving from a larger category or grouping to a smaller one).

You could use all four types of reasoning if you believe that displaying the Ten Commandments is a violation of the principle of separation of church and state. You might appeal to the sympathy of Christian jurists by asking them how they would feel if this had been a statue inscribed with Hindu scripture (analogical reasoning). You could argue that the display creates a hostile environment that undermines the confidence of people of other religious traditions in the court system (causal reasoning). You might suggest that leaving the monument in place would encourage other judges and politicians to disobey laws they don't like (inductive reasoning). You could also point out that the Alabama ruling is only the latest in a series of decisions banning religious displays on public property (deductive reasoning).

At the same time you formulate your position, you need to identify and attack the weaknesses in the positions of other participants. This process is often neglected in group discussions. Group communication experts Dennis Gouran and Randy Hirokawa found that undetected errors are the primary cause of poor-quality decisions.[22] These errors include incomplete data, accepting bad information as fact, selecting only that information that supports a flawed choice, rejecting valid evidence, poor reasoning, and making unreasonable inferences from the facts. Be on the lookout for the common errors in evidence and reasoning found in Box 8.3. According to Gouran and Hirokawa, all groups make mistakes, but members of successful groups catch their errors and get the group back on track through corrective communication called *counteractive influence.*[16] An excellent example of counteractive influence is found earlier in this chapter in Box 8.1, Leadership Ethics at the Movies Case: *Twelve Angry Men.*

Box 8.3

Common Fallacies

Faulty Evidence

   Unreliable and biased sources

   Source lacking proper knowledge and background

   Inconsistency (disagrees with other sources, source contradicts him or herself)

   Outdated evidence

   Evidence appears to support a claim but does not

   Information gathered from secondhand observers

   Inaccurate citation of sources

   Uncritical acceptance of statistical data

Faulty Reasoning

   Comparing two things that are not alike (false analogy)

   Drawing conclusions based on too few examples or examples that aren't typical of the population as a whole (hasty generalization)

(Continued)

Box 8.3 *(Continued)*

Believing that the event that happens first always causes the event that happens second (false cause)

Arguing that complicated problems have only one cause (single cause)

Assuming without evidence that one event will inevitably lead to a bad result (slippery slope)

Using the argument to support the argument (circular reasoning)

Failing to offer evidence that supports the position (non sequitur)

Attacking the person instead of the argument (ad hominem)

Appealing to the crowd/popular opinion (bandwagon effect)

Resisting change based on past practices (appeal to tradition)

Attacking a weakened version on an opponent's argument (straw argument)

Arguing that a claim is right just because it hasn't been demonstrated to be wrong (appeal to ignorance)

Reducing choices down to two either/or alternatives (false alternatives)

Believing that an exception to a rule establishes its truth rather than challenging its truth (exception to the rule)

SOURCES: Compiled from Warnick, B., & Inch, E. S. (1994). *Critical thinking and communication: The use of reason in argument.* New York: Macmillan.

Conway, D. A., & Munson, R. (1990). *The elements of reasoning.* Belmont, CA: Wadsworth.

Implications and Applications

- As a leader, much of your work will be done in committees, boards, task forces, and other small groups. Making ethical choices is one of a team's most important responsibilities. Your task is to foster the conditions that promote effective, ethical decisions.
- An overemphasis on group cohesion is a significant threat to ethical decision making. Be alert for the symptoms of groupthink. These include (a) signs of overconfidence (illusion of invulnerability, belief in the inherent morality of the group), (b) signs of closed-mindedness (collective rationalization, stereotypes of outside groups), (c) pressure on dissenters (self-censorship, illusion of unanimity, self-appointed mindguards).
- Adopting teamthink strategies is one way to resist the temptation to put agreement ahead of reasoned problem solving. Encourage your group to visualize successful outcomes, avoid pressure tactics, and challenge faulty assumptions.
- Groups stumble when they falsely believe that everyone supports a decision that, in reality, everyone opposes. The best way to avoid the Abilene Paradox is

to overcome your fears of being separated from the rest of the group and state your honest opinion.

- Despite group pressures, you are ultimately responsible for your individual choices and behaviors.
- A dialogic approach to communication, one that treats others as humans rather than as objects, lays the groundwork for productive group interaction.
- If you want a healthy group that makes effective ethical decisions, engage productive or enlightened communication patterns and encourage followers to do the same. Enlightening communication skills and tactics include comprehensive, critical listening; supportive messages; productive conflict management; and effective argumentation.

For Further Exploration, Challenge, and Self-Assessment

1. Interview a leader at your school or in another organization to develop a "meeting profile" for this person. Find out how much time this person spends in meetings during an average week and if this is typical of other leaders in the same organization. Identify the types of meetings she or he attends and her or his role. Determine if ethical issues are part of these discussions. As part of your profile, record your reactions. Are you surprised by your findings? Has this assignment changed your understanding of what leaders do?

2. Have you ever been part of a group that was victimized by groupthink? Which symptoms were present? How did they affect the group's ethical decisions and actions? Does the Abilene Paradox offer a better explanation for what happened?

3. Evaluate a recent ethical decision made by one of your groups. Was it a high-quality decision? Why or why not? What factors contributed to the group's success or failure? Which of the keys to effective ethical problem solving were present? Absent? How did the leader (you or someone else) shape the outcome, for better or worse? How would you evaluate your performance as a leader or team member?

4. Develop a plan for becoming a better listener in a group. Implement your plan and then evaluate your progress.

5. Pair off with a partner and discuss your argumentativeness scores. What experiences and attitudes contribute to your willingness or unwillingness to argue? Are you more willing to argue in some situations than in others? How could you increase your argumentativeness score?

6. Identify forms of faulty evidence and reasoning in an argument about an ethical issue. Draw from talk shows, newspaper editorials, speeches, interviews, debates, congressional hearings, and other sources. Possible topics might include capital punishment, profanity on television, tightening bankruptcy laws, and cloning.

7. With other team members, develop a conflict covenant. Determine how you will enforce this code.

8. Fishbowl discussion: In a fishbowl discussion, one group discusses a problem while the rest of the class looks on and then provides feedback. Assign a group to the Ten Commandments Goes to Court case—Case 8.1 at the beginning of this chapter—or the Chapter End Case: Death Row Organ Transplants. Make sure that each discussant has one or more observers who specifically note his or her behavior. When the discussion is over, observers should meet with their "fish." Then the class as a whole should give its impressions of the overall performance of the team. Draw on chapter concepts when evaluating the work of individual participants and the group.

CASE STUDY 8.2

Chapter End Case: Death Row Organ Transplants

Longer prison sentences, aging inmates, and state budget cuts have created a medical crisis in the nation's correctional systems. Jail officials are required by law to provide prisoners (who get sicker as they get older) with adequate care. At the same time, state legislatures are cutting back on medical care for the poor, raising the very real possibility that inmates could receive better treatment than law-abiding citizens.

Organ transplants for prisoners further heighten the ethical controversy surrounding prison medical care. A California convict recently died after receiving a heart transplant costing nearly $2 million. A former prostitute serving a life sentence for murder in Nebraska may be put on the waiting list for a new liver. In the most unusual case, an Oregon prisoner on death row applied to be considered for a kidney transplant. His request was denied, but the cost for his current dialysis treatments (over $100,000 a year while he awaits execution) will total more than the cost of a transplant operation ($80–120,000).

Many politicians and citizens are outraged at the thought of organ transplants for death row inmates and other convicts. Legislators in Louisiana have passed a law outlawing transplants for convicted murderers and rapists. Some potential donors who learn of prisoners receiving transplants are threatening to tear up their organ donation cards in protest. Part of this anger stems from the fact that there are a limited number of organs available for transplant. Fifty-six thousand Americans are awaiting a kidney operation, for example, and 17 die daily before they receive an organ. The thought of a death row convict receiving a liver at the expense of a model citizen is troubling, to say the least. In Oregon, low-income patients have been kept off the organ recipient list because they wouldn't be able to pay for the antirejection drugs that an inmate would receive free.

Resolving the inmate transplant dilemma will not be easy. Prison officials must follow court mandates. Transplants, as in the case of the Oregon death row prisoner, may actually save states money. In addition, doctors are obligated to help patients, no matter what their legal status. University of Toronto ethicist Bernard Dickens points out that inmates are people, too:

> Prisoners are human beings with full entitlement. Although he (the Oregon prisoner) is paying the price for his wrongs, he is entitled to medical treatment indicated for his medical condition, not his moral condition. We don't treat people in accordance with their moral worth. We treat them in accordance with their health needs.[23]

DISCUSSION PROBES

1.   Should prisoners be entitled to the same medical treatment as law-abiding citizens? Should there be limits to the amount of health care that inmates receive?

238 SHAPING ETHICAL CONTEXTS

2. Is there ever a time when an inmate should receive a transplant?

3. What ethical principles can be applied when deciding whether or not to pay for transplants for prisoners?

4. As a doctor, would you perform a transplant on a prisoner serving a sentence for murder?

5. What leadership lessons do you draw from this case?

REFERENCES

Anderson, E. (2003, June 21). Bill denies transplants to killers, rapists. *The Times-Picayune* National, p. 7.

Gustafson, A. (2003, May 5). Dialysis keeps death row inmate alive: Expensive treatments prompt ethical questions. *Seattle Post-Intelligencer,* p. B2.

Higgins, M. (2003, May 28). Death-row inmate up for transplant: Murderer may get kidney. *National Post,* p. A3.

Podger, P. J. (2002, December 18). Prisoner with transplanted heart dies. *San Francisco Chronicle,* p. A25.

Spencer, C. (2003, June 12). Panel denies transplant for inmate on death row but issue remains. *The Oregonian,* p. B1.

Thiessen, M. (2003, February 28). Convicted killer in Nebraska may get liver transplant. *Associated Press.* Retrieved from LexisNexis (www.lexisnexis.com/).

CASE STUDY 8.3

Chapter End Case Study: Groupthink and Faulty Reasoning: NASA's Recipe for Disaster

On January 31, 2003, America's space program suffered its second shuttle disaster when the *Columbia* disintegrated on reentry into the earth's atmosphere. All seven aboard died in the explosion. The accident occurred nearly 17 years to the day after the *Challenger* explosion. That disaster also took the lives of seven astronauts, including the first teacher headed into space.

Space shuttle *Columbia's* troubles began when a piece of foam the size of a flat screen television broke off the propellant tank and hit the spacecraft 82 seconds after liftoff. The debris struck with a ton of force and likely caused a 6- to 10-inch hole. This opening allowed superheated gas to enter the craft when it came back to earth.

The day after the launch, NASA officials reviewed tracking videos. This footage showed the debris strike but didn't reveal any damage because the pictures couldn't pick up details smaller than 2 feet in size. Five days after launch, the mission control team in charge of the *Columbia* flight first discussed the possibility that a piece of insulating foam might have damaged the shuttle's left wing. Mission project leader Linda Ham downplayed the likelihood that the shuttle had been seriously compromised. She pointed out that the group had earlier concluded that foam, which routinely comes off during shuttle launches, wouldn't do any significant damage. Foam damage was considered a minor maintenance problem that could be taken care of between trips.

Other engineers and managers at NASA were not convinced that the foam strike was insignificant. Bryan O'Connor, NASA's top safety official, ordered a hazard assessment. Those carrying out the assessment requested permission to ask for additional satellite images from the Pentagon to determine if there was damage to the orbiting ship. Ham denied their request in part because the shuttle would have to slow in order to position the wing for a photograph. This maneuver would disrupt the mission. The hazard assessment group was then forced to depend on the conclusions of a team of Boeing engineers. These experts used a computer program that determined there was potential for "significant tile damage" but not a complete "burn-through." Their analysis, however, was flawed. The group's software was not designed for use in making in-flight decisions. Also, Boeing engineers assumed that the reinforced carbon carbon (RCC) material around the strike area was as damage-resistant as the glassy tiles on the rest of the ship. It was not.

During the same period, a group of low-level NASA engineers launched their own independent investigation. Their requests for photos were denied because they didn't come through proper channels. Senior structural engineer Rodney Rocha then drafted e-mail pointing out the "grave hazards" caused by the foam. Sadly, he never sent the message to Ham, claiming: "I was too low down here in the organization, and she's way up here. I just couldn't do it."[24]

Meanwhile, members of the mission control team continued to express concern about possible damage to the shuttle but backed down when pressured by Ham. Dissenters lacked hard data to establish that the shuttle had been damaged. When the group met for the final time, engineers did not even discuss possible dangers to the shuttle. Instead, they talked about how eager they were to review the astronauts' launch day photos after the shuttle landed to determine exactly where the foam had come off the tank. Mission control informed the astronauts that debris had hit their craft. However, controllers noted that the problem was "not even worth mentioning" except that a reporter might ask them about it.

After the explosion, the Columbia Accident Investigation Board, chaired by Admiral Harold Gehman (USN, retired), wrote a scathing report that placed much of the blame on NASA's culture. Board members accused the agency of becoming overconfident after years of flying safely. Safety, which was elevated to top priority after the first disaster, became less important as years passed and space budgets were cut. NASA administrator Sean O'Keefe and other top managers were more interested in keeping the shuttles flying in order to complete the space station by February 2004. Engineers also lost sight of the fact that a space shuttle is a highly risky experimental craft. Communication between teams, departments, and organizational levels broke down. Nobody, including the leadership of NASA, seems clear about the agency's mission after the success of the manned moon landing and the unmanned Mars probes.

Although flawed culture drew most of the headlines describing the Columbia board's final report, groupthink and faulty reasoning were just as much to blame. Mission control team members displayed many groupthink symptoms. They rationalized that shredding foam was only a routine problem, and team leader Ham pressured dissenters. Individuals eventually kept their doubts to themselves and thus gave the appearance that everyone in the group solidly backed its conclusions. The hazard assessment task force and Boeing engineers fell prey to shaky logic. These groups relied on a flawed computer model and assumed that all materials covering the spacecraft were equally durable.

There is no guarantee that the Columbia crew could have been rescued even if NASA officials had recognized the danger. Shuttle astronauts had a limited amount of food, water, and air and couldn't go to the space station for repairs. Any attempt to launch a rescue shuttle would have endangered another crew, because the second shuttle would face the same risk of a fatal foam strike as the first. Nonetheless, by falling victim to both groupthink and faulty assumptions, leaders at NASA eliminated any chance that the Columbia crew would make it safely back to Earth.

DISCUSSION PROBES

1.   Should NASA fire the Columbia mission leaders? Why or why not?

2.   How much blame do you assign to those who questioned the safety of the mission but either kept their doubts to themselves or failed to communicate them to NASA's top management?

3. What advice would you give to NASA teams to help them better resist groupthink?

4. How can NASA do a better job of challenging widely held assumptions?

5. What advice would you give to group members (like those on the mission control team) who have doubts but lack the evidence to support their position?

6. If you were the head of NASA, would you have launched a rescue shuttle if you had identified the damage to the Columbia? Why or why not?

7. What can NASA leaders do to prevent a similar disaster from happening again?

8. What leadership lessons do you draw from this case?

REFERENCES

Barrett, J. (2003, July 18). Q&A: Clearly there is a problem here. *Newsweek* (Web Exclusive). Retrieved September 2, 2003, from LexisNexis (www.lexisnexis.com/).

Glanz, W. (2003, August 27). NASA ignored dangers to shuttle, panel says. *The Washington Times,* p. A1.

Grose, T. K. (2003, September 1). Can the manned space program find a new, revitalizing mission in the wake of the Columbia tragedy? *U.S. News & World Report,* p. 36.

Hilzenrath, D. S. (2003, September 2). Rescue of Columbia a hindsight dream. *The Washington Post,* p. A8.

Mishra, R. (2003, August 27). Probe hits NASA in crash of shuttle. *The Boston Globe.* Retrieved September 2, 2003, from LexisNexis (www.lexisnexis.com/).

Sawyer, K. (2003, August 24) Shuttle's "smoking gun" took time to register. *The Washington Post,* p. A1.

Notes

1. Palmer, P. (1996). Leading from within. In L. C. Spears (Ed.), *Insights on leadership: Service, stewardship, spirit, and servant-leadership* (pp. 197–208). New York: Wiley, p. 200.

2. Rothwell, J. D. (1998). *In mixed company: Small group communication* (3rd ed.). Fort Worth, TX: Harcourt Brace, p. 2.

3. Tropman, J. (2003). *Making meetings work: Achieving high quality group decisions* (2nd ed.). Thousand Oaks, CA: Sage, p. 196.

4. Dukerich, J. M., Nichols, M. L., Elm, D. R., & Voltrath, D. A. (1990). Moral reasoning in groups: Leaders make a difference. *Human Relations, 43,* 473–493; Nichols, M. L., & Day, V. E. (1982). A comparison of moral reasoning of groups and individuals on the "defining issues test." *Academy of Management Journal, 24,* 201–208.

5. Janis, I. (1971, November). Groupthink: The problems of conformity. *Psychology Today,* 271–279; Janis, I. (1982). *Groupthink* (2nd ed.). Boston, MA: Houghton Mifflin; Janis, I. (1989). *Crucial decisions: Leadership in policymaking and crisis management.* New York: Free Press.

6. Moorhead, G., Neck, C. P., & West, M. S. (1998). The tendency toward defective decision making within self-managing teams: The relevance of groupthink for the 21st century. *Organizational Behavior and Human Decision Processes, 73,* 327–351.

7. See, for example, the following:

Chen, A., Lawson, R. B., Gordon, L. R., & McIntosh, B. (1996). Groupthink: Deciding with the leader and the devil. *Psychological Record, 46,* 581–590.

Esser, J. K. (1998). Alive and well after 25 years: A review of groupthink research. *Organizational Behavior and Human Decision Processes, 73,* 116–141.

Flippen, A. R. (1999). Understanding groupthink from a self-regulatory perspective. *Small Group Research, 30,* 139–165.

Street, M. D. (1997). Groupthink: An examination of theoretical issues, implications, and future research suggestions. *Small Group Research, 28,* 72–93.

8. Manz, C. C., & Neck, C. P. (1995). Teamthink: Beyond the groupthink syndrome in self-managing work teams. *Journal of Managerial Psychology, 10*(1), 7–15; Manz, C. C., & Sims, H. P. (1989). *Superleadership: Leading others to lead themselves.* Upper Saddle River, NJ: Prentice Hall.

9. Harvey, J. (1988). *The Abilene Paradox and other meditations on management.* New York: Simon & Schuster. See also Harvey, J. B. (1999). *How come every time I get stabbed in the back my fingerprints are on the knife?* San Francisco: Jossey-Bass.

10. Harvey (1988), *Abilene Paradox,* p. 15.

11. Buber, M. (1970. *I and thou.* (R. G. Smith, Trans.) New York: Charles Scribner's Sons; Johannesen, R. L. (2002). *Ethics in human communication* (5th ed.). Prospect Heights, IL: Waveland Press, ch. 4.

12. Cissna, K. N., & Anderson, R. (1994). Communication and the ground of dialogue. In R. Anderson, K. N. Cissna, & R. C. Arnett (Eds.), *The reach of dialogue: Confirmation, voice, and community* (pp. 9–30). Cresskill, NJ: Hampton Press.

13. Czubaroff, J. (2000). Dialogical rhetoric: An application of Martin Buber's philosophy of dialogue. *Quarterly Journal of Speech, 2,* 168–189.

14. Wolvin, A. D., & Coakley, G. C. (1993). A listening taxonomy. In A. D. Wolvin & C. G. Coakley (Eds.), *Perspectives in listening* (pp. 15–22). Norwood, NJ: Ablex.

15. Johnson, J. (1993). Functions and processes of inner speech in listening. In A. D. Wolvin & C. G. Coakley (Eds.), *Perspectives in listening* (pp. 170–184). Norwood, NJ: Ablex.

16. Barker, L., Johnson, P., & Watson, K. (1991). The role of listening in managing interpersonal and group conflict. In D. Borisoff & M. Purdy (Eds.), *Listening in everyday life: A personal and professional approach* (pp. 139–157). Lanham, MD: University Press of America.

17. Gibb, J. R. (1961). Defensive communication. *Journal of Communication, 11-12,* 141–148.

18. See, for example, the following:

Bell, M. A. (1974). The effects of substantive and affective conflict in problem-solving groups. *Speech Monographs, 41,* 19–23.

Bell, M. A. (1979). The effects of substantive and affective verbal conflict on the quality of decisions of small problem-solving groups. *Central States Speech Journal, 30,* 75–82.

Johnson, D. W., & Tjosvold, D. (1983). *Productive conflict management.* New York: Irvington.

19. Moscovici, S., Mugny, G., & Van Avermaet, E. (Eds.). (1985). *Perspectives on minority influence.* Cambridge, UK: Cambridge University Press; Maas, A., & Clark, R. D. (1984). Hidden impact of minorities: Fifteen years of minority influence research. *Psychological Bulletin, 95,* 428–450; Nemeth, C., & Chiles, C. (1986). Modeling courage: The role of dissent in fostering independence. *European Journal of Social Psychology, 18,* 275–280.

20. Schultz, B. (1982). Argumentativeness: Its effect in group decision making and its role in leadership perception. *Communication Quarterly, 30,* 368–375.

21. Infante, D., & Rancer, A. (1996). Argumentativeness and verbal aggressiveness: A review of recent theory and research. In B. Burleson (Ed.), *Communication yearbook 19* (pp. 319–351). Thousand Oaks, CA: Sage; Infante, D. (1988). *Arguing constructively.* Prospect Heights, IL: Waveland Press.

22. Gouran, D. S., Hirokawa, R. Y., Julian, K. M., & Leatham, G. B. (1993). The evolution and current status of the functional perspective on communication in decision-making and problem-solving groups. *Communication Yearbook 16,* 573– 600; Gouran, D. S., & Hirokawa, R. Y. (1986). Counteractive functions of communication in effective group decision making. In R. Y. Hirokawa & M. S. Poole (Eds.), *Communication and group decision making* (pp. 81–90). Beverly Hills, CA: Sage.

23. Higgins, M. (2003, May 28). Death-row inmate up for transplant: Murderer may get kidney. *National Post,* p. A3.

24. Sawyer, K. (2003, August 24) Shuttle's "smoking gun" took time to register. *The Washington Post,* p. A1.

9

Creating an Ethical Organizational Climate

Bad ethics is bad business.

Anonymous

What's Ahead

Organizations that cast light act with integrity (ethical soundness, wholeness, and consistency) emphasize that goals must be achieved through moral means or processes and reinforce ethical behavior through their structures. This chapter outlines ways to build ethical organizational climates, paying particular attention to shared values, codes of ethics, and continuous ethical improvement.

Organizational Light or Shadow

The distinction between ethical and unethical organizations can be as sharp as the contrast between moral and immoral leaders. Some organizations, like humanitarian relief agencies and socially responsible businesses, shine brightly. Others, such as corrupt police departments and authoritarian political regimes, are cloaked in darkness.

Few of us will experience the oppression of truly dark organizations. Destructive behaviors are an all too common fact of organizational life, however. Common shadow casting actions include the following:[1]

Lying and withholding information	Stealing
Scapegoating and blaming	Protecting turf
Overconforming	Playing it safe
Sabotage	Manipulation for personal gain
Verbal abuse	Gossiping
Wasting resources	Playing favorites
Undermining change	Sexual harassment
Endangering coworkers	Violence
Refusing to help others	Slowing down production

Forming and maintaining a positive ethical climate that discourages the behaviors listed above is one of the most important responsibilities we assume when we take on a leadership role in an organization. All members help to shape the collective ethical atmosphere, but leaders exert the most influence.[2] Followers will look to us for moral guidance. They'll scrutinize our words and actions for information about mission, values, standards, and organizational priorities. They'll want answers to such questions as "What happens to those who break the rules?" "How should I treat suppliers and customers?" "What's most important—making a profit or doing the right thing?" "Am I expected to be an active member of the larger community?"

Don't assume that shaping climate is easy. Leaders are just as likely to be corrupted by the existing moral atmosphere as followers, turning a blind eye to questionable practices because "it's always been done that way." Further, as the Air Force Academy case at the end of the chapter demonstrates, entrenched attitudes and practices are highly resistant to change.

Ethical Climates

Ethical climate is best understood as part of an organization's culture. From the cultural vantage point, an organization is a tribe. As tribal members gather, they develop their own language, stories, beliefs, assumptions, ceremonies, and power structures. These elements combine to form a unique perspective on the world referred to as the organization's culture.[3] How an organization responds to ethical issues is a part of this mix. Every organization will face a special set of ethical challenges, create its own set of values and norms, develop guidelines for enforcing its ethical standards, honor particular ethical heroes, and so on.

ETHICAL ORIENTATIONS

Management professors Bart Victor and John Cullen argue that ethical climates can be classified according to (a) the criteria members use to make moral choices and (b) the groups that members refer to when making ethical determinations.[4] Victor and Cullen identify five climate types. *Instrumental* climates follow the principle of ethical egotism. Ethical egotists make decisions based on selfish interests that serve the individual and his or her immediate group and organization. *Caring* climates emphasize concern or care for others. *Law and order* climates are driven by external criteria like professional codes of conduct. *Rules* climates are governed by the policies, rules, and procedures developed within the organization. *Independent* climates give members wide latitude to make their own decisions.

Leaders would do well to know the particular ethical orientation of their organizations.[5] To begin, each of the five climate types poses unique ethical challenges. Members of instrumental organizations often ignore the needs of others, whereas those driven by a care ethic are tempted to overlook the rules to help out friends and colleagues. Leaders and followers in law and order cultures may be blind to the needs of coworkers because they rely on outside standards for guidance. On the other hand, those who play by organizational rules may be blinded to societal norms. Independence produces the best results when members have the knowledge and skills they need to make good decisions.

Orientation also has an impact on ethical change efforts, a topic we will examine in more depth later in the chapter. Ethical appeals in instrumental cultures must speak to self-benefits by emphasizing how the individual and group will profit from ethical behavior. Caring-oriented individuals are motivated by rationale that emphasizes benevolence or benefits to others. They will not respond well to detailed codes and regulations. Members of law and order cultures want to see how the opinions of outside experts can be applied to their specific situation. Rules-oriented followers look to their leaders for guidance on how to behave and rely heavily on manuals and written regulations. Independent-oriented thinkers need time to reflect on ethical issues and will feel most comfortable when they are able to justify their choices.

SIGNS OF HEALTHY ETHICAL CLIMATES

There is no "one size fits all" approach to creating an ethical climate. Rather, we need to identify principles and practices that characterize positive ethical climates. Then we have to adapt these elements to our particular organizational setting. Key markers of highly ethical organizations include integrity, a focus on process, and structural reinforcement.

Integrity

Integrity refers to ethical soundness, wholeness, and consistency.[6] All units and organizational levels share a commitment to high moral standards, backing up their ethical "talk" with their ethical "walk." Consistency increases the level of trust, encouraging members and units to be vulnerable to one another. They are more willing to share undistorted information, negotiate in good faith, take risks, share authority for making decisions, collaborate, and follow through on promises.[7]

According to business ethicist Lynn Sharp Paine, managers who act with integrity see ethics as "a driving force of an enterprise." These leaders recognize that ethical values largely define what an organization is and what it hopes to accomplish. They keep these values in mind when making routine decisions. Their goal? To help constituents learn to govern their own behavior following these same principles. Paine believes that any effort to improve organizational integrity must include the following elements:[8]

There are sensible, clearly communicated values and commitments. These values and commitments spell out the organization's obligations to external stakeholders (customers, suppliers, neighbors) while appealing to insiders. In highly ethical organizations, members take shared values seriously and don't hesitate to talk about them.

Company leaders are committed to and act on the values. Leaders consistently back the values, use them when making choices, and determine priorities when ethical obligations conflict with one another. For example, former Southwest Airlines president Herb Kelleher put a high value both on the needs of his employees and on customer service. However, it's clear that his workers came first. He didn't hesitate to take their side when customers unfairly criticized them. Such principled leadership was missing at accounting firm Arthur Andersen, which is profiled at the end of the chapter.

The values are part of the routine decision-making process and are factored into every important organizational activity. Ethical considerations shape such activities as planning and goal setting, spending, the gathering and sharing of information, evaluation, and promotion.

Systems and structures support and reinforce organizational commitments. Systems and structures, such as the organizational chart, how work is processed, budgeting procedures, and product development, serve the organization's values. (I'll have more to say about the relationship between ethics and structure later in the chapter.)

Leaders throughout the organization have the knowledge and skills they need to make ethical decisions. Organizational leaders make ethical choices every day. To demonstrate integrity, they must have the necessary skills, knowledge, and experience (see our discussion of ethical development in Chapter 2). Ethics education and training must be part of their professional development.

Paine and other observers warn us not to confuse integrity with compliance. Ethical compliance strategies are generally responses to outside pressures like media scrutiny or the U.S. Sentencing Commission guidelines. Under these federal guidelines, corporate executives can be fined and jailed not only for their ethical misdeeds but also for failing to take reasonable steps to prevent the illegal behavior of employees. Although compliance tactics look good to outsiders, they don't have a lasting impact on ethical climate.[9] Consider, for example, the ethics programs of many *Fortune 1000* companies. Nearly all of the nation's largest firms have ethical strategies in place, including formal ethics codes and policies, ethics officers, and systems for registering and dealing with ethical concerns and complaints. However, most of these programs have minimal influence on company operations. Many ethics officials devote only a small portion of their time to their ethical duties and some complaint hotlines are rarely used. CEOs typically discuss ethical topics with their ethics officers only once or twice a year, attend no meetings focusing primarily on ethics, and rarely communicate to employees about ethics. Followers generally don't receive more than one ethical message annually, and one fifth to one third of lower-level workers receive no ethics training at all in a given year.[10] A similar compliance focus is found in Canadian firms.[11]

The contrast between compliance and integrity is reflected in the model of corporate moral development offered by Eric Reidenbach and Donald Robin.[12] These theorists argue that organizations can be classified according to their level of ethical progress. Stage I *amoral organizations* occupy the lowest level on the hierarchy. Such companies largely ignore ethical concerns, focusing solely on productivity and profit. To them, fines and penalties are the cost of doing business. Dishonest telemarketing firms fall into this category. Next up are Stage II *legalistic organizations,* in which leaders equate ethics with following societal rules and want to protect their organizations from harm. Large tobacco companies, such as R. J. Reynolds, Philip Morris, and Brown & Williamson (see Box 9.1), are Stage II organizations that believe that there is nothing wrong with selling cigarettes because such activity is not prohibited by law.

Responsive organizations (Stage III) are concerned about external stockholders and with being seen as responsible corporate citizens. Yet they often find themselves reacting to ethical problems rather than anticipating them before they occur. Proctor & Gamble's reaction to the toxic shock syndrome of the 1980s is typical of responsive organizations. When notified of the possible link between Rely tampons and toxic shock, the company bought back all unsold products

---

Box 9.1

Leadership Ethics at the Movies: *The Insider*

Key Cast Members: Russell Crowe, Al Pacino, Christopher Plummer

Synopsis: Russell Crowe plays Jeffrey Wigand, a former research executive at the Brown & Williamson tobacco company, who wrestles with the decision of whether or not to go public with what he knows about the industry's cover-up of the health risks of smoking. If he does, he will lose his pension and health benefits as well as any hope of continuing his career in business. *60 Minutes* producer Lowell Bergman (Al Pacino) coaxes him to come forward, but executive producer Don Hewitt, under pressure from CBS lawyers, betrays Wigand by deciding not to air the interview. Belatedly, Hewitt and Mike Wallace (Christopher Plummer) realize that their journalistic integrity has been compromised and they air the segment. Wigand's wife divorces him, and he becomes a science teacher. Bergman resigns from CBS.

Rating: R for language

Themes: the costs of whistle blowing, courage and cowardice, personal integrity, following through on choices, manipulation of the media

---

and sponsored research into the disease at the Centers for Disease Control. *Emergent ethical organizations* (Stage IV) are more advanced than their Stage III counterparts because these groups actively manage their cultures to improve ethical climate. They create a variety of ethical vehicles (handbooks, policy statements, ombudspersons) to shape and communicate important values and standards. Johnson & Johnson and Sara Lee are Stage IV organizations that go to great lengths to emphasize that ethics and not just profits should guide corporate activities.

The highest level of moral development is the Stage V *ethical organization.* Groups in this stage model integrity. Company officers and employees select core values and use these principles in everything from strategic planning to hiring and firing. Further, they try to anticipate ethical problems that might arise. Examples of contemporary Stage V corporations are hard to find, but Reidenbach and Robin point to Sir Adrian Cadbury as a model of how to incorporate ethics into organizational operations. The founder of Britain's Cadbury's chocolates was confronted with the choice of whether or not to supply Christmas tins to English soldiers during the Boer War. Cadbury (a Quaker) opposed the war but realized that his employees as well as the soldiers would be hurt if he turned down the contract. He resolved the problem by producing the chocolates at cost. His employees were then paid, but Sir Adrian didn't benefit personally from the contract.[13]

Process Focus (Concern for Means and Ends)

Concern for how an organization achieves its goals is another important indicator of a healthy ethical climate. In far too many organizations, leaders set demanding performance goals but intentionally or unintentionally ignore how these objectives are to be reached. Instead, they pressure employees to produce sales and profits by whatever means possible. Followers then feel powerless and alienated, becoming estranged from the rest of the group. Sociologists use the term *anomie* to refer to this sense of normlessness and unease that results when rules lose their force.[14] Anomie increases the likelihood that group members will engage in illegal activities and reduces their resistance to demands from authority figures who want them to break the law. Loss of confidence in the organization may also encourage alienated employees to retaliate against coworkers and the group as a whole.

Leaders can address the problem of anomie by making sure that goals are achieved through ethical means. False promises cannot be used to land accounts, all debts must be fully disclosed to investors, kickbacks are prohibited, and so on. They can also make a stronger link between means and ends through ethics programs that address all aspects of organizational ethical performance.

Structural Reinforcement

An organization's structure shouldn't undermine the ethical standards of its members but, as I noted in our discussion of integrity, should encourage higher ethical performance on the part of both leaders and followers. Three elements of an organization's structure have a particularly strong impact on moral behavior:

1. Monetary and nonmonetary reward systems. Organizations often encourage unethical behavior by rewarding it.[15] Consider the case of the software company that paid programmers $20 to correct each software bug they found. Soon programmers were deliberately creating bugs to fix! A visit to the local 10-minute oil change shop provides another example of the impact of misplaced rewards. Some lube and oil franchises pay managers and employees based in part on how many additional services and parts they sell beyond the basic oil change. As a consequence, unscrupulous mechanics persuade car owners to buy unneeded air filters, transmission flushes, and wiper blades. It is not always easy to determine all the consequences of a particular reward system. However, ethical leaders make every effort to ensure that desired moral behaviors are rewarded, not discouraged.

2. Performance and evaluation processes. Performance and evaluation processes need to reflect the balance between means and ends described earlier, monitoring both *how* and *if* goals are achieved. Ethically insensitive monitoring processes fail to detect illegal and immoral behavior and may actually make such practices more likely. When poor behavior goes unpunished, followers may assume that leaders condone and expect such actions. Salomon, Inc., described at the end of Chapter 2, is a case in point. Failure to swiftly punish "star" performers Paul Mozer and Jack Grubman cost the company millions and eventually led to its demise.[16]

3. Decision-making rights and responsibilities. Ethical conduct is more likely when workers are responsible for ethical decisions and have the authority to choose how to respond. Leaders at ethical organizations do all they can to ensure that those closest to the process or problem can communicate their concerns about ethical issues. These managers also empower followers to make and implement their choices. Unfortunately, employees with the most knowledge are often excluded from the decision-making process or lack the power to follow through on their choices. Such was the case in the *Columbia* shuttle explosion profiled in the last chapter. Higher-ranking NASA officials dismissed the concerns of lower-level managers.

Discovering Core Values

Identifying and applying ethical values is an important step to creating a highly moral climate. Leaders promoting integrity first define and then focus attention on central ethical values. I noted in Chapter 3 that comparing responses on a standardized values list can be a way to clarify group and organizational priorities. In this section, I will introduce additional strategies specifically designed to reveal shared values, purposes, and assumptions.

CORE IDEOLOGY

Management experts James Collins and Jerry Porras use the term "core ideology" to refer to the central identity or character of an organization. The character of outstanding companies remains constant even as these firms continually learn and adapt. According to Collins and Porras, "Truly great companies understand the difference between what should never change and what should be open for change, between what is genuinely sacred and what is not."[17]

Core values are the first component of core ideology. Most companies have between three and five such values (see Box 9.2 for some examples). Firms that come up with more than five or six are probably confusing essential values with business tactics and strategies. One way to determine if a value is sacred to your organization is to ask "What would happen if we were penalized for holding this standard?" If you can't honestly say that you would keep this value if it cost your group market share or profits, then it shouldn't show up on your final list. To determine who should be involved in spelling out core values, Collins and Porras recommend the Mars Group technique described in Box 9.3.

Box 9.2

Core Values

Nordstrom

- Service to the customer above all else
- Hard work and individual productivity
- Never be satisfied
- Excellence in reputation; being part of something special

Sony

- Elevation of the Japanese culture and national status
- Being a pioneer—not following others; doing the impossible
- Encouraging individual ability and creativity

Walt Disney

- No cynicism
- Nurturing and promulgation of "wholesome American values"
- Creativity, dreams, and imagination
- Fanatical attention to consistency and detail
- Preservation and control of the Disney magic

SOURCE: Collins, J. C., & Porras, J. I. (1996, September-October). Building your company's vision. *Harvard Business Review, 74*(5), 65–77.

Core purpose makes up the second part of an organization's ideology. *Purpose* is the group's reason for being that reflects the ideals of its members. Examples of effective purpose statements include the following:

To strengthen the social fabric by continually democratizing home ownership (Federal National Mortgage or "Fannie Mae")

To solve unsolved problems innovatively (3M)

To provide a place for people to flourish and to enhance the community (Pacific Theatres)

Asking the "Five Whys" is one way to identify organizational purpose. Start with a description of what your organization does and then ask why that activity is important five separate times. Each "why?" will get you closer to the fundamental mission of your group.

Your organization's purpose statement should inspire members. (Don't make high profits or stock dividends your goal because they don't motivate individuals at every level of the organization.) Your purpose should also serve as an organizational anchor. Every other element of your organization (business plans, expansion efforts, buildings, products) will come and go, but your purpose and values will remain.

Box 9.3

Self-Assessment

MARS GROUP TECHNIQUE

Imagine that you have been asked to re-create the very best attributes of your organization (school, business, nonprofit) on another planet. There are only enough seats on the rocket ship for five to seven people, so select highly credible, competent individuals to go with you on the trip. Meet as a group and work from personal to organizational values by considering these questions:

What core values (values that you would hold regardless of whether or not they were rewarded) do you personally bring to your work?

What values would you tell your children that you hold at work and that you hope they will hold as working adults?

If you woke up tomorrow morning with enough money to retire, would you continue to live with those core values? Can you envision them being as valid for you 100 years from now as they are today?

Would you want to hold these core values even if one or more of them became a competitive *dis*advantage?

If you were to start a new organization in a different line of work, what core values would you build into the new organization regardless of industry?

Summarize your conclusions and present them to others in your class or organization. Compare your values with those of other groups traveling on other spaceships. Conclude by reflecting on what you've learned about yourself and your organization from this exercise. How well do your values match those of the larger group?

SOURCE: Collins, J. C., & Porras, J. I. (1996, September-October). Building your company's vision. *Harvard Business Review, 74*(5), 65–77.

VALUES ADOPTION PROCESS (VAP)

Wife-and-husband team Susan and Thomas Kuczmarski believe that everyone in an organization ought to be involved in the values identification process, not just a select group.[18] Their organizationwide approach is called the *values adoption process* (VAP). In Stage 1, the CEO or designated facilitator kicks off the process in face-to-face conversations or public meetings. Members record their personal values, ones that they would want to be shared in the workplace. These values are then collected, prioritized, and segmented into department or topic groups (manufacturing, research and development, workplace relationships, product quality, innovation). In Stage 2, groups of followers and leaders meet to identify the most important categories and develop a list of specific values for adoption. Roughly 20 values should be identified (10 as "must have" and 10 as "would like to have").

In Stage 3, all members develop a "People Values Pledge" and an "Organization Values Pledge." The People Values Pledge summarizes how each individual should act toward others in the organization (e.g., "have a sense of humor," "set egos aside," "respect diversity"). The Organization Values Pledge reflects the commitment of top leaders to members, for instance: "recognize and reward excellence," "encourage risk taking," "honor teamwork." Both value statements are distributed to members through cards, plaques, annual reports, newsletters, and other means.

In Stage 4, the organization translates internal values to outside audiences. It surveys customers to determine (a) what values they see the organization conveying through its product, market position, and service; (b) what values they would want the organization to communicate; (c) which value should have top priority; and (d) what new value the organization should adopt. This information is then communicated to employees who create a "Customer Values Pledge." These values guide the development of new products and services and efforts to market them. For example, Rubbermaid puts a high priority on durability. Everyone from industrial design engineers to salespeople recognizes that any new product must withstand considerable punishment.

Once collective values have been identified, organizations ought to give careful thought to how their values will be translated into action. To this end, the Kuczmarskis encourage individuals and then small groups to identify and to analyze current group norms. Which norms should be dropped? added? Leaders should make sure an organization's norms support its values, paying particular attention to the following:

- People systems (training, pay, evaluation, promotion)
- Policies and practices (selection and recruiting, management style and decision making, degree of employee participation)
- Physical systems (organization structure, job descriptions, communication and information systems)

Codes of Ethics

Codes of ethics are among the most common ethics tools. Nearly all large corporations have them (see the Fortune 1000 study cited earlier). The same is true for government departments, professional associations, social service agencies, and schools. However, formal ethics statements are as controversial as they are popular. Skeptics make these criticisms:[19]

- Codes are too vague to be useful.

- Codes may not be widely distributed or read.

- Most codes are developed as public relations documents designed solely to improve an organization's image.

- Codes don't improve the ethical climate of an organization or produce more ethical behavior.

- Codes often become the final word on the subject of ethics.

- Codes are hard to apply across cultures and in different situations.

- Codes frequently lack adequate enforcement provisions.

- Codes often fail to spell out which ethical obligations should take priority, or they put the needs of the organization ahead of those of society as a whole.

- Adherence to codes frequently goes unrewarded.

The experience of Enron highlights the shortcomings of formal ethical statements. Company officials had a "beautifully written" code of ethics that specifically prohibited the off-the-books financial deals that led to its bankruptcy (see Chapter 1).[20] Unfortunately, these same executives convinced the board of directors to waive this prohibition.

Defenders of ethical codes point to their potential benefits: One, a code describes an organization's ethical stance both to members and to the outside world. Newcomers, in particular, look to the code for guidance about an organization's ethical standards and potential ethical problems they may face in carrying out their duties. Two, a formal ethics statement can improve the group's image while protecting it from lawsuits and further regulation. In the case of wrongdoing, an organization can point to the code as evidence that the unethical behavior is limited to a few individuals and not the policy of the company as a whole. Three, referring to a code can encourage followers and leaders to resist unethical group and organizational pressures. Four, a written document can have a direct, positive influence on ethical behavior. Students who sign honor codes, for example, are significantly less likely to plagiarize and cheat on tests.[21] (See Case Study 9.1 for a closer look at the problem of academic cheating.)

CASE STUDY 9.1

Cutting Corners at the University

Academic cheating—claiming someone else's work as your own—has reached epidemic proportions among America's high school and college students. Eighty percent of top high school students admit that they cheat to get ahead. Eighty-seven percent of college students cheat on papers, and 70% have cheated at least once on a test. Cheating appears to be a means to an end, enabling ambitious high school seniors to get into prestigious universities and helping undergraduates get better jobs and to make it into graduate school. Offenders often go unpunished. Those who don't cheat are at a disadvantage and may be seen as naive because they won't manipulate the system.

Many students think of cheating as a personal matter. They don't believe that copying test questions or downloading material from the Internet is a problem for others. However, officials at the Educational Testing Service point out that widespread cheating reduces the value of every degree granted by an institution and dishonest habits established in school can carry over after graduation. There have been reports of police recruits and paramedics using notes and stolen exams to pass CPR and emergency medical tests. Coast Guard personnel have been charged with cheating on pilot license exams.

Alarmed by the rise in academic dishonesty, your college or university president has created an Integrity Task Force to come up with a plan for reducing cheating among students at your school. The president has asked you to serve as a representative on this panel. What suggestions would you make to the rest of the group?

REFERENCES

Cheating is a personal foul. (n.d.). Retrieved September 25, 2001, from www.nocheating .org/adcouncil/research/cheatingbackgrounder.html
Universities retreat in war on cheating. (2000, August 25). Retrieved September 25, 2000, from www.ncpa.org/pi/edu/jan890.html

There's no doubt that a code of ethics can be a vague document that has little impact on how members act. A number of organizations use these statements for purposes of image, not integrity. They want to appear concerned about ethical issues while protecting themselves from litigation. Just having a code on file, as in the case of Enron, doesn't mean that it will be read or used. Nonetheless, creating an ethical statement can be an important first step on the road to organizational integrity. Although a code doesn't guarantee moral improvement, it is hard to imagine an ethical organization without one. Codes can focus attention on important ethical standards, outline expectations, and help individuals act more appropriately. They have the most impact when senior executives make them a priority and follow their provisions while, at the same time, rewarding followers who do the same.

Communication ethicist Richard Johannsen believes that many of the objections to formal codes could be overcome by following these guidelines:[22]

1. Distinguish between ideals and minimum conditions. Identify which parts of the statement are goals to strive for and which are minimal or basic ethical standards.

2. Design the code for ordinary circumstances. Members shouldn't have to demonstrate extraordinary courage or make unusual sacrifices in order to follow the code. Ensure that average employees can follow its guidelines.

3. Use clear, specific language. Important abstract terms like "reasonable," "distort," and "falsify" should be explained and illustrated.

4. Prioritize obligations. Which commitments are most important to the client? the public? the employer? the profession?

5. Protect the larger community. Don't protect the interests of the organization at the expense of the public. Speak to the needs of outside groups.

6. Focus on issues of particular importance to group members. Every organization and profession will face particular ethical dilemmas and temptations. Lawyers, for instance, must balance duties to clients with their responsibilities as officers of the court. Doctors try to provide the best care while HMOs pressure them to keep costs down. The code should address the group's unique moral issues.

7. Stimulate further discussion and modification. Don't file the code away or treat it as the final word on the subject of collective ethics. Use it to spark ethical discussion and modify its provisions when needed.

8. Provide guidance for the entire organization and the profession to which it belongs. Spell out the consequences when the business or nonprofit as a whole acts unethically. Who should respond and how? What role should outside groups (professional associations, accrediting bodies, regulatory agencies) play in responding to the organization's ethical transgressions?

9. Outline the moral principles behind the code. Explain *why* an action is right based on ethical standards (communitarianism, utilitarianism, altruism) like those described in Chapter 5.

10. Encourage widespread input. Draw on all constituencies, including management, union members, and professionals, when developing the provisions of the code.

11. Back the code with enforcement. Create procedures for interpreting the code and applying sanctions. Ethics offices and officers should set up systems for reporting problems, investigating charges, and reaching conclusions. Possible punishments for ethical transgressions include informal warnings, formal reprimands that are entered into employment files, suspensions without pay, and terminations.

An extensive collection of ethics statements is found in *The Executive's Handbook of Model Business Conduct Codes.*[23] Compiler Walter Manley examined 276 firms and over 10,000 pages of material. He divides code provisions into the 19 categories found in Box 9.4. If you're interested in developing or refining a code of ethics, you can use these examples as models.

Box 9.4

Ethics Codes: A Sampler

Walter Manley divides the provisions of ethical codes into the following categories. His typology is a good starting point for any group interested in developing its own ethics statement. Your organization may not need to address all of these issues, but reading his survey should keep you from overlooking any important areas.

- Business dealings and relationships (competition, gifts, lobbying, purchasing)
- International business relationships and practices (foreign investment, record keeping)
- Management responsibilities (travel, duties to shareholders, member development)
- Rights and responsibilities of employers and employees (commitment, rights, privacy)
- Fundamental honesty (laws and criminal acts)
- Protecting proprietary and confidential information (patents, copyrights, security, espionage and sabotage)
- Internal communications
- Equal employment (nondiscrimination, equal employment)
- Sexual and nonsexual harassment
- Substance abuse
- Workplace safety, consumer protection, and product quality (employee safety, product safety and quality, testing)
- Ethics in marketing and advertising
- Compliance with antitrust laws
- Managing computer-based information systems (proper use of computers, computer security, use of software)

(Continued)

Box 9.4   *(Continued)*

- Ethical duties of accountants
- Expense accounts, credit cards, and entertaining
- Insider trading and securities laws
- Corporate citizenship and responsibility to society (community involvement, charitable activities)
- Protecting the environment

Sample Provisions

Proper Use of Computer Systems (Aetna)

Management has the responsibility to ensure that computer resources are used to further Aetna's business. You should not allow computers to be used for amusement or other trivial purposes because that is a misuse of a valuable company asset. Private benefit or gain is strictly prohibited. Misappropriation, destruction, misuses, abuse, or unauthorized modification of computer resources are offenses for which dismissal will be considered. (Manley, 1991, pp. 159–160)

Proper Marketing Practices (Lockheed)

All marketing and related practices that infringe on business ethics or could cause embarrassment to Lockheed are strictly forbidden, and violations will not be tolerated. Employees are responsible for adhering to ethical behavior, regardless of any perceived justification for deliberate infractions. (Manley, 1991, pp. 144–145)

Health and Safety in the Workplace (PPG)

Assuring the health and safety of PPG personnel is a top corporate priority, worldwide.

An important component of this strategy is assuring that both our own personnel and those living near us are clearly informed about the nature of the materials used at our facility.

It is PPG's goal to completely eliminate the incidence of work-related illness or injury. To achieve that goal, the Company has developed a series of emergency response procedures as well as corporatewide policies related to the safe operation of PPG's equipment, the proper handling of materials, limits on exposure to potentially hazardous substances, and other matters affecting employee health and safety on the job. (Manley, 1991, pp. 133–134)

SOURCE: Manley, W. W., II. (1991). *Executive's handbook of model business conduct codes.* Englewood Cliffs, NJ: Prentice Hall.

Continuous Ethical Improvement

THE NEED FOR CONTINUOUS ETHICAL LEARNING

Total quality management (TQM) is a buzzword at thousands of firms in Japan, the United States, and other countries. TQM describes a continuous improvement process designed to reduce product defects, improve response times, and eliminate waste. The TQM movement is founded on the belief that organizations, like individuals, learn through experience, observation, training, and other means. Although all organizations learn, some learn faster and more efficiently than others, a characteristic that gives them a competitive edge. Those that learn quickly produce better products in less time while responding to demographic shifts and technological advances. High-tech firms are particularly aware of the importance of rapid learning. They scramble to stay ahead in the development of memory chips, cell phones, software, and other products.

Organizations ought to be as concerned about continuous ethical improvement, what I'll call "total ethical management" (TEM), as they are about improving products and services.[24] Three factors should encourage ongoing ethical learning: risk, lingering ethical weaknesses, and change. Let's take a closer look at each.

Risk. As we've seen, serious ethical misbehavior can threaten the very survival of an organization. Accounting fraud is a quick path to corporate bankruptcy; malfeasance in government agencies leads to budget reductions; contributions dry up when the leaders of social service agencies and religious groups live like royalty. Managerial misconduct (whether motivated by poor judgment or criminal intent) is now the leading cause of business crises.[25] No type of organization, be it religious, humanitarian, business, government, or military, is exempt from ethical failure.

On a more positive note, there is evidence to suggest that moral organizations can be extremely effective. The Body Shop, Ben & Jerry's, Tom's of Maine, the Herman Miller Company, and ServiceMaster are highly successful as well as highly ethical. Shared values can increase productivity by focusing the efforts of employees and by encouraging supervisors to empower their subordinates. Having a good reputation attracts customers, clients, and investors and forms the basis for long-term relationships with outside constituencies.[26] Merck & Company, profiled at the end of Chapter 3, is one example of a successful company that has prospered while helping others.

Ethical weakness. Organizations can never claim to have "arrived" when it comes to ethical development. There will always be room for improvement. In addition, the same inconsistencies that plague individual leaders are found in the climate of entire organizations. Starbucks, for example, has been praised for its commitment to its employees (they make higher-than-average wages and part-timers are covered by the company's health insurance plan). However, activists complain that the firm doesn't pay coffee growers enough and that valuable rain forest has been destroyed in order to grow its coffee beans.

Change. Organizational leaders must recognize that they operate in constantly shifting environments. Competitors, suppliers, government regulations, and public tastes are always changing. Each change, in turn, brings new ethical challenges. Take the case of genetically altered foods. Opponents are raising moral objections to these products. They worry about their safety and their impact on the environment. Critics believe that biotechnology companies are putting the health of consumers, as well as the future of native plants and animals, at risk. Leaders of biotech companies must now publicly acknowledge and respond to these arguments.

Like the environments in which they live, organizations themselves are in a constant process of transformation. New employees join, divisions reorganize, companies become publicly owned, products and services are added or dropped. Once again, each change alters the ethical landscape. Consider the impact of a changing workforce, for instance. As more women and minorities join an organization, leaders need to focus more attention on diversity issues. They must consider such questions as "How do we make diverse individuals feel like valued team members?" "How do we ensure that everyone has an equal chance of being promoted, regardless of background?" "How far do we go to meet the needs of subgroups (working mothers, nonnative speakers, and religious minorities)?

ENHANCING ORGANIZATIONAL ETHICAL LEARNING

Like other forms of organizational learning, ethical development is more likely under the right conditions. Organization development consultants Anthony DiBella and Edwin Nevis identify 10 practices that enhance organizational learning. Taken together, these elements, called *facilitating factors,* determine the learning potential of an organization.[27] DiBella and Nevis are most interested in the kinds of learning that improve quality. Nonetheless, the same factors also spur continuous ethical improvement.

1. Scanning imperative. Ethical learners look outside the immediate group for information. They continually scan the environment for emerging ethical issues that might affect the organization in the future. They monitor newspapers and trade journals to identify questionable industry practices and consider the ethical impact of entering a new market or introducing a new product (see our earlier discussion of genetically altered foods). In addition, continuous learners take a close look at what other organizations do to prevent and to manage ethical problems. Organizational learning theorists refer to this process as benchmarking. In benchmarking, groups identify outstanding organizations and isolate the practices that make them so effective. They then adapt these practices to their own organizations.[28]

Information on effective ethical practices can be found in a variety of sources. You may want to draw on these as you identify ethical benchmarks. Managerial texts and business ethics books include examples of moral and immoral behavior, sample ethics codes, and case studies. There are also two academic journals—the *Journal of Business Ethics* and *Business Ethics Quarterly*—devoted exclusively to ethics in the workplace.

2. Performance gap. A performance gap is the distance between where an organization is and where it would like to be. Martin Marietta is one example of an organization that recognized its ethical failings and took steps to correct them. The defense contractor, under investigation for improper billings in the mid-1980s, responded by highlighting its code of conduct, starting an ethics training program, developing a system for reporting ethical concerns, and rewarding executives for moral behavior. As a result, the company improved its compliance with federal regulations and reduced the number of ethical complaints filed by employees. The firm also prevented a number of potential crises stemming from bad management, safety problems, and discrimination.

Some organizations turn their moral failures into case studies. At West Point, Army instructors use the massacre of civilians at My Lai during the Vietnam War to teach ethical principles to cadets. Organizations don't have to wait for an ethical disaster to strike to identify performance gaps, of course. Potential problems can be identified through surveys (see below), ethics hotlines, and focus groups.

3. Concern for measurement. Organizational priorities are reflected in what leaders pay attention to. For instance, executives at a delivery company that prides itself on on-time service will reward those who reach delivery targets and discipline those who don't. In a similar fashion, followers won't take ethics seriously unless leaders measure ethical performance and then use that information to improve ethical climate. Ethics audits (surveys that measure employee perceptions of values and corporate behavior) and focus groups track the moral climate of the group as a whole. Ethics items on performance appraisal forms provide data on individual performance.

4. Organizational curiosity. Learning organizations are populated with individuals who act like experimental scientists or curious children. They tinker with products and systems, continually trying out new ideas. At Wal-Mart, for example, there are some 250 minor experiments being conducted on any given day. Ethical learning organizations demonstrate the same creative spirit. They don't hesitate to try out new strategies for better identifying and resolving ethical issues. They experiment with better ways to track ethical complaints, to identify ethical problems, and to encourage adherence to federal regulations.

5. *Climate of openness.* Openness refers, first of all, to the free flow of information. In open organizations, leaders make a conscious effort to reduce barriers of all kinds between individuals and units. In this environment, new ideas are more likely to develop and then to be shared throughout the group as a whole. Learning leaders put few restrictions on what can be shared, rotate individuals between divisions, set up forums for sharing ideas, and form multidepartment task forces. In addition, they create formal (companywide forums, idea fairs) and informal (employee cafeterias, celebrations) settings where members can meet and share information about projects, procedures, and ethics.

Openness also refers to the type of communication that occurs between group members. In learning organizations, individuals engage in dialogue (see Chapter 8). They recognize that they can glean important information from anyone regardless of status. When they interact, members treat others as equals and are more interested in understanding than in being understood. They work together to create shared meaning.

Ethical dialogue can be facilitated through designated dialogue sessions. In these gatherings, members meet to engage in open communication about moral questions. Dialogue sessions work best when attendees complete assigned readings in advance, meet in a quiet setting, convene at a round table or in a circle to emphasize equality, and suspend their opinions and judgments.[29]

6. *Continuous education.* Continuous education reflects the organizationwide commitment to the never ending process of learning. Organizations that value learning will make it a priority everywhere, not just in the training department. These groups (a) support on-the-job training (such as when an experienced worker helps a new hire resolve an ethical problem), (b) hold retreats, (c) encourage networking and dialogue, and (d) send individuals to conferences, classes, and workshops to learn more about ethics.

7. *Operational variety.* There is more than one way to reach work goals. By using a variety of strategies, an organization can better adapt to unforeseen problems. At one mutual fund group, managers use three different approaches to making investment choices. Employees of Semco, a Brazilian firm, decide if they would rather work for a straight salary, be paid according to incentives, or operate as independent contractors. Innovative organizations also set up entirely new operations to try out alternative procedures. This strategy allows them to test unproven ideas without having to give up their current systems.

Similar tactics can nurture ethical improvement. Organizations may use different types of ethics training or use a variety of media (video, forums, bulletin boards, newsletters) to communicate ethics messages to members. They may also want to conduct an "ethical experiment" in one location before making wholesale changes. For example, a manufacturer might give work teams in one location more freedom to make ethical choices. If these groups adhere to organizational values, the corporation might empower all work teams to enforce moral standards.

8. Multiple advocates. New ideas aren't widely adopted unless championed by significant numbers of people throughout an organization. Effective champions are respected individuals who promote an idea at the same time they model its use. The Motorola Corporation identified 300 individuals and enlisted them as advocates in a quality improvement campaign. Continuous ethical improvement requires the same type of support. Influential leaders of every organizational rank must support ethics initiatives and put them into action.

9. Involved leadership. Leaders play a critical role in driving continuous ethical improvement. The key is hands-on involvement. Involved leaders are students. They encourage the learning of others by first learning themselves. If they want to promote diversity, for instance, they are the first to take diversity training. They continue to be involved in the learning process by interacting with followers, visiting job sites, and holding forums on ethical issues.

10. Systems perspective. The systems perspective refers to seeing the big picture, to recognizing that organizations are highly interdependent. Ongoing ethical learners try to anticipate the ethical implications of their decisions for those in other divisions. A big-picture leader may be tempted to "dump" an incompetent employee onto another department but recognizes that this strategy benefits her unit at the expense of another. The productivity of the organization as a whole suffers because this ineffective individual is still on the payroll. With this in mind, she confronts the problem employee immediately.

The open communication climate described earlier facilitates systems thinking. Communicating across boundaries helps members (a) develop a better understanding of the ethical problems faced by other units, and (b) learn how their actions may result in moral complications for others.

Implications and Applications

- Creating a positive ethical climate is one of the most important challenges you'll face when you take on a leadership role in an organization.
- Organizations have varying ethical orientations that affect how they make ethical choices and respond to ethical change initiatives.

- Integrity develops through clearly communicated values and commitments, leaders who are committed to these values, application of the values to routine decisions, systems and structures that support organizational commitments, and members who are equipped to make wise ethical choices.
- Don't confuse compliance with integrity. Compliance protects an organization from regulation and public criticism but has little impact on day-to-day operations. Integrity is at the center of an organization's activities, influencing every type of decision and activity.
- Pay close attention to how your organization achieves its goals. Failure to do so will create anomie and undermine ethical performance.
- Reinforce ethical commitments in your organization through the design of monetary and nonmonetary reward systems, performance and evaluation processes, and allocation of decision-making authority.
- Shared values are essential to any healthy ethical climate. Help your organization identify these values through the use of task forces, employee meetings, and other means.
- Useful codes of ethics can play an important role in shaping ethical climate. Make sure they define and illustrate important terms and address the problems faced by the members of your particular organization. View ethics statements as discussion starters, not as the final word on the topic of organizational morality.
- Risk, lingering ethical weaknesses, and constant change create a demand for continuous organizational ethical development.
- The ethical learning capacity of your organization will be determined by the presence or absence of such factors as ethical benchmarking, measurement, open communication, organizational curiosity, and systems thinking.

For Further Exploration, Challenge, and Self-Assessment

1. Analyze the ethical climate of your organization. In your paper, consider the following questions:
   How would you classify its ethical orientation?
   What stage of moral development is it in?
   Overall, would you characterize the climate as positive or negative? Why?
   What factors shape the moral atmosphere?
   What role have leaders played in its formation and maintenance?
   Does the organization consider both means and ends?
   How does the group's structure reinforce (or fail to reinforce) espoused values and ethical behavior?
   What inconsistencies do you note?

2. Discuss each of the following statements in a group or, as an alternative, argue for and against each proposition in a formal debate. Your instructor will set the rules and time limits. Refer to Box 8.2 (Argumentativeness Scale) and Box 8.3 (Common Fallacies) in the previous chapter for more information on constructing effective arguments.

Pro or con: Organizations are less ethical now than they were 10 years ago.

Pro or con: Formal codes of ethics do more harm than good.

Pro or con: Ethical businesses are more profitable over the long term.

Pro or con: Organizational values can't be developed; they must be uncovered or discovered instead.

Pro or con: An organization's purpose has to be inspirational.

Pro or con: An organization can change everything except its core values and purpose.

3. Compare and contrast an organization that has a climate of integrity with one that pursues ethical compliance.

4. Describe a time when you experienced anomie in an organization. What factors led to your feelings of powerlessness and alienation? How did anomie influence your behavior?

5. Develop a shared set of values for your class using strategies presented in the chapter.

6. Evaluate an ethical code based on chapter guidelines. What are its strengths and weaknesses? How useful would it be to members of the organization? How could the code be improved? What can we learn from this statement?

7. Design a total ethics management (TEM) program for your organization that incorporates the 10 facilitating factors that make up ethical learning potential.

CASE STUDY 9.2

Chapter End Case: Agenda for Change at the Air Force Academy

U.S. service academies attract many of the nation's top high school students who hope to become the next generation of military leaders. Cadets are nominated by members of their congressional delegations and must be fit as well as smart. Once enrolled, they combine strenuous physical training with a demanding academic program. Plebes pledge to follow stringent honor codes that prohibit such behaviors as drinking, drug use, cheating, and breaking curfew.

Unfortunately, would-be leaders at the service academies don't always live up to their lofty reputations or follow the codes of ethics of their institutions. Nowhere is this more apparent than at the Air Force Academy. Over the past decade, crime at the academy has reached an all-time high. Cadets have been punished for a variety of offenses ranging from ATM theft to drug dealing. The most serious allegations involve rapes of female cadets by their male colleagues. In 2000, current and former female cadets approached Colorado congressional representatives and the Air Force with complaints that academy officers mishandled charges of sexual assault. Not only did officials fail to prosecute the rapists, these women claimed, but those who filed reports were punished for minor rules infractions. Investigations were shoddy, with complainants facing retribution from their immediate superiors and shunning by fellow plebes. In some cases, the victims dropped out of school while the offenders were promoted.

Allegations of widespread sexual crimes against women sparked three investigations and led to the replacement of four top academy officials, including Superintendent General John Dallager and Commander of Cadets, Brigadier General Taco Gilbert. Investigators report the following:

1. The academy has been a "hostile" environment for women since female cadets were first admitted in 1981. The academy is male dominated, shows little concern for the welfare of female officers, and seldom puts women in leadership positions. Retention rates for female cadets are lower, even though women on average have higher grades than their male counterparts. For years, a sign reading "Bring Me Men" greeted visitors to the school.

2. The problem of sexual assault is widespread. Fifty-six cases were investigated in the past 10 years with many more going unreported. Forty cadets have been punished for sexual misconduct. At least 60 women have complained about rapes and assaults to lawyers and members of Congress.

3. Changes introduced after a gang rape in 1993, which were designed to make it easier for women to come forward after an attack, may have had the opposite effect. Under this system, victims were guaranteed confidentiality unless they filed a formal complaint. Some counselors advised against filing reports for fear that victims

would find their Air Force careers cut short. As a result, the number of rape cases was underreported. Top officials were unaware that abuse was so widespread.

4. Academy legal officials lacked a clear understanding of what constitutes sexual assault.

The Air Force is taking a number of steps called the "Agenda for Change" to root out sexual crime at the academy and to restore the school's luster. In addition to removing top officials and instituting the policy that protected the confidentiality of victims, the academy has taken down the offensive Bring Me Men sign and renewed its emphasis on character. Minor infractions are now covered by a "blanket amnesty." This means that, for example, a victim won't be punished for drinking if the rape took place at a drinking party. Counselors are given better training, and cadets attend 4 days of briefings on military law, gender sensitivity, sexual assault, and honor codes. Colonel Debra Gray was named vice commandant, making her the first woman to occupy a top spot at the academy.

If the past is any indication, the Agenda for Change faces an uphill battle. Machismo remains deeply rooted in academy culture; layers of hierarchy make it difficult for top officers to keep in touch with what is happening in the ranks. Forcing women to reveal their identities when victimized may make it less likely that they will report abuse.

DISCUSSION PROBES

1. Should we expect cadets at service academies to behave more ethically than students at other colleges or universities? Is such an expectation realistic?

2. Cadets at the academy are in violation of the honor code if they fail to report violators. Is this requirement ethical?

3. Do you blame top leaders for being unaware of the extent of the sexual assault problem on campus? Why or why not?

4. Will the Agenda for Change significantly reduce sexual crime at the academy? What additional steps should the school take, if any?

5. What leadership lessons do you take from this case?

REFERENCES

Air force's top officers say academy problems endemic. (2003, June 2). *The Colorado Springs Gazette*. Retrieved July 21, 2003, from http:web12.epnet.com/citation

Crime by Air Force Academy cadets at a 10-year high. (2002, January 27). *The Colorado Springs Gazette*. Retrieved July 21, 2003, from http://web12.epnet.com/citation

Janofsky, M. (2003, March 8). Top Air Force officer, at academy, issues warning. *The New York Times*, p. A13.

Janofsky, M. (2003, April 1). Academy's top general apologizes to cadets. *The New York Times*, p. A14.

O'Driscoll, P., & Kenworthy, T. (2003, June 27). Cadets march into new academy. *USA Today*, p. 6A.

Schemo, D. J. (2003, May 22). Women at West Point face tough choices on assaults. *The New York Times,* p. A16.

Schemo, D. J. (2003, June 7). Policy shift on handling of complaints at academy. *The New York Times,* p. A10.

Schemo, D. J. (2003, July 12). Ex-superintendent of Air Force Academy is demoted in wake of rape scandal. *The New York Times,* p. A7.

Schemo, D. J. (2003, July 13). Academy cadet chief backs rape report disclosures. *The New York Times,* p. A16.

Study concluded Air Force Academy hostile to women for 25 years. (June 16, 2003). *The Colorado Springs Gazette.* Retrieved July 21, 2003, from http://epnet.com/citation

CASE STUDY 9.3

Chapter End Case: The Fall of Arthur Andersen

Arthur Andersen was the most respected accounting firm in America for much of its history. Founder Andersen (who started the company in 1913) and his successor Leonard Spacek (who led the firm during the 1950s) didn't hesitate to drop clients they thought were violating generally accepted accounting principles. When railroads refused to depreciate their rails, ties, and other property, Andersen resigned all of its railroad accounts except for two firms that agreed to change their accounting practices. The company also escaped the scandals of the savings and loan crisis because it refused to work for S & Ls that artificially boosted their earnings.

Andersen's reputation for integrity was shattered by a series of scandals that began in the 1990s. In case after case, Andersen clients—Waste Management, Boston Chicken, Qwest, Global Crossing, Sunbeam, WorldCom, the Baptist Foundation of Arizona—were found guilty of accounting fraud. Andersen itself (referred to as "the Firm" by employees) was convicted of obstruction of justice in June 2002 for shredding Enron accounting documents. Shortly thereafter, the Firm's managing partners dissolved the corporation.

Barbara Ley Toffler explores the reasons why Arthur Andersen went from ethical paragon to ethical pariah in her book *Final Accounting* (2003). Toffler is uniquely qualified to comment on the ethical climate at Andersen. She was a professor of business ethics at Harvard and an independent ethics consultant before she took a job as partner-in-charge of Ethics & Responsible Business Practices consulting services at Andersen. She spent 4 frustrating years with the firm (1995–1999) before resigning to return to teaching.

Toffler puts much of the blame for Andersen's collapse on the company's culture. Arthur Andersen was known for carefully shaping new employees to the requirements of the Firm. New employees or "androids" were chosen for their ability to play by the rules and were given weeks of intensive training at a special facility near the company's Chicago headquarters. They were expected to follow a strict dress code (even casual days were carefully regulated), to behave professionally (no dining at fast-food restaurants), and to follow such rules as help others and don't stand out. Lower-level employees could expect to be dismissed or humiliated if they challenged their superiors.

Toffler notes that Andersen's hierarchical, lockstep culture was functional when managed by ethical leaders. Andersen clients all over the world could expect the same high-quality, reputable service. Unfortunately, when the Firm's values and leadership changed for the worse, the "don't question" attitude at Andersen led to disaster. Partners shifted their focus from serving investors by producing reliable numbers to generating as much income as possible. In this new climate, success depended on racking up as many billable hours as possible. Employees competed with one another to sell potential customers a wide variety of consulting services (tax advice, surveys, business plans). Often these services were overpriced or poorly done. Instead of "firing" companies who cooked their books, Andersen auditors ignored serious violations in order to hold on to lucrative clients like Enron and WorldCom. Androids didn't question the decisions of partners because to do so would cost them their jobs.

Andersen might still be operating had strong leaders with good values emerged to guide the Firm back to its ethical roots. Exercising forceful leadership is more difficult in a worldwide partnership (where individuals have equal voting rights) than in the typical corporation. Nonetheless, Arthur Andersen and Leonard Spacek had succeeded in unifying the Firm behind one moral vision that included core values like integrity and serving the public. During most of the 1990s, however, Andersen leaders like Steve Samek and Joe Berardino focused instead on battling the competition and raising revenues.

Toffler and other insiders warned of possible risks and outlined steps to address potential scandals. Their concerns were largely ignored; no one at Andersen stepped forward to make the tough decisions that could have saved the Firm.

> Looking back, I think this was a critical juncture for the Firm, a point at which great leadership could truly have made a difference. Yet I also acknowledge the other pressures on the partners. Becoming a tougher audit firm might have meant losing some major clients, and that would have had a direct financial impact on their livelihood. So the leaders did what, unfortunately, many leaders do when times are tough: They punted the ball. They released a few warning memos and essentially crossed their fingers and hoped everything would work out. It didn't—not for the Firm, not for its thousands of worldwide employees, not for its clients, and not for the investors, who trusted that the numbers they read were accurate. Yes, it would have taken a special leader to stand up to all of these groups and his own partners and acknowledge that something was spinning out of control. Such leaders are indeed rare. At Arthur Andersen, they didn't exist.[30]

DISCUSSION PROBES

1. Could the Firm have been saved from ruin if the right leader had emerged? Why or why not?

2. What were the signs of an unhealthy ethical climate at Andersen?

3. As an ethics consultant, what suggestions would you have made to the partners at Arthur Andersen?

4. How much are lower-level androids to blame for what happened at Arthur Andersen?

5. Can you think of examples of other organizations that failed when their leaders decided to ignore ethical risks and hoped instead that they would go away?

6. What leadership lessons do you draw from this case?

REFERENCE

Toffler, B. L., & Reingold, J. (2003). *Final accounting: Ambition, greed, and the fall of Arthur Andersen.* New York: Broadway Books.

Notes

1. Robinson, S. I., & Bennett, R. (1995). A typology of deviant workplace behaviors: A multidimensional scaling study. *Academy of Management Journal, 38,* 555–572; Ashforth, B. E., & Lee, R. T. (1990). Defensive behavior in organizations: A preliminary model. *Human Relations, 43,* 621–648; Grover, S. L. (1993). Lying, deceit, and subterfuge: A model of dishonesty in the workplace. *Organization Science, 4,* 478–495.

2. Mumford, M. D., Gessner, T. L., Connelly, M. S., O'Conner, J. A., & Clifton, T. (1993). Leadership and destructive acts: Individual and situational influences. *Leadership Quarterly, 4,* 115–147.

3. Pacanowsky, M. E., & O'Donnell-Trujillo, N. (1983). Organizational communication as cultural performance. *Communication Monographs, 50,* 126–147.

4. Victor, B., & Cullen, J. B. (1988). The organizational bases of ethical work climates. *Administrative Science Quarterly, 33,* 101–125.

5. Victor, B., & Cullen, J. B. (1990). A theory and measure of ethical climate in organizations. In W. C. Frederick & L. E. Preston (Eds.), *Business ethics: Research issues and empirical studies* (pp. 77–97). Greenwich, CT: JAI; Victor, B., Cullen, J., & Boynton, A. (1993). Toward a general framework of organizational meaning systems. In C. Conrad (Ed.), *The ethical nexus* (pp. 193–215). Norwood, NJ: Ablex.

6. A number of authors use the term "integrity" to describe ideal managers and organizations. See, for example, the following:

Pearson, G. (1995). *Integrity in organizations: An alternative business ethic.* London: McGraw-Hill.
Petrick, J. A. (1998). Building organizational integrity and quality with the four Ps: Perspectives, paradigms, processes, and principles. In M. Schminke (Ed.), *Managerial ethics: Moral management of people and processes* (pp. 115–131). Mahwah, NJ: Erlbaum.
Solomon, R. C. (1992). *Ethics and excellence: Cooperation and integrity in business.* New York: Oxford University Press.
Srivastva, S. (Ed.). (1988). *Executive integrity.* San Francisco: Jossey-Bass.

7. Kramer, R. M., & Tyler, T. R. (Eds.). (1996). *Trust in organizations: Frontiers of theory and research.* Thousand Oaks, CA: Sage.

8. Paine, L. S. (1996, March-April). Managing for organizational integrity. *Harvard Business Review,* 106–117.

9. Weaver, G. R., Trevino, L. K., & Cochran, P. L. (1999). Integrated and decoupled corporate social performance: Management commitments, external pressures, and corporate ethics practices. *Academy of Management Journal, 42,* 539–552.

10. Weaver, G. R., Trevino, L. K., & Cochran, P. L. (1999). Corporate ethics practices in the mid-1990s: An empirical study of the Fortune 1000. *Journal of Business Ethics, 18,* 283–294.

11. Lindsay, R. M., & Irvine, V. B. (1996). Instilling ethical behavior in organizations: A survey of Canadian companies. *Journal of Business Ethics, 15,* 393–407.

12. Reidenbach, R. E., & Robin, D. P. (1991). A conceptual model of corporate moral development. *Journal of Business Ethics, 10,* 273–284.

13. Cadbury, A. (1987, September-October). Ethical managers make their own rules. *Harvard Business Review,* 69–73.

14. Cohen, D. V. (1993). Creating and maintaining ethical work climates: Anomie in the workplace and implications for managing change. *Business Ethics Quarterly, 3,* 343–358.

15. James, H. S. (2000). Reinforcing ethical decision making through organizational structure. *Journal of Business Ethics, 28,* 43–58.

16. Useem, M. (1998). *The leadership moment.* New York: Times Business, ch. 7.

17. Collins, J. C., & Porras, J. I. (1996, September-October). Building your company's vision. *Harvard Business Review,* 66.

18. Kuczmarski, S. S., & Kuczmarski, T. D. (1995). *Values-based leadership.* Englewood Cliffs, NJ: Prentice Hall.

19. For more information on the pros and cons of codes of conduct, see the following:

Darley, J. M. (2001). The dynamics of authority influence in organizations and the unintended action consequences. In J. M. Darley, D. M. Messick, & T. R. Tyler (Eds.), *Social influences on ethical behavior in organizations* (pp. 37–52). Mahwah, NJ: Erlbaum.

Mathews, M. C. (1990). Codes of ethics: Organizational behavior and misbehavior. In W. C. Frederick & L. E. Preston (Eds.), *Business ethics: Research issues and empirical studies* (pp. 99–122). Greenwich, CT: JAI.

Metzger, M., Dalton, D. R., & Hill, J. W. (1993). The organization of ethics and the ethics of organizations: The case for expanded organizational ethics audits. *Business Ethics Quarterly, 3*(1), 27–43.

Trevino, L. K., Butterfield, K. D., & McCabe, D. L. (1998). The ethical context in organizations: Influences on employee attitudes and behaviors. *Business Ethics Quarterly, 8,* 447–476.

Wright, D. K. (1993). Enforcement dilemma: Voluntary nature of public relations codes. *Public Relations Review, 19,* 13–20.

20. Countryman, A. (2001. December 7). Leadership key ingredient in ethics recipe, experts say. *The Chicago Tribune,* pp. B1, B6.

21. McCabe, D., & Trevino, K. L. (1993). Academic dishonesty: Honor codes and other contextual influences. *Journal of Higher Education, 64,* 522–569.

22. Johannsen, R. L. (2002). *Ethics in human communication* (5th ed.). Prospect Heights, IL: Waveland Press, ch. 10.

23. Manley, W. W., II. (1991). *Executive's handbook of model business conduct codes.* Englewood Cliffs, NJ: Prentice Hall.

24. For more information on the link between learning and organizational integrity see the following:

Kolb, D. A. (1988). Integrity, advanced professional development, and learning. In S. Srivastva (Ed.), *Executive integrity: The search for high human values in organizational life.* San Francisco, CA: Jossey-Bass.

Petrick, J. A. (1998). Building organizational integrity and quality with the four Ps: Perspectives, paradigms, processes, and principles. In M. Schminke (Ed.), *Managerial ethics: Moral management of people and processes* (pp. 115–131). Mahwah, NJ: Erlbaum.

25. Millar, D. P., & Irvine, R. B. (1996, November). *Exposing the errors: An examination of the nature of organizational crises.* Paper presented to the meeting of the National Communication Association, San Diego, CA.

26. Paine, L. S. (1997). *Cases in leadership, ethics, and organizational integrity: A strategic perspective.* Boston, MA: Irwin McGraw-Hill, pt. 1.

27. DiBella, A., & Nevis, E. C. (1998). *How organizations learn: An integrated strategy for building learning capability.* San Francisco: Jossey-Bass; DiBella, A. J., Nevis, E. C., & Gould, J. M. (1996). Organizational learning as a core capability. In B. Moingeon & A. Edmondson (Eds.), *Organizational learning and competitive advantage* (pp. 38–55). London: Sage.

28. Camp, R. C. (1989). *Benchmarking: The search for industry best practices that lead to superior performance.* Milwaukee, WI: Quality Press.

29. Brown, J. (1995). Dialogue: Capacities and stories. In S. Chawla & J. Renesch (Eds.), *Learning organizations: Developing cultures for tomorrow's workplace* (pp. 153–164). Portland, OR: Productivity Press.

30. Toffler, B. L., & Reingold, J. (2003). *Final accounting: Ambition, greed, and the fall of Arthur Andersen.* New York: Broadway Books, pp. 167–168.

10

Meeting the Ethical Challenges of Cultural Diversity

Human beings draw close to one another by their common nature, but habits and customs keep them apart.

Confucian saying

What's Ahead

In this chapter, we examine the problems and opportunities posed by cultural differences. Mastering the ethical challenges of leadership in a global society begins with acknowledging the dark side of globalization and recognizing the impact of ethical diversity. Leaders must then overcome ethnocentrism and prejudice, understand the relationship between cultural values and ethical choices, seek synergistic solutions, and find ethical common ground.

The Dark Side of Globalization

Globalization may be the most important trend of the twenty-first century. We now live in a global economy shaped by multinational corporations, international travel, the Internet, immigration, and satellite communication systems. Supporters of globalization point to its benefits. Free trade produces new wealth by opening up international markets, they argue. At the same time, the costs of goods and services drop. Cheaper, faster means of communication and travel encourage unprecedented cross-cultural contact.[1] The greater flow of information and people puts pressure on repressive governments to reform.

Critics of globalization paint a much bleaker picture. They note that global capitalism encourages greed rather than concern for others. Ethical and spiritual values have been overshadowed by the profit motive. Local cultural traditions and the environment are being destroyed in the name of economic growth. The gap between the rich and poor keeps growing.[2]

Debate over whether the benefits of globalization outweigh its costs is not likely to end anytime soon. This much is clear, however: as leaders, we need to give serious consideration to the dark side of the global society in order to help prevent ethical abuse. With that in mind, let's take a closer look at how leaders cast the shadows I outlined in Chapter 1 in a global environment.

THE GLOBAL SHADOW OF POWER

In the modern world, a leader's power is no longer limited by national boundaries. Increasing interdependence brought about by the integration of markets, communication systems, computers, and financial institutions means that the actions of one leader or nation can have a dramatic impact on the rest of the world. Pulitzer Prize–winning foreign affairs correspondent Thomas Friedman points to the collapse of Thailand's currency in 1997 as an example of just how integrated the international economy has become.[3] When the value of the Thai baht plunged, Southeast Asia went into a deep recession that drove down world commodity prices. The Russian economy, which is heavily based on exports of oil and other commodities, then collapsed. Investors sold off their holdings to cover their losses in Southeast Asia and Russia. This massive sell-off forced the Brazilian government to raise interest rates as high as 40% to retain economic capital. Some frightened investors sought safety in U.S. treasury bonds, driving down interest rates and undermining the financial standing of many U.S. mutual funds and banks.

Ethical leadership in the multinational context must take into account the potential, far-ranging consequences of every choice. Shadows fall when leaders forget this fact. For example, the U.S. government's decision to relax mileage requirements for trucks and automobiles increases gas consumption, contributing to global warming. Saudi Arabia's unwillingness to ban terrorist groups contributed to the World Trade Center and Bali bombings.

Concentration of power is a by-product of globalization that increases the likelihood of abuse. The United States is a case in point. Critics accuse the world's only superpower of throwing its political and military weight around. Corporations also wield great influence in the global marketplace. If Wal-Mart were a nation, for example, its economy would rank fifteenth among free-market democracies.[4] Other retailers must reduce wages and other expenses in order to compete with this economic giant.

THE GLOBAL SHADOW OF PRIVILEGE

As noted earlier, globalization appears to be increasing, not decreasing, the gap between the haves and have-nots. Between 1960 and 1995, the income gap between the world's richest and poorest people more than doubled.[5] So far, leaders of wealthy nations have been more interested in promoting the sale of their goods than in opening up their markets to poorer countries (see Box 10.1). Privileged nations also consume more, which leads to environmental damage in the form of logging, oil drilling, and mineral extraction. This damage has a disproportionate impact on the disadvantaged. Whereas the wealthy can move to cleaner areas, they cannot. Instead, poor citizens must deal with the loss of hunting and fishing grounds, clean air, and safe water.

Leaders will continue to cast shadows unless they take steps to make globalization more equitable. To do so, they must (a) put the common (international) good above private gain or self or national interest, (b) create a global economy that recognizes the interconnectedness of all peoples as well as the importance of sustaining the environment, (c) practice restraint and moderation in the consumption of goods, and (d) seek justice and compassion by helping marginalized groups.[6]

CASE STUDY 10.1

Rich Nations, Poor Nations: The Ethics of Farm Subsidies

Since the World Trade Organization (WTO) was founded in 1995 to create international trade agreements, poor nations have sparred with their wealthy trading partners over the generous farm subsidies given out by the governments of the European Union, Japan, the United States, and other developed countries. Farm subsidies in the world's industrialized nations totaled $320 billion in 2002, compared with $50 billion given out in assistance to Third World countries. Government aid enables growers from industrialized lands to sell their rice, cotton, corn, sugar, and other products at below cost. Farmers in poorer regions can't compete even though their labor costs are much lower. Wealthy countries also impose high tariffs and quotas that close off their lucrative markets to their poorer neighbors.

Conflict over agricultural aid is the major obstacle to reaching a global trade treaty—the long-term objective of the WTO. Talks at the group's 2003 meeting in Cancun, Mexico, collapsed over the farm aid issue. Developing countries, including Brazil, China, and India, banded together to lobby against farm subsidies and high tariffs, but encountered resistance from wealthy nations anxious to reduce trade deficits and to protect their own farmers. Both sides were bitter about the tone of the failed negotiations. Third World nations vowed not to take any more bullying from developed countries; U.S. trade representative Robert Zoellick accused some developing countries of using "tactics of inflexibility and inflammatory rhetoric" (Carl, 2003, p. C1).

Poorer nations appear to occupy the moral high ground when it comes to the farm aid debate. Subsidies, tariffs, and quotas have driven hundreds of thousands of peasants off the land, contributing to urban sprawl, poverty, hunger, and death. According to former Philippines president Fidel Ramos, "Poor countries cannot afford to be on the short end of this deal for long. People are in real need. People are dying" (Harvesting poverty, 2003, p. 10). Editors at the *New York Times* called current international trade agreements "rigged" and "morally depraved" (Harvesting poverty, 2003, p. 10).

There is still hope for an international agreement on reducing farm subsidies. The 146 members of the WTO were reviewing such a proposal when their talks in Cancun broke down. Governments of rich nations, however, face considerable pressure to continue their generous agricultural policies. Farmers make up a small percentage of the populations of industrialized nations (2.5% in the United States, for example) but remain a potent political force. They are a well-organized, vocal minority supported by large agribusinesses that sell them goods and services and market their products. After the failed Cancun conference, the EU trade commissioner pointed out just how hard it is to convince wealthy farm producers to accept lower subsidies: "The benefits of trade opening are spread over millions of people who don't know it. The costs of trade opening are concentrated over a few constituencies who have a lot of complaining capacity" (Carl, 2003, C3).

DISCUSSION PROBES

1. Are the farm subsidies, tariffs, and import quotas of wealthy countries "morally depraved?" Why or why not?

2. Is there any ethical justification for keeping high farm subsidies?

3. Should leaders in industrialized nations abandon attempts to protect their farmers? What might happen to them if they did?

4. How do you determine if and when the needs of domestic groups should take priority over the needs of people of other countries?

5. Do you think that poor and wealthy countries can reach an agreement on farm trade policies? What needs to happen for this to occur?

6. What leadership lessons do you draw from this case?

REFERENCES

Becker, E., & Thompson, G. (2003, September 11). Poorer nations plead farmers' case at trade talks. *The New York Times,* p. A3.

Carl, T. (2003, September 16). WTO leaders work to keep plans for global trade treaty on course. *The Oregonian,* pp. C1, C3.

Harvesting poverty: Inching toward trade fairness. (2003, August 15). *The New York Times,* p. A28.

Geitner, P. (2003, August 13). EU, U.S. agree on common stance to ease talks with poor nations on cutting farm subsidies at WTO. *Associated Press.* Retrieved September 15, 2003, from LexisNexis (www.lexisnexis.com/).

Koppel, N. (2003, September 13). WTO drafts proposal for major cuts in farming subsidies. *Associated Press.* Retrieved September 15, 2003, from LexisNexis (www.lexisnexis.com/).

Lacey, M. (2003, September 10). Africans' burden: West's farm subsidies. *The New York Times,* p. A9.

Lazio, R. (2003, August 12). Ditching farm subsidies would do America a service. *The New York Times,* Opinion, p. 6.

THE GLOBAL SHADOW OF DECEIT

Deceit is all too common on the international stage. Nations routinely spy on each other for economic and military purposes and do their best to deceive their enemies. Businesses from industrialized countries frequently take advantage of consumers in economically depressed regions. Take the marketing of infant formula, for example. UN experts estimate that the lives of a million and

282 SHAPING ETHICAL CONTEXTS

a half babies could be spared every year if they were adequately breast-fed rather than bottle-fed.[7] As an added benefit, poor households could then spend their money on other pressing needs. Despite the adoption of the International Code of Marketing Breast-milk Substitutes in 1981, formula manufacturers continue to engage in a variety of deceptive sales practices. These include (a) stressing that baby formula is equal to or better than breast-feeding, (b) playing on women's fears that they won't produce enough milk, (c) representing healthy, thriving babies on packaging (in impoverished countries, babies often sicken and die when formula is mixed with polluted water), (d) disguising salespersons as health workers, and (e) gaining medical endorsement by providing free samples to hospitals and gifts to doctors.

In addition to casting shadows through deception, global leaders also cast shadows by withholding information. They don't feel as much obligation to share information about safety problems and environmental hazards with foreign nationals as they do with their own citizens. They are guilty of extracting information from poor countries, giving little in return. Clinical drug trials in Third World regions, for example, produce data that goes back to company headquarters in Europe or the United States. Weaker countries are given little support in their efforts to develop their own research facilities.[8]

THE GLOBAL SHADOW OF INCONSISTENCY

Economic and social disparities make it hard for leaders of multinational firms and nonprofits to act consistently. For instance, what are "fair" wages and working conditions in a Third World nation? Do these workers deserve the same safety standards as employees in an industrialized country? Should drugs that are banned in the United States for their undesirable side effects be sold in countries where their potential health benefits outweigh their risks? Should a multinational follow the stringent pollution regulations of its home country or the lower standards of a host nation? All too often global leaders answer these questions in ways that cast shadows on disadvantaged world citizens. They pay the bare minimum to Third World workers, pay less attention to safety and environmental problems in overseas locations, dump dangerous products they can't sell in their homelands, and so on.

The shadow of inconsistency grows deeper and longer when leaders ignore human rights abuses and buy the favor of corrupt officials in order to benefit from the status quo. Such was the case with Shell Nigeria. Nigeria has huge oil reserves (24–25 billion gallons) that account for 80–90% of its exports. Such natural bounty should bring prosperity, but it does not. The country's political and military leaders (rated as some of the most corrupt in the world) siphon off most oil revenue; little goes to its poor and indigenous peoples. When dissidents demanded that a larger share of oil revenue return to communities around drilling sites, Shell Nigeria leaders supported government efforts to repress the rebellion. They refused to intervene when two ethnic leaders were falsely convicted and hung by the military regime.[9]

THE GLOBAL SHADOW OF MISPLACED AND BROKEN LOYALTIES

Traditional loyalties are eroding in an integrated world. In the past, national leaders were expected to meet the needs of their citizens. Now, because their actions affect the lives of residents of other nations, they must consider their duties to people they may never meet. Failure to do so produces shadow in the form of environmental damage, poverty, hunger, and the widening income gap.[10]

Broken loyalties cast shadows in a global society just as they do in individual leader-follower relationships. Many poorer world citizens feel betrayed by the shattered promises of globalization. Trade barriers remain in place, special interests in wealthy nations continue to receive favored treatment, and so on. Economic exploitation adds to this sense of betrayal. Low labor costs drive the investments of many multinational companies. Executives at these firms are continually on the lookout for cheaper labor, so they continually transfer production to even more economically depressed regions.

THE GLOBAL SHADOW OF IRRESPONSIBILITY

Globalization increases the breadth of leaders' responsibilities because they are accountable for the actions of followers in many different geographic locations. Like local leaders, they can't be blamed for all the misdeeds of their followers. Yet they should be held to the same set of responsibility standards outlined in our discussion of the shadow side of leadership in Chapter 1. In order to cast light instead of shadow, global leaders must do the following:

1. Take reasonable efforts to prevent followers' misdeeds. Fostering a consistent, ethical organization climate in every location can prevent many moral abuses. Integrity and a clear set of guiding values should be as characteristic of branch offices as they are of headquarters. This can be done by (a) clearly stating organizational values, (b) communicating these values to all branches through print and electronic media as well as training programs, (c) letting business partners know about standards, and (d) translating ethical behavior into performance standards and then evaluating followers based on those criteria.[11]

2. Acknowledge and address ethical problems wherever they occur. Geographic and cultural distance makes it easy for global leaders to deny responsibility for the misbehavior of followers. Subcontractors often get the blame for low wages and poor working conditions at foreign manufacturing facilities. More responsible firms acknowledge their duty to adequately supervise the activities of their contractors.

3. *Shoulder responsibility for the consequences of their directives.* Wise global leaders recognize that in trying to do the right thing, they might end up producing some unintended negative consequences. Take well-intentioned efforts to eliminate child labor, for instance. Removing children from the factory floor in developing countries can do significant harm. Poor children are an important source of income for their families. When fired from their manufacturing jobs, they often are forced into prostitution or begging. Levi Strauss realized that eliminating child laborers from its Bangladesh plants could do damage to both the children and their families. After identifying workers under age 14 (the international standard for child labor), company officials asked their contractors to remove these children from the production line while continuing to pay their wages. Levi Strauss covered the kids' school costs (tuition, uniforms, books) and agreed to rehire them when they reached age 14.[12]

4. *Admit their duties to followers.* Multinational leaders have obligations to all their followers, regardless of citizenship or ethnic and cultural background, as well as to the communities where they operate. Shell Nigeria tried to deny any responsibility for human rights abuses, claiming that it had no right to interfere in local affairs. However, the company regularly intervened in Nigerian politics in order to try to reduce the amount of oil royalties it owed the government.

5. *Hold themselves to the same standards as followers.* Leaders are not above the values, rules, and codes of conduct they impose on their global organizations. At the same time they hold diverse followers to consistent standards, ethical leaders also live up to the same guidelines.

Leadership and Ethical Diversity

Along with taking stock of the potential moral pitfalls of globalization, leaders need to recognize that cultural diversity makes the difficult process of ethical decision making even harder. Every ethnic group, nation, and religion approaches moral dilemmas from a different perspective. What is perfectly acceptable to members of one group may raise serious ethical concerns for another. Consider, for example, the differing responses to these common ethical problems.[13]

Bribery. Spurred by reports that ExxonMobil had paid $59 million to Italian politicians in order to do business in that country, Congress passed the

Foreign Corrupt Practices Act of 1977, which forbids U.S. corporations from exchanging money or goods for something in return. Those guilty of bribery can be fined and sent to prison. Malaysia has even stricter bribery statutes, executing corporate officers who offer and accept bribes. On the other hand, bribery is a common, acceptable practice in many countries in Africa, Asia, and the Middle East. In recognition of this fact, small payments to facilitate travel and business in less developed nations are permitted under the Corrupt Practices Act.

False information. Mexico and the United States might be geographic neighbors, but citizens of these countries react differently to deception. In one encounter, American businessmen were offended when their Mexican counterparts promised to complete a project by an impossible deadline. The Mexicans, on the other hand, viewed their deception as a way to smooth relations between the two sides while protecting their interests.

Intellectual property rights. Copyright laws are rigorously enforced in many Western nations but are less binding in many Asian countries. In fact, piracy is legal in Thailand, Indonesia, and Malaysia.

Gender equality. Treatment of women varies widely. Denmark and Sweden have done the most to promote gender equality whereas Japan and Saudi Arabia offer some of the stiffest resistance to women's rights. In Japan, women are expected to care for the home and are excluded from leadership positions in government and business. In Saudi Arabia, women (who must wear traditional garb) aren't allowed to drive or form relationships with non-Moslem men.

Cultural differences can cause leaders to cast some serious shadows. Ethnocentric leaders often impose their cultural values on followers, either consciously or unconsciously. *Ethnocentrism* is the tendency to see the world from our cultural group's point of view. From this vantage point, our customs and values then become the standard by which the rest of the world is judged. Our cultural ways seem natural; those of other groups fall short. According to cross-cultural communication experts William Gudykunst and Young Yun Kim, a certain degree of ethnocentrism is inevitable.[14] Ethnocentrism can help a group band together and survive in the face of outside threats. Ethnocentrism is a significant barrier, however, to cross-cultural communication and problem solving. High levels of ethnocentrism can lead to the following problems:

- Inaccurate attributions about the behavior of strangers (we interpret their behavior from our point of view, not theirs)

- Expressions of disparagement or animosity (ethnic slurs, belittling nicknames)

- – Reduced contact with outsiders
- – Indifference and insensitivity to the perspectives of strangers
- – Pressure on other groups to conform to our cultural standards
- – Justification for war and violence as a means of expressing cultural dominance

Examples of ethnocentrism abound. For many years the Bureau of Indian Affairs made assimilation its official policy, forcing Native Americans to send their children to reservation schools where they were punished for speaking their tribal languages. Government officials in Australia kidnapped aboriginal children and placed them with white families (see the Leadership Ethics at the Movies Case: *Rabbit-Proof Fence,* Box 10.1). In other instances, well-meaning individuals assume that their values and practices are the only "right" ones. Many early missionaries equated Christianity with Western lifestyles and required converts to dress, live, think, and worship like Europeans or North Americans.

Prejudice is the prejudgment of out-group members, based on prior experiences and beliefs. Prejudice, like ethnocentrism, is universal (most of us prefer to socialize with those of our own age and ethnic group, for example). However, the degree of prejudice will vary from person to person, ranging from slight bias to extreme prejudice like that displayed by racist skinheads. Negative prejudgments can be dangerous because they produce discriminatory behavior. For instance, police in many urban areas believe that African Americans are more likely to commit crimes. As a consequence, officers are more likely to stop and question black citizens, particularly young males, and to use force if they show the slightest sign of resistance.[15]

The challenges posed by cultural variables can discourage leaders from making reasoned moral choices. They may decide to cling to their old ways of thinking or blindly follow local customs. Cultural relativism ("When in Rome do as the Romans do") is an attractive option for many. Nevertheless, being in a new culture or working with a diverse group of followers doesn't excuse leaders from engaging in careful ethical deliberation. Just because a culture has adopted a practice doesn't make it right. Female circumcision may still be carried out in parts of Africa, but the vast majority of Americans are appalled by this custom.

Fortunately, we can expand our capacity to act ethically in a global society and, in so doing, brighten the lives of diverse groups of followers. To do so, we first need to come to grips with our ethnocentrism and prejudice. Next, we need to deepen our understanding of the relationship between cultural differences and ethical values. Third, we should strive for cultural-ethical synergy when interacting with individuals of different cultural backgrounds. Fourth, we need to reject cultural relativism and search instead for moral common ground.

Box 10.1

Leadership Ethics at the Movies: *Rabbit-Proof Fence*

Key Cast Members: Everlyn Sampi, Tianna Sansbury, Laura Monaghan, Kenneth Branagh

Synopsis: Until 1970, mixed-race children in Australia were removed from their homes and raised to be "white." They were placed in boarding schools where officials tried to remove all traces of their aboriginal culture while training them for lives as farm laborers and domestic servants. This film tells the true story of three girls who rebelled against the system in 1931. Fourteen-year-old Molly (Sampi), her eight-year-old sister Daisy (Sansbury), and their 10-year-old cousin Gracie (Monaghan) escape from boarding school. Following a rabbit-proof fence that runs the length of Australia, Molly and Daisy find their way back home after a 9-week, 1,500-mile trek (Gracie is recaptured). Branagh plays the part of A. O. Neville, who holds the title of Chief Protector of the Aboriginal People. At one point, he declares that "the native must be helped in spite of himself."

Rating: PG for mature subject matter and intense emotional scenes

Themes: ethnocentrism, bureaucratic evil, racism, courage, perseverance, love

---

Overcoming Ethnocentrism and Prejudice

As I noted earlier, ethnocentric tendencies and negative prejudices are the cause of a great number of moral abuses. Confronting these tendencies can go a long way toward improving the ethical atmosphere of multicultural groups.

According to Gudykunst and Kim, we can reduce our levels of ethnocentrism and negative prejudice by committing ourselves to the following:

Mindfulness. In most routine encounters, we tend to operate on "autopilot" and perform our roles mechanically, without much reflection. When we're engaged in such mindless interaction, we're not likely to challenge the ethnocentric assumption that ours is the only way to solve problems. Mindfulness is the opposite of mindlessness. When we're mindful, we pay close attention to our attitudes and behaviors. Three psychological processes take place.[16]

The first is *openness to new categories*. Being mindful makes us more sensitive to differences. Instead of lumping people into broad categories based on age, race, gender, or role, we make finer distinctions within these classifications.

We discover that not all student government officers, retirees, professors, Japanese exchange students, and professors are alike.

The second psychological process involves *openness to new information.* Mindless communication closes us off to new data, and we fail to note the kinds of cultural differences I described earlier. We assume that others hold the same ethical values. In mindful communication, we pick up new information as we closely monitor our behavior along with the behavior of others.

The third psychological process is *recognizing the existence of more than one perspective.* Mindlessness results in tunnel vision that ignores potential solutions. Mindfulness, on the other hand, opens our eyes to other possibilities. As we'll see later in our discussion of cultural-ethical synergy, there can be more than one way to make and implement ethical choices.

2. *Dignity and integrity.* Dignity and integrity ought to characterize all of our interactions with people of other cultures. We maintain our own dignity by confronting others who engage in prejudicial comments or actions; we maintain the dignity of others by respecting their views. Respect doesn't mean that we have to agree with another's moral stance. But when we disagree, we need to respond in a civil, sensitive manner.

3. *Moral inclusion.* As we saw in Chapter 4, widespread evil occurs when groups have been devalued or dehumanized. This sanctioning process is referred to as "moral exclusion."[17] Exclusionary tactics include biased evaluation of women and minorities, hostility, contempt, condescension, and double standards (one for insiders, another for outsiders). Moral inclusiveness rejects exclusionary tactics of all kinds. If we're dedicated to inclusiveness, we'll apply the same rules, values, and standards to strangers as well as neighbors.

By committing ourselves as leaders to mindful communication, the dignity of others, and moral inclusion, we can reduce ethnocentrism and prejudice in the group as a whole. Using morally inclusive language and disputing prejudiced statements, for instance, improves ethical climate because followers will be less likely to attack other groups in our presence. However, if we don't speak out when followers disparage members of out-groups, the practice will continue. We'll share some of the responsibility for creating a hostile atmosphere like the one described in the Mitsubishi case at the end of the chapter.

Cultural Differences and Ethical Values

DEFINING CULTURE

The same factors that make up an organization's culture—language, rituals, stories, buildings, beliefs, assumptions, power structures—also form the cultures of communities, ethnic groups, and nations. Cultures are comprehensive, incorporating both the visible (architecture, physical objects, nonverbal behavior) and the invisible (thoughts, attitudes, values). In sum, a culture is "the total way of life of a people, composed of their learned and shared behavior patterns, values, norms, and material objects."[18]

There are several features of cultures that are worth noting in more detail. These elements include the following:

- *Created.* Ethnocentrism would have us believe that ours is the only way to solve problems. In fact, there are countless ways to deal with the environment, manage interpersonal relationships, produce food, and cope with death. Each cultural group devises its own way of responding to circumstances.
- *Learned.* Elements of culture are passed on from generation to generation and from person to person. Cultural conditioning is both a formal and informal process that takes place in every context—homes, schools, playgrounds, camps, games. The most crucial aspects of a culture, like loyalty to country, are constantly reinforced. Patriotism in the United States is promoted through high school civics classes, the singing of the national anthem at sporting events, flags flying on everything from pickup trucks to skyscrapers, and Fourth of July and Memorial Day programs.
- *Shared.* The shared nature of culture becomes apparent when we break the rules that are set and enforced by the group. There are negative consequences for violating cultural norms of all types. Punishments vary depending on the severity of the offense. You might receive a cold stare from your professor, for example, when your cell phone goes off in class. You may face jail time, however, if you break drug laws.
- *Dynamic.* Cultures aren't static but evolve. Over time, the changes can be dramatic. Compare the cultural values of the *Leave It to Beaver* television show with those found in modern situation comedies. The world of the Cleavers (a wholesome, two-parent family with a well-dressed, stay-at-home mom) has been replaced by portrayals of unmarried friends, single parents, blended families, and gay partners.

CULTURAL VALUES ORIENTATIONS

Ethical decisions and practices are shaped by widely held cultural values. Although each culture has its own set of ethical priorities, researchers have discovered that ethnic groups and nations hold values in common. As a result, cultures can be grouped according to their values orientations. These orientations help explain ethical differences and enable leaders to predict how members of other cultural groups will respond to moral dilemmas. In this section of the chapter, I'll describe two widely used cultural classification systems. Before we examine them, however, there are four cautions to keep in mind. First, all categories are gross overgeneralizations. They describe what most people in that culture value. Not all U.S. residents are individualistic, for example, and not all

Japanese citizens are collectivists. However, *in general,* more Americans put the individual first, whereas more Japanese emphasize group relations. Second, scholars may categorize the same nation differently and have not studied some regions of the world (such as Africa) as intensively as others (Europe, Asia, and the United States). Three, political and cultural boundaries aren't always identical. The Basque people, for instance, live in both France and Spain. Four, as we noted earlier, cultures are dynamic, so values change. A society may change its ethical priorities, making older values rankings obsolete.

Programmed Value Patterns

Gert Hofstede of the Netherlands conducted an extensive investigation of cultural value patterns.[19] According to Hofstede, important values are "programmed" into members of every culture. He surveyed over 100,000 IBM employees in 50 countries and three multicountry regions to uncover these value dimensions. He then checked his findings against those of other researchers who studied the same countries. Four value orientations emerged:

Power distance. The first category describes the relative importance of power differences. Status differences are universal, but cultures treat them differently. In high power distance cultures, inequality is accepted as part of the natural order. Leaders enjoy special privileges and make no attempt to reduce power differentials; they are, however, expected to care for the less fortunate. The wealthy landowner in the Philippines must respond to the neighboring peasant who comes to him or her for help. Low power distance cultures, in contrast, are uneasy with large gaps in wealth, power, privilege, and status. Superiors tend to downplay these differences and strive for a greater degree of equality.

High Power Distance Nations	*Low Power Distance Nations*
Philippines	Ireland
Mexico	New Zealand
Venezuela	Denmark
India	Israel
Singapore	Austria

Individualism/collectivism. Hofstede's second values category divides cultures according to their preference for either the individual or the group. Individualistic cultures put the needs and goals of the person and her or his immediate family first. Members of these cultures see themselves as independent actors. In contrast, collectivistic cultures give top priority to the desires of the larger group (extended family, tribe, community). Members of these societies stress connection instead of separateness, putting a high value on their place in the collective. Think back to your decision to attend your current college or university. As a resident of Canada or the United States, you probably asked friends, high school counselors, and family members for advice, but in the end, you made the choice. In a collectivistic society, your family or village might well make this decision for you. There's no guarantee that you would have even gone to college. Families with limited resources can only afford to send one child to school. You might have been expected to go to work to help pay for the education of a brother or sister.

High Individualism	*Low Individualism*
United States	Taiwan
Australia	Peru
Great Britain	Pakistan
Canada	Colombia
Netherlands	Venezuela

Masculinity/femininity. The third dimension reflects attitudes toward the roles of men and women. Highly masculine cultures maintain clearly defined sex roles. Men are expected to be decisive, assertive, dominant, ambitious, and materialistic; women are encouraged to serve. They are to care for the family, interpersonal relationships, and the weaker members of society. In feminine cultures, the differences between sexes are blurred. Both men and women can be competitive and caring, assertive and nurturing. These cultures are more likely to stress interdependence, intuition, and concern for others.

Masculine	*Feminine*
Japan	Finland
Austria	Denmark
Venezuela	Netherlands
Italy	Norway
Switzerland	Sweden

Uncertainty avoidance. This dimension describes the way that cultures respond to uncertainty. Three indicators measure this orientation: (1) anxiety level, (2) widely held attitudes about rules, and (3) employment stability. Members of high uncertainty avoidance societies feel anxious about uncertainty and view it as a threat. They believe in written rules and regulations, engage in more rituals, and accept directives from those in authority. In addition, they are less likely to change jobs and view long-term employment as a right. People who live in low uncertainty avoidance cultures are more comfortable with uncertainty, viewing ambiguity as a fact of life. They experience lower stress and are more likely to take risks like starting a new company or accepting a new job in another part of the country. These individuals are less reliant on written regulations and rituals and are more likely to trust their own judgments instead of obeying authority figures.

High Uncertainty Avoidance	Low Uncertainty Avoidance
Greece	Ireland
Portugal	Hong Kong
Belgium	Sweden
Japan	Denmark
Peru	Singapore

Hofstede argues that value patterns have a significant impact on ethical behavior.[20] For example, masculine European countries give relatively little to international development programs but invest heavily in weapons. Feminine European nations do just the opposite. Strong uncertainty avoidance cultures are prone to ethnocentrism and prejudice because they follow the credo, "What is different is dangerous." Weak uncertainty avoidance cultures follow the credo, "What is different is curious," and are more tolerant of strangers and new ideas.

Of the four value dimensions, individualism/collectivism has attracted the most attention. Scholars have used this dimension to explain a variety of cultural differences, including variations in ethical behavior. Management professors Stephen Carroll and Martin Gannon report that individualistic countries prefer universal ethical standards like Kant's categorical imperative.[21] Collectivistic societies take a more utilitarian approach, seeking to generate the greatest good for in-group members. Citizens of these nations are more sensitive to elements of the situation. To see how these orientations affect ethical decisions, let's return to the four dilemmas I introduced earlier in the chapter.

- *Bribery.* Payoffs tend to be more common in collectivistic nations and may be a way to meet obligations to the community. In some cases, there are laws against the practice, but they take a backseat to history and custom. Individualistic nations view bribery as a form of corruption; payoffs destroy trust and benefit some companies and people at the expense of others.
- *False information.* Individualists are more likely to lie in order to protect their privacy; collectivists are more likely to lie in order to protect the group or family. This accounts for the conflict between the Mexican and U.S. businesspeople

described earlier. Mexicans, who tend to have a collectivistic orientation, promise what they can't deliver in order to reduce tensions between their in-group and outsiders. Americans (among the world's most individualistic peoples) condemn this practice as deceptive and therefore unethical. Individualists and collectivists also express disagreement differently. Germans and Americans, for instance, don't hesitate to say "no" directly to another party. Japanese may answer by saying "that will be difficult" rather than by offering an out-and-out refusal. This indirect strategy is designed to save the "face" or image of the receiver.

- *Intellectual property rights.* Whereas individuals own the rights to their creative ideas in individualistic societies, they are expected to share their knowledge in collectivistic nations. Copyright laws are a Western invention based on the belief that individuals should be rewarded for their efforts.
- *Gender equality.* Resistance to gender equality is strongest in collectivistic nations such as Saudi Arabia and Japan. Women are seen as an out-group in these societies. Many men fear that granting women more status (better jobs, leadership positions) would threaten group stability. Individualistic nations are more likely to have laws that promote equal opportunity, though in many of these countries (such as the United States) women hold fewer leadership positions than men and continue to earn less.

In addition to shaping our moral choices, both individualism and collectivism create "ethical blind spots." Being self- or group-focused can make us particularly susceptible to certain types of ethical abuses. Turn to Box 10.2 below for one list of the ethical problems associated with individualism and collectivism.

Box 10.2

Ethical Disadvantages of Collectivism and Individualism

University of Illinois psychology professor Harry Triandis argues that there are ethical strengths and weaknesses associated with collectivism and individualism. In general, collectivism is better for interpersonal relationships but poses a danger when members deal with outsiders. Individualism promotes human rights, creativity, and achievement but undermines social connections. Some of the specific ethical disadvantages of collectivism and individualism are outlined below:

Ethical Disadvantages of Collectivism

Suppression of individual thought and innovation

Undermining of self-esteem of some members

Encouragement of blind obedience to authoritarian groups and leaders

Harsh treatment of out-groups (discrimination, ethnic cleansing, etc.)

(Continued)

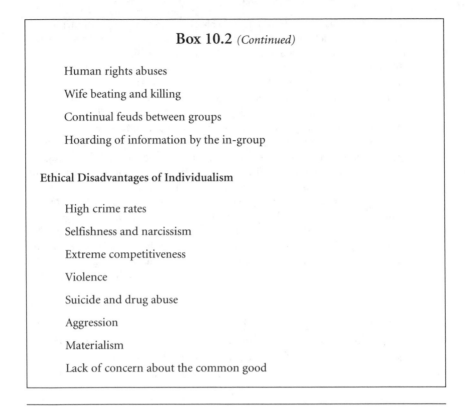

Box 10.2 *(Continued)*

Human rights abuses

Wife beating and killing

Continual feuds between groups

Hoarding of information by the in-group

Ethical Disadvantages of Individualism

High crime rates

Selfishness and narcissism

Extreme competitiveness

Violence

Suicide and drug abuse

Aggression

Materialism

Lack of concern about the common good

SOURCE: Triandis, H. C. (1995). *Individualism and collectivism.* Boulder, CO: Westview Press, ch. 7.

Seven Cultures of Capitalism

Charles Hampden-Turner and Alfons Trompenaars call the creation of wealth "a moral act." To flourish, capitalism must be supported by cultural values that (a) support the production and sale of products, and (b) encourage people to work together to create these goods. Corporations also make a series of value judgments as they conduct business. The authors surveyed 15,000 managers and discovered that leaders of capitalist organizations must balance seven sets of contrasting values. Hampden-Turner and Trompenaars focus their attention on corporations, but leaders of governments and nonprofits must also weigh the importance of these competing values.[22]

1. Universalism versus particularism. Universalist societies emphasize standards and obedience to the rules. There is strong resistance to creating exceptions to established guidelines out of fear that the system will collapse. Particularist

---

Box 10.3

Self-Assessment

A DRIVING DILEMMA

You are riding in a car driven by a close friend. He hits a pedestrian. You know he was going at least 35 miles per hour in an area of the city where the maximum allowed speed is 20 miles per hour. There are no witnesses. His lawyer says that if you testify under oath that he was only driving 20 miles per hour, it may save him from serious consequences.

What right has your friend to expect you to protect him?

---

nations focus on the present circumstances, opting to break the rules based on friendship, family connections, and other factors. Universalists don't think they can trust particularists who put their friends ahead of the rules; particularists don't trust universalists who won't help a friend in need. A moral dilemma that illustrates the difference between these two perspectives is found in Box 10.3, the Self-Assessment.

Over 90% of respondents from Canada, the United States, Australia, and northern Europe would refuse to lie in the situation described in Box 10.3. Respondents from South Korea, Venezuela, and Russia, on the other hand, are much more likely to lie on the stand. The greater the consequences of the incident, the more the two groups diverge. Universalists believe that the more serious the accident, the more important it is to obey the law, to uphold principles. Particularists are convinced that the friend deserves even more help when the pedestrian's injuries are severe. After all, he could lose his license, be fined, or serve jail time.

2. Individualism versus communitarianism. This dimension appears to be identical to Hofstede's individualism/collectivism values cluster. Canadian, American, and Norwegian managers are most individualistic; Nepalese, Kuwaitis, and Egyptians are most communitarian.

3. Analyzing versus integrating. Members of analytical cultures (United States, Canada, Belgium) prefer to break products and operations down in order to identify and correct defects. They focus on tasks, numbers, facts, and units. Members of integrative cultures (Japan, France, Singapore) look for the whole pattern and emphasize relationships.

4. *Inner-directed versus outer-directed orientation.* Inner-directed leaders are guided by their own judgments and commitments and expect their followers to be self-directed as well. Outer-directed leaders are more interested in responding to the environment. They're sensitive to business and cultural trends and adjust to these changes. The United States, Germany, Canada, and Austria tend to be inner-directed cultures, whereas Belgium, Sweden, Singapore, and Japan are more outer-directed.

5. *Achieved status versus ascribed status.* Status can be granted on the basis of individual achievement or bestowed (ascribed) to organizational members based on some other characteristic like age, seniority, gender, or education. Business leaders from the United States, Austria, and Canada are more likely to emphasize achievement. Their counterparts from Singapore, Japan, and Korea give more weight to ascribed status.

6. *Time as sequence versus time as synchronization.* Sequential individuals view time as a linear process. They try to complete their tasks quickly and efficiently by following a series of steps. To them, time is a precious commodity that is carefully measured and managed. Sequential thinkers have a short-term perspective and tend to be future oriented. Synchronizing people, on the other hand, see time more as a cycle than as a straight line. To them, time is a friend, one that will come again. Synchronic thinkers have a long-term perspective and are more likely to honor the past and present. Less concerned about punctuality, they try to coordinate several tasks at once (i.e., talking on the phone and checking on stock quotes while conducting an interview). The United States, Great Britain, and the Netherlands are sequential societies, whereas many Latin American, African, and Middle Eastern cultures are synchronic.

7. *Equality versus hierarchy.* Followers can be given a great deal of freedom to make their own decisions (equality), or they may be required to carry out the wishes of their bosses (hierarchy). West Germany, the United States, and the Netherlands are most equalitarian; Pakistan, Venezuela, and China most hierarchical.

No organization or society can adhere to one value to the exclusion of its contrasting value. For example, a business couldn't function without at least some common standards and procedures (universalism). Yet no set of guidelines can cover every contingency, so the corporation must learn to deal with exceptional situations (particularism). Leaders must acknowledge *both* values in each set if they and the groups they lead are to prosper in a multicultural world. Further, there is more than one way to succeed. Instead of one capitalist culture (U.S.), there are many (French, British, Japanese, Dutch). We can learn from the choices of other cultures. In the words of Hampden-Turner and Trompenaars,

You can combine the traditions of excellence from many nations, provided you can manage cultural diversity and not allow it to descend into a Tower of Babel. In the same way you can also learn, and make your own, the strategies and thought processes behind these traditions of excellence.[23]

Our cultural values may not generate the best response to a particular ethical dilemma. Analysis can be counterproductive in cultural settings that stress connection and relationships. Being inner-directed can blind us to important environmental factors. Honoring achievement may work well in the United States but backfire in status-conscious societies.

Cultural-Ethical Synergy

The belief that leaders and followers can learn from the insights of other cultural groups is the foundation of *cultural-ethical synergy.* Synergy refers to creating an end product that is greater than the sum of its parts. In cultural-ethical synergy, diverse decision makers come up with a better than anticipated solution to a moral dilemma by drawing on the perspectives of a variety of cultures. They combine their insights to generate highly ethical, creative solutions.

According to cross-cultural management expert Nancy Adler, culturally synergistic problem solving is a four-step process.[24] The first step, situation description, is to identify the problem facing a dyad or group. This is far from easy. Due to differing cultural perspectives, one party may not realize that there is a problem. As we saw earlier, lying to maintain harmony seems "normal" for many members of collectivistic societies but is perceived as unethical by many individualists. Bribery is a criminal offense in some cultures but an accepted way of life in others. Even when parties acknowledge that a problem exists, they may define it differently. For example, negotiations between a Canadian and an Egyptian executive broke off when the Canadian insisted on meeting the next day with lawyers to finalize contract details. When the Egyptian party never showed up, the Canadian wondered if his counterpart was expecting a counteroffer or couldn't locate attorneys. In reality, the Egyptian was offended by the presence of lawyers. Lawyers marked the end of successful negotiations for the Canadian (a universalist) but symbolized distrust to the Egyptian (a particularist) who had given his binding verbal commitment.

The second step, cultural interpretation, is to determine why people of other cultures think and act as they do. This step is based on the assumption that people act rationally from their culture's point of view but that we misinterpret their logic based on our cultural biases. Accurate interpretation depends on identifying similarities and differences while taking multiple perspectives. Cultural classification systems help in this process. If you can determine a culture's value orientations (individualistic or collectivistic, for example), you'll have a much better chance of predicting how members of that group will respond to ethical problems.

The third step, cultural creativity, is driven by the question, "What can people of one culture contribute to people of another culture?" In this stage, problem solvers generate alternatives and then come up with a novel solution, one that incorporates the cultural perspectives of all group members but transcends them.

The fourth step, implementation, puts the solution into effect. Whenever possible, give the other parties as much leeway as possible in implementing decisions. As a leader of a transnational organization, empower local personnel to implement changes, distribute awards, and punish ethical misbehavior.

The process of cultural-ethical synergy is demonstrated in the following case: An international relief agency appointed a new program director in a Latin American country who, after assuming his position, discovered that his treasurer had stolen $50,000 from the organization. He reported the theft to his supervisor, the vice president of program development at the organization's U.S. headquarters. The vice president wanted to fire the embezzler immediately and to bring charges against him. The national director advised otherwise. There was no chance of recovering the money, he argued, and the country's labor laws made it extremely difficult to fire the thief. Government authorities were likely to side with the treasurer and pressing charges would make the new director's job harder. Needy citizens might suffer if the agency's relationships with the government and local communities deteriorated. In the end, the director went to the thief in private, confronted him with his crime, and then negotiated a settlement. This solution acknowledged the perspectives of both cultures while combining elements of each. The embezzler was fired for his crime (the goal of the individualistically oriented vice president) but in a manner that was suitable to the host country's collectivistic culture. The national director preserved harmony, avoided a protracted legal battle, and was free to concentrate on his new responsibilities.

Standing on Moral Common Ground

Confronted with a wide range of ethical values and standards, a number of philosophers, business leaders, anthropologists, and others opt for ethical relativism. In ethical relativism, there are no universal moral codes or standards. Each group and society is unique. Therefore, members of one culture can't pass moral judgment on members of another group.

I'll admit that, at first glance, ethical relativism is appealing. It avoids the problem of ethnocentrism while simplifying the decision-making process. We can concentrate on fitting in with the prevailing culture and never have to pass judgment. On closer examination, however, the difficulties of ethical relativism become all too apparent.[25] Without shared standards, there's little hope that the peoples of the world can work together to address global problems. There may be no basis on which to condemn the evil of notorious leaders who are popular in their own countries. Further, the standard of cultural relativism obligates us to follow (or at least not to protest against) abhorrent local practices like the killing of brides by their in-laws in the rural villages of Pakistan. Without universal rights and wrongs, we have no basis on which to contest such practices.

I believe that there is ethical common ground that can help us address the dark side of globalization. In fact, the existence of universal standards has enabled members of the world community to punish crimes against humanity and to create the United Nations and its Universal Declaration of Human Rights. Responsible multinational corporations like Merck & Company, The Body Shop, and Levi Strauss adhere to widely held moral principles as they conduct business in a variety of cultural settings. In this final section, I'll describe four different approaches to universal ethics, any one of which could serve as a worldwide standard. As you read each description, look for commonalties. Then decide for yourself which approach or combinations of approaches best captures the foundational values of humankind (see question 7, For Further Exploration, Challenge, and Self-Assessment). Apply these principles and standards to resolving the ethical issues outlined in the scenarios found at the end of the chapter.

A GLOBAL ETHIC

Many of the world's conflicts center around religious differences: Hindu versus Moslem, Protestant versus Catholic, Moslem versus Jew. However, these hostilities didn't prevent 6,500 representatives from a wide range of religious faiths from reaching agreement on a global ethic.[26] A council of former heads of state and prime ministers then ratified this statement. Delegates of both groups agreed on two universal principles. First, every person must be treated humanely regardless of language, skin color, mental ability, political beliefs, or national or social origin. Second, every person and group, no matter how powerful, must respect the dignity of others. These two foundational principles, in turn, lead to these ethical directives or imperatives:

- Commitment to a culture of nonviolence and respect for all life

- Commitment to a culture of solidarity and a just economic order (do not steal, deal fairly and honestly with others)

- Commitment to a culture of tolerance and truthfulness

– Commitment to a culture of equal rights and partnership between men and women (avoid immorality; respect and love members of both genders)

EIGHT GLOBAL VALUES

Rushworth Kidder and his colleagues at the Institute for Global Ethics identify eight core values that appear to be shared the world over. They isolated these values after conducting interviews with 24 international "ethical thought leaders."[27] Kidder's sample included UN officials, heads of states, university presidents, writers, and religious figures drawn from such nations as the United States, Vietnam, Mozambique, New Zealand, Bangladesh, Britain, China, Sri Lanka, Costa Rica, and Lebanon. Each interview ran from 1 to 3 hours and began with this question: "If you could help create a global code of ethics, what would be on it?" These global standards emerged:

1. *Love.* Spontaneous concern for others, compassion that transcends political and ethnic differences

2. *Truthfulness.* Achieving goals through honest means, keeping promises, being worthy of the trust of others

3. *Fairness (justice).* Fair play, evenhandedness, equality

4. *Freedom.* The pursuit of liberty, right of free expression and action and accountability

5. *Unity.* Seeking the common good; cooperation, community, solidarity

6. *Tolerance.* Respect for others and their ideas; empathy, appreciation for variety

7. *Responsibility.* Care for self, the sick and needy, the community, and future generations; responsible use of force

8. *Respect for life.* Reluctance to kill through war and other means

Kidder and his fellow researchers don't claim to have discovered the one and only set of universal values, but they do believe that they have established ethical common ground. Kidder admits that the eight values are ordinary rather than unique. Yet that the list contains few surprises is evidence these standards are widely shared.

THE PEACE ETHIC

Communication professor David Kale argues that peace ought to be the ultimate goal of all intercultural contact because living in peace protects the worth and dignity of the human spirit.[28] Conflicts are inevitable. Nevertheless, with the help of those in leadership roles, peoples and nations can learn to value the goals of other parties even in the midst of their differences. There are four principles of the Peace Ethic:

Principle 1: Ethical communicators address people of other cultures with the same respect they desire themselves. Verbal and psychological violence, like physical violence, damages the human spirit. Demeaning or belittling others makes it hard for individuals to live at peace with themselves or their cultural heritage.

Principle 2: Ethical communicators describe the world as they see it as accurately possible. Perceptions of what is truth vary from culture to culture, but all individuals, regardless of their cultural background, should be true to the truth as they perceive it. Lying undermines trust that lays the foundation for peace.

Principle 3: Ethical communicators encourage people of other cultures to express their cultural uniqueness. Individuals and nations have the right to hold and to express different values and beliefs, a principle enshrined in the United Nations Universal Declaration of Human Rights. As leaders, we shouldn't force others to adopt our standards before allowing them to engage in dialogue.

Principle 4: Ethical communicators strive for identification with people of other cultures. We should seek mutual understanding and common ethical ground whenever possible. Incidents of racial harassment at colleges and universities are unethical, according to this principle, because they lead to division rather than peace.

INTERNATIONAL RIGHTS

Philosopher Thomas Donaldson believes that multinational corporations should recognize that citizens of every culture have the 10 fundamental rights listed below.[29] Each of these rights protects something of great value that can be taken away from individuals.

1. The right to freedom of physical movement
2. The right to ownership of property
3. The right to freedom from torture
4. The right to a fair trial
5. The right to nondiscriminatory treatment (freedom from discrimination on the basis of race or sex or other characteristics)
6. The right to physical security

302 SHAPING ETHICAL CONTEXTS

7. The right to freedom of speech and association

8. The right to minimal education

9. The right to political participation

10. The right to subsistence

Honoring these 10 rights imposes certain duties or responsibilities. At the very least, business leaders have a responsibility to do no harm. They shouldn't enslave workers or deliberately injure them. Leaders of corporations and other international organizations, however, may need to take a more active stance, actively protecting fundamental rights. This might mean

- Establishing nondiscriminatory policies in cultures that discriminate according to caste, sex, age, or some other factor

- Maintaining the highest safety standards for all employees in every nation

- Refusing to hire children if this prevents them from learning how to read or write

- Paying a decent wage, even if not required by a country's laws

- Protesting government attempts to take away the rights of free speech and association

THE CAUX PRINCIPLES

The Caux Round Table is made up of business executives from the United States, Japan, and Europe, who meet every year in Caux, Switzerland. Round Table members hope to set a world standard by which to judge business behavior. Their principles are based on twin ethical ideals. The first is the Japanese concept of *kyosei*, which refers to living and working together for the common good. The second is the Western notion of human dignity—the sacredness and value of each person as an end rather than as a means to someone else's end.[30]

Principle 1. The responsibilities of corporations: Beyond shareholders toward stakeholders. Corporations have a responsibility to improve the lives of everyone they come in contact with, starting with employees, shareholders, and suppliers, and then extending out to local, national, regional, and global communities.

Principle 2. The economic and social impact of corporations: Toward innovation, justice, and world community. Companies in foreign countries should not only create jobs and wealth but also foster better social conditions (education, welfare, human rights). Corporations have an obligation to enrich the world community through innovation, the wise use of resources, and fair competition.

Principle 3. Corporate behavior: Beyond the letter of law toward a spirit of trust. Businesses ought to promote honesty, transparency, integrity, and keeping promises. These behaviors make it easier to conduct international business and to support a global economy.

Principle 4. Respect for rules: Beyond trade friction toward cooperation. Leaders of international firms must respect both international and local laws in order to reduce trade wars and to promote the free flow of goods and services.

Principle 5. Support for multilateral trade: Beyond isolation toward world community. Firms should support international trading systems and agreements and eliminate domestic measures that undermine free trade.

Principle 6. Respect for the environment: Beyond protection toward enhancement. A corporation ought to protect and, if possible, improve the physical environment through sustainable development and cutting back on the wasteful use of natural resources.

Principle 7. Avoidance of illicit operations: Beyond profit toward peace. Global business leaders must ensure that their organizations aren't involved in such forbidden activities as bribery, money laundering, support of terrorism, drug trafficking, and organized crime.

After spelling out general principles, the Caux accord applies them to important stakeholder groups. Leaders following these standards hope to (a) treat customers and employees with dignity, (b) honor the trust of investors, (c) create relationships with suppliers based on mutual trust, (d) engage in just behavior with competitors, and (e) work for reform and human rights in host communities.

Implications and Applications

- Acknowledging the dark side of globalization reduces the likelihood of ethical abuse on the world stage. As a leader in a global environment, you must take additional care to avoid casting shadows of power, privilege, deceit, inconsistency, misplaced and broken loyalties, and irresponsibility.
- Cultural differences make ethical decisions more difficult. Nevertheless, resist the temptation to revert to your old ways of thinking or to blindly follow local customs. Try instead to expand your capacity to act ethically in multicultural situations.
- Ethnocentrism and prejudice lead to a great many moral abuses. You can avoid casting cross-cultural shadows if you commit yourself to mindfulness, human dignity, and moral inclusiveness.
- Understanding the relationship between cultural differences and ethical values can help you predict how members of that group will respond to moral questions.

Two popular cultural values classification systems are (a) programmed values (power distance, individualism/collectivism, masculinity/femininity, uncertainty avoidance), and (b) capitalistic values (universalism versus particularism, individualism versus communitarianism, analyzing versus integrating, inner-directed versus outer-directed, achieved versus ascribed status, time as sequence versus time as synchronization, equality versus hierarchy).

- No culture has a monopoly on the truth. In your role as a leader, you can learn from the strengths of other cultures and help others do the same.
- Strive for cultural-ethical synergy, combining insights from a variety of cultures to create better than expected ethical solutions.
- Universal standards can help you establish common ground with diverse followers. These shared standards can take the form of religious commitments, global values, a commitment to peace, international rights, or world business standards.

For Further Exploration, Challenge, and Self-Assessment

1. Form groups and debate the following proposition: "Overall, globalization does more harm than good."

2. Brainstorm a list of the advantages and disadvantages of ethical diversity. What conclusions do you draw from your list?

3. Using the Internet, compare press coverage of an international ethical issue from a variety of countries. How does the coverage differ and why?

4. Rate yourself on one or both of the cultural classification systems described in the chapter. Create a values profile of your community, organization, or university. How well do you fit in?

5. Analyze the cultural values that likely influenced the ethical decision of a prominent leader.

6. Create a synergistic solution for a cross-cultural ethical dilemma of your choice. Write up your findings.

7. Is there a common morality that peoples of all nations can share? Which of the global codes described in the chapter best reflects these shared standards and values? If you were to create your own declaration of global ethics, what would you put on it?

CASE STUDY 10.2

Chapter End Case: Sexual Intimidation at Mitsubishi

Japanese automakers have become a major force in the U.S. market by producing high-quality products and marketing them through a series of savvy ad campaigns. These manufacturers have demonstrated that they can adapt to American customs, laws, and tastes. In light of this success, it is hard to understand how one major Japanese car company—Mitsubishi—did nearly everything wrong when confronted with charges of sexual harassment.

In 1992, four women from Mitsubishi's plant in Normal, Illinois, filed a lawsuit alleging sexual harassment with the Equal Employment Opportunity Commission (EEOC). Four years later, after an extensive investigation, the EEOC filed charges against the company, alleging a widespread pattern of discrimination. The commission estimated that 400 male employees participated in sexual intimidation. Among the charges were these:

- Women were called "inferior" at new employee orientation.

- Managers sent to training in Japan attended sex bars where they and their Japanese hosts had sex with prostitutes on stage.

- Sexual graffiti (sexual comments, gestures, organs) were affixed to cars as they moved down the assembly line at the Normal plant.

- Women were referred to as "whores and "bitches" and some men exposed themselves to their female coworkers.

- Male employees and managers brought and displayed pornographic pictures.

- Females were attacked physically and verbally through threatening phone calls, assaults in cars, and unwanted touching and rubbing.

- Local sex parties were organized by plant managers on company time.

- Complaints had to be made first to immediate supervisors (often those doing the harassing).

- Only three male employees had been fired for their sexual behavior; most were given only the mildest of rebukes.

When the EEOC suit became public, Mitsubishi began a counterattack. Top officials denied all allegations, calling them "outrageous," and employees were urged to use any means possible (phone calls, the Internet, petitions) to influence public opinion. In its most dramatic act of defiance, the company paid 3,000 workers to demonstrate in front of the EEOC's Chicago offices.

Soon the National Organization of Women announced plans to picket dealerships, and the Reverend Jesse Jackson called for a boycott of Mitsubishi products. The company then softened its position, hiring an outside consultant (former Secretary of Labor Lynn Martin) to help it improve working conditions for women. A few months later the Mitsubishi Motor Company's board of directors replaced the firm's chairman. Nearly 2 years after the EEOC filed its case, the company agreed to pay $34 million in damages and to allow the agency to monitor working conditions for 3 years. In addition, the firm instituted "zero tolerance" policies and improved complaint procedures.

Cultural differences clearly contributed to the problems at Mitsubishi. After-hours sex parties are much more common in Japan. Women who work play a subservient role as "office ladies" and are expected to quit after they marry. Yet other Japanese firms have been careful to comply with U.S. regulations, and Mitsubishi never once raised a moral objection to equal opportunity laws. Instead, the firm denied that problems existed. Ultimately, the failure was an ethical one. Company executives denied the humanity and dignity of their female workers.

Not all the blame can be placed on Japanese ownership. There were only 70 Japanese managers at the Normal plant, and they were in upper management positions. Middle managers and employees were U.S. residents. Hundreds of U.S. men participated in and condoned the intimidating behavior. Said one EEOC attorney, "I've been doing sexual harassment litigation for years and I don't think any culture's got a lock on it."[31]

DISCUSSION PROBES

1. Who deserves most of the blame for what happened at the Normal plant? Top executives in Japan? The Japanese managers working at the plant? Male American managers and employees?

2. Why do you think Mitsubishi made so many mistakes?

3. What U.S. business practices might seem unethical to Japanese leaders? Why?

4. What steps can leaders and organizations take to prevent sexual discrimination and intimidation in the workplace?

5. What leadership lessons can we draw from Mitsubishi's ethical miscues?

REFERENCE

Paul, E. F. (1999). Strangers in a strange land: The Mitsubishi sexual harassment case. In T. T. Machan (Ed.), *Business ethics in the global market* (pp. 87–136). Stanford, CA: Stanford University Press.

CASE STUDY 10.3

Chapter End Case: Ethical Diversity Scenarios

THE CASE OF THE DISGUISED LEADER

You are the new director of overseas operations for a small cargo airline. The company's most profitable international contract is with the government of Kuwait. You are planning your first visit to that country to see Kuwaiti operations firsthand. The problem is that you are a female traveling to a male-dominated Moslem society. Kuwaiti officials object to women in leadership roles. The CEO of your firm suggests that you let your male deputy act as the leader (meeting with government authorities and company employees, conducting negotiations) when you travel to the Middle East. That way, the Kuwaitis won't be offended and the contract will likely be renewed. You, of course, would resume your regular duties when you left the region.

Would you take the CEO's advice? Why or why not?

ASBESTOS USA

Asbestos is a known cancer-causing agent and the U.S. government requires strict safeguards for employees who make it. These standards greatly increase the cost of manufacturing. Rather than shut down completely, Asbestos USA decided to move its manufacturing plant to Mexico where safety standards and costs are lower. The firm continues to ship to the American market. Company officials see a win-win situation. Not only does the company stay in operation (benefiting shareholders), but American consumers also have the option to purchase asbestos products from a U.S.-owned manufacturer. Mexican workers are warned of the increased cancer risk and are paid somewhat higher wages than other workers in the region. Critics of the company contend that Mexican employees are forced to accept jobs at the plant because there is little other work. Wages, although higher, don't seem to be enough to compensate for the increased danger. Without new safety equipment, Mexican laborers are likely to have the same high cancer rates as the company's former American employees.

Is it immoral for Asbestos USA to manufacture asbestos in Mexico under its current operating procedures? How could it behave more ethically?

REFERENCE

DeGeorge, R. T. (1995). *Business ethics* (4th ed.). Englewood Cliffs, NJ: Prentice Hall, ch. 18.

THE REGIME CHANGE

You are the plant manager at a large clothing manufacturing facility in a small Central American country. Your Canadian company has invested heavily in the plant over the past decade and offers the best wages and working conditions in this impoverished region. Recently the host nation's parliamentary democracy was overthrown in a military coup. The new president has assured you that your plant can continue to operate without government interference. At the same time, he is moving aggressively against his opponents by shutting down newspapers, jailing dissidents, and placing former government officials under house arrest. Upcoming trials could mean lengthy sentences for the accused and, in some cases, death sentences.

Should your plant continue to operate under the new regime? What recommendation would you make to company officials at company headquarters?

TAINTED AMNESTY

The dictator of a small, war-torn African nation has agreed to go into exile and let opposition forces take power. His departure will not only end the fighting but also open the door to international humanitarian aid and investment for a country that has largely been reduced to rubble. The dictator will only leave if the international community will assure him that he will never be prosecuted by an international court of law for crimes committed during his regime. News sources report that thousands of citizens were kidnapped and killed during his reign of terror. He will be relocating with millions looted from the state treasury.

As a diplomat, would you encourage your national government to agree to the dictator's demand for amnesty?

Notes

1. Tavis, T. (2000). The globalization phenomenon and multinational corporate developmental responsibility. In O. F. Williams (Ed.), *Global codes of conduct: An idea whose time has come* (pp. 13–36). Notre Dame, IN: University of Notre Dame Press; Dunning, J. H. (2003). Overview. In J. H. Dunning (Ed.), *Making globalization good: The moral challenges of global capitalism* (pp. 11–40). Oxford, UK: Oxford University Press.

2. Muzaffar, C. (2002). Conclusion. In P. F. Knitter & C. Muzaffar (Eds.), *Subverting greed: Religious perspectives on the global economy* (pp. 154–172). Maryknoll, NY: Orbis Books; Ritzer, G. (2004). *The globalization of nothing.* Thousand Oaks, CA: Pine Forge; Dunning, J. H. (2000). Whither global capitalism? *Global Focus, 12,* 117–136.

3. Friedman, T. (2000). *The lexus and the olive tree* (expanded ver.). New York: Anchor Books.

4. Nielsen, S. (2003, November 2). At Wal-Mart, a world power runs the sale bins. *The Oregonian*, pp. E1–E2.

5. Statistics taken from Singer, P. (2002). *One world: The ethics of globalization*. New Haven, CT: Yale University Press.

6. Muzaffar (2002), Conclusion.

7. Richter, J. (2001). *Holding corporations accountable: Corporate conduct, international codes and citizen action*. London: Zed Books.

8. Karim, A. (2000, June 23). Globalization, ethics, and AIDS vaccines. *Science*, pp. 21–29.

9. Manby, B. (1999). The role and responsibility of oil multinationals in Nigeria. *Journal of International Affairs*, 281–301; Murphy, C. (1999, March 15). The most twisted economy on the planet. *Fortune*, pp. 42–43.

10. Ethicist Peter Singer believes that loyalty to traditional nation state is obsolete. See Singer, P. (2002). *One world: The ethics of globalization*. New Haven, CT: Yale University Press.

11. Solomon, C. M. (2001). Put your ethics to a global test. In M. H. Albrecht (Ed.), *International HRM: Managing diversity in the workplace* (pp. 329–335). Oxford, UK: Blackwell.

12. Donaldson, T. (1996, September-October). Values in tension: Ethics away from home. *Harvard Business Review*, 48–57.

13. Carroll, S. J., & Gannon, M. J. (1997). *Ethical dimensions of management*. Thousand Oaks, CA: Sage.

14. Gudykunst, W. B., & Kim, Y. Y. (1997). *Communicating with strangers: An approach to intercultural communication* (3rd ed.). New York: McGraw-Hill; Gudykunst, W. B., Ting-Toomey, S., Suydweeks, S., & Stewart, L. P. (1995). *Building bridges: Interpersonal skills for a changing world*. Boston, MA: Houghton Mifflin.

15. Drummond, T. (2000, April 3). Coping with cops. *Time*, pp. 72–73.

16. Langer, E. J. (1989). *Mindfulness*. Reading, MA: Addison-Wesley.

17. Opotow, S. (1990). Moral exclusion and injustice: An introduction. *Journal of Social Issues*, 46(1), 1–20. Opotow provides an extensive list of what she calls direct and indirect exclusionary tactics.

18. Rogers, E. M., & Steinfatt, T. M. (1999). *Intercultural communication*. Prospect Heights, IL: Waveland Press, p. 79.

19. Hofstede, G. (1984). *Culture's consequences*. Beverly Hills: Sage; Hofstede, G. (1991). *Cultures and organizations: Software of the mind*. London: McGraw-Hill.

20. Hofstede, G. (2001). Difference and danger: Cultural profiles of nations and limits to tolerance. In M. H. Albrecht (Ed.), *International HRM: Managing diversity in the workplace* (pp. 9–23). Oxford, UK: Blackwell.

21. Carroll and Gannon (1997), *Ethical dimensions of management*.

22. Hampden-Turner, C., & Trompenaars, A. (1993). *The seven cultures of capitalism*. New York: CurrencyDoubleday; Trompenaars, F. (1993). *Riding the waves of culture: Understanding diversity in global business*. Burr Ridge, IL: Irwin.

23. Hampden-Turner & Trompenaars (1993), *The seven cultures of capitalism*, p. 17.

24. Adler, N. J. (2002). *International dimensions of organizational behavior* (4th ed.). Cincinnati, OH: South-Western. See also Moran, R. T, & Harris, P. R. (1982). *Managing cultural synergy.* Houston Gulf.

25. Talbot, M. (1999). Against relativism. In J. M. Halstead & T. H. McLaughlin (Eds.), *Education in morality* (pp. 206–217). London: Routledge.

26. Kung, H. (1998), *A global ethic for global politics and economics.* New York: Oxford University Press; Kung, H. (1999). A global ethic in an age of globalization. In G. Enderle (Ed.), *International business ethics: Challenges and approaches* (pp. 109–127). Notre Dame, IN: University of Notre Dame Press; Kung, H. (2003). An ethical framework for the global market economy. In J. H. Dunning (Ed.), *Making globalization good: The moral challenges of global capitalism* (pp. 146–158). Oxford, UK: Oxford University Press.

27. Kidder, R. M. (1994). *Shared values for a troubled world: Conversations with men and women of conscience.* San Francisco: Jossey-Bass.

28. Kale, D. W. (1994). Peace as an ethic for intercultural communication. In Samovar, L. A., & Porter, R. E. (Eds.), *Intercultural communication: A reader* (7th ed., pp. 435–440). Belmont, CA: Wadsworth.

29. Donaldson, T. (1989). *The ethics of international business.* New York: Oxford University Press.

30. Caux Round Table (2000). Appendix 26: The Caux principles. In O. F. Williams (Ed.), *Global codes of conduct: An idea whose time has come* (pp. 384–388). Notre Dame, IN: Notre Dame University Press.

31. Paul, E. F. (1999). Strangers in a strange land: The Mitsubishi sexual harassment case. In T. T. Machan (Ed.), *Business ethics in the global market* (pp. 87–136). Stanford, CA: Stanford University Press, p. 123.

Epilogue

It's only fair to tell you fellows now that we're not likely to come out of this.

Captain Joshua James speaking to his
crew during the hurricane of 1888

Captain Joshua James (1826–1902) is the "patron saint" of the search and rescue unit of the U.S. Coast Guard. James led rescue efforts to save sailors who crashed off the shores of Massachusetts. When word came of shipwreck, James and his volunteer crew would launch a large rowboat into heavy seas. James would keep an eye out for the stricken vessel as his men rowed, steering with a large wooden rudder. During his career, he never lost a crewman or a shipwrecked person who had been alive when picked up. The captain's finest hour came during a tremendous storm in late November 1888. Over a 24-hour period, James (62 years old at the time) and his men rescued 29 sailors from five ships.

Philip Haillie, who writes about James in his book *Tales of Good and Evil, Help and Harm,* argues that we can only understand James's courageous leadership as an extension of his larger community. James lived in the town of Hull, a tiny, impoverished community on the Massachusetts coast. Most coastal villages of the time profited from shipwrecks. Beachcombers would scavenge everything from the cargo to the sunken ship's timbers and anchors. Unscrupulous individuals called "mooncussers" would lure boats aground. On dark, moonless nights, they would hang a lantern from a donkey and trick sea captains into sailing into the rocks.

Unlike their neighbors up and down the coast, the people of Hull tried to stop the carnage. They built shelters for those who washed ashore, cared for the sick and injured, protested against shipping companies and insurers who sent inexperienced captains and crews into danger, and had their lifeboat always at the ready. During the storm of 1888, citizens burned their fences to light the way for Captain James, his crew, and victims alike. According to Haillie,

Many of the other people of Hull tore up some picket fences near the crest of the hill and built a big fire that lit up the wreck and helped the lifesavers to avoid the flopping, slashing debris around the boat. The loose and broken spars of a ruined ship were one of the main dangers lifesavers had to face. But the sailors on the wrecked ship needed the firelight too. It showed them what the lifesavers were doing, and what they could do to help them. And it gave them hope: It showed them that they were not alone.[1]

The story of Captain James and his neighbors is a fitting end to this text. In their actions they embodied many of the themes introduced earlier: character, values, good vs. evil, altruism, transformational and servant leadership, and purpose. The captain, who lost his mother and baby sister in a shipwreck, had one mission in life—saving lives at sea. Following his lead, residents took on nearly insurmountable challenges at great personal cost. They recognized that "helpers often need help." By burning their fences, these followers (living in extremely modest conditions) cast a light that literally made the difference between life and death. But, like other groups of leaders and followers, they were far from perfect. In the winter hurricane season, the village did its best to save lives. In the summer, pickpockets (helped by a corrupt police force) preyed on those who visited the town's resorts. The dark side of Hull shouldn't diminish the astonishing feats of Captain James and his neighbors, however. Haillie calls what James did during the storm of 1888 an example of "moral beauty."

And moral beauty happens when someone carves out a place for compassion in a largely ruthless universe. It happened in the French village of Le Chambon during the war, and it happened in and near the American village of Hull during the long lifetime of Joshua James.

It happens, and it fails to happen, in almost every event of people's lives together—in streets, in kitchens, in bedrooms, in workplaces, in wars. But sometimes it happens in a way that engrosses the mind and captivates memory. Sometimes it happens in such a way that the people who make it happen seem to unify the universe around themselves like powerful magnets. Somehow they seem to redeem us all from deathlike indifference. They carve a place for caring in the very middle of the quiet and loud storms of uncaring that surround—and eventually kill—us all.[2]

Notes

1. Haillie, P. (1997). *Tales of good and evil, help and harm.* New York: HarperCollins, p. 146.
2. Haillie (1997), *Tales of good and evil,* p. 173.

Index

About the Author

Craig E. Johnson is professor of leadership studies at George Fox University, Newberg, Oregon, where he teaches graduate and undergraduate courses in leadership, ethics, and communication. He is coauthor with Michael Z. Hackman of *Leadership: A Communication Perspective* and his research findings have been published in the *Journal of Leadership Education, Selected Proceedings of the International Leadership Association, Journal of Leadership Studies, Communication Quarterly, Communication Reports,* and *Communication Education.* He has held a variety of volunteer leadership positions in religious and nonprofit organizations and has participated in educational and service trips to Kenya, New Zealand, Brazil, and Honduras.